Boston

A Topographical History

NON
POTEST
CIVITAS
ABSCONDI
SUPRA
MONTEM
POSITA

BOSTON
A Topographical History

Walter Muir Whitehill

Second edition, enlarged

THE BELKNAP PRESS OF HARVARD UNIVERSITY PRESS

CAMBRIDGE, MASSACHUSETTS 1968

DISTRIBUTED IN GREAT BRITAIN BY
OXFORD UNIVERSITY PRESS
LONDON

Copyright 1959, 1968, by the President and Fellows of Harvard College
Library of Congress Catalog Card Number 69–13769

Manufactured in the United States of America

Typeset by the Harvard University Printing Office
Printed by offset lithography by the Meriden Gravure Company
Bound by the Stanhope Bindery, Typography by Burton L. Stratton

Second edition, enlarged

To
The Memory of

FRANCIS HENRY TAYLOR
(1903–1957)

and

PETER OLIVER
(1901–1959)

Preface to the First Edition

ONLY RESIDENTS of Essex County and Maine and New Hampshiremen, traveling by car, approach Boston with any decency. From the upper deck of the Mystic River Bridge, particularly in the early morning, a marvelous panorama of the city in Monet-like blues and grays unfolds itself. Great bridges are one of the few indisputable triumphs of twentieth-century America, yet their builders — so skilful in spans and stresses — seem to take a perverse delight in placing guard rails so exactly at eye level that the traveler is almost invariably denied even a glimpse of the river or bay that he is crossing. This is doubtless deliberate. Pedestrians are prohibited by numerous signs on many bridges; so is parking or even stopping, for the great bridge is part of a tacit conspiracy to get the motorist out of one state into another before he has a chance to determine the difference, if any, between them. The designers of the Mystic River Bridge did their best to conform to this new orthodoxy, yet somehow, in spite of their efforts, the individuality of Boston imposes itself. As one climbs above the unmitigated nastiness of Chelsea, one may have a fleeting glimpse of a tanker being nosed into a Mystic River berth by tugs, while the brief pause for change at the toll-bar allows a moment to enjoy the profile of Boston. On the right, the outsize obelisk of Bunker Hill Monument provides a great vertical accent. At nine of a sunny morning one of its granite faces is in brilliant light; another cloaked in chiaroscuro that would have delighted Piranesi. Below on the left is the Boston Naval Shipyard, with flight decks of immobilized carriers, great machine shops, a destroyer perhaps backing into the stream, and, suddenly for one instant, the masts and spars of a full-rigged ship. For here in Boston the United States Navy, quietly and inexorably occupied, as it must be, with atomic submarines and guided missiles, preserves, cheek by jowl with its contemporary concerns, the frigate *Constitution*. Beyond, a variety of blue-gray buildings, tall for Boston, suggests the illusion of a miniature Manhattan. To the left, sunlight glitters on a great expanse of water, as one looks down the harbor toward the sea. To the right lies a more constricted body of water, the Charles River Basin, that was created of ugly and smelly mudflats half a century ago by judicious damming. The roadway dips and rises, and as it momentarily changes direction the prospect is altered. For a moment the white spire of Christ Church, Salem Street, dominates the North End. For another moment one catches sight of the gold dome of the State House. A stranger would hardly realize that this dome rises above the highest land in Boston, so closely have tall buildings ringed about and obscured the outline of Beacon Hill. *Non potest civitas abscondi supra montem posita*, yet Boston *has* by cutting down its chief hill and sprawling far beyond its traditional boundaries succeeded in hiding itself save to those who approach by sea or over the Mystic River Bridge. Even from the bridge one gets only a momentary hint of the shape and pattern of Boston, for with the pressure of fast-moving lines of traffic suddenly one is in the city. The brief happiness of the distant prospect is over. Unless one succumbs to the wiles of the traffic engineer and continues on out of town to the southward, one must come down from the heights and crawl through crowded streets.

David McCord has spoken of "the images which the walker in Boston remembers more clearly than the man behind the wheel." Furthermore he uses the word "walker" advisedly, remarking that "a pedestrian is a man in danger of his life; a walker is a man in possession of his soul." But even the pedestrian, who weaves his way through traffic with a lordly and individualistic disregard of

lights and paternalistic regulations, sees more of Boston than the
motorist. Sensible people only bring cars into the city if obliged
to transport heavier loads than they can comfortably carry in their
hands. That is why, in spite of determined efforts by railroads to
discourage passenger traffic, so many men and women debouch
from the North and South Stations every weekday morning between eight and nine.

My own normal daily entry to Boston is from the North Station.
Arriving, with luck, at eight forty from Andover, the obvious course
to the Athenæum is on foot. Most commuters work on the same
principle, save for students heading for Boston University or other
tolerably distant colleges or schools. On rainy mornings stenogra-
phers and state employees huddle together in little groups hoping
for a cab, but in general, rain or shine, a solid stream of walkers
emerges from the North Station, following routes to their places
of business that include, if possible, an alleyway. No right-minded
Bostonian would dream of walking along a street if he could by
any chance cut through an alley headed even approximately in the
direction he is going.

There is not much to be said, scenically or architecturally, for
the region between the North Station and the business district.
Originally it was a mill pond. When the top of Beacon Hill was
dumped into it in the first quarter of the last century, it built up
into an area of melancholy dreariness that has not been alleviated
by the random introduction of elevated tracks and overhead highways. Only when one crosses Hanover Street and comes within
sight of Faneuil Hall does the neighborhood become in any way
sympathetic.

Hanover Street, from the settlement of Boston until very recent
years, was the road that linked the North End with the rest of the
Boston peninsula. Now it is bisected by the artery leading from
the Mystic River Bridge. Thus the North End has become almost
an island, separated from the rest of the city, that concerns chiefly
its numerous Italian residents and the visitors who go there in
search of historic monuments. The streets of the North End do
not lend themselves to through traffic, but they are admirably

suited to the celebration of the festivals of saints esteemed in the neighborhood. Narrow enough to permit their spanning by arches of electric lights on appropriate occasions, they are lined by shops rich in cheeses, squids, sausages, strings of garlic free of cellophane, pastries and other good things denied to the outside world. The Mathers, whose church was once in North Square, might have taken a dim view of all this; so doubtless do the occupants of sight-seeing buses who are being carted on historic tours. But Paul Revere, whose house in the same square is the destination of thousands of these commercially-propelled visitors, would, one feels sure, approve of his present-day neighbors, for he was, as his friend and patron John Singleton Copley portrayed him, a French silversmith, working, like any honest craftsman, in his shirt sleeves. Like the present-day walkers, who are not above admiring good displays of comestibles in the shops they pass, Paul Revere would have liked the North End in its current manifestation.

The surroundings of Faneuil Hall have suffered from the exigencies of traffic. Ever since Mayor Josiah Quincy built in 1826 the noble granite market that bears his name, people have been pulling down adjacent buildings to permit the freer passage of men and vehicles. Although the approaches to the Sumner Tunnel and the overhead highways have stripped the old market house of its accustomed surroundings, both indoors and out old habits survive. In December the pavement surrounding Faneuil Hall is fragrant with the piles of spruce trees brought by trucks from the forests of northern New England, while a season later lines of yews, willows and nursery stock crowd the sidewalks as messengers of spring. At any season the pleasing sight of sides of beef and crates of vegetables being unloaded from trucks reminds the passer-by of the vitality of an unbroken historical tradition that still serves a valued purpose in the present-day life of Boston.

A block away State Street continues to be the financial center of the city. The harbor was once nearer, for here, more than anywhere else in downtown Boston, land has encroached upon water. Much of today's State Street was once the Long Wharf, jutting into Town Cove. What one could see of the harbor a few years ago is now obscured by the omnipresent overhead highway, but the east wind still brings the Bostonian from the sea, as David McCord has remarked, "its cooling quality and the faint and, to him, quite pleasing smell of distant fish." In the colonial period the intersection of State and Washington Streets was the nerve centre of Boston.

Although butchers and bankers have kept to their traditional stands, the press has deserted the stretch of Washington Street between the Old State House and the Old South Meeting House that was its stamping ground for many decades. *Transcript* and *Post* have vanished completely, while the still flourishing *Globe* has moved to modern quarters on the southern outskirts of the city. Beyond the Old South Meeting House one enters the area devastated by the great fire of 1872. At the point in Washington Street where Winter Street turns into Summer are the chief department stores. Consequently this intersection is probably the most frequented one in the present city. I recall how, when I was a child, my mother once absent-mindedly referred to something that she had seen at "the four corners." My father and I instantly recognized the spot that she meant. Men normally eschew this region, lest they be trampled under foot by wild herds of suburban shoppers, attracted, among other delights, by the phenomenal bargains of Filene's basement.

In one sense Boston is a series of contiguous villages, whose villagers rarely cross the invisible boundaries that separate them from wholly different worlds. If I pause on the doorstep of the Athenæum for a few minutes, the passers-by and their destinations are as clearly recognizable as they would be in a small town in northern New England, for the stretch of Beacon Street from the State House to King's Chapel is on the direct route between public and private offices, courts, clubs, and Beacon Hill and Back Bay houses and apartments. Thus the same walkers pass again and again, at highly predictable hours, as they do on the residential streets of Beacon Hill. The same is doubtless true in other regions that are off my beat, but each man has his particular area, the bounds of which develop from personal accident.

My first acquaintance with Boston streets began on Sundays
some fifty years ago when my parents took me to the Church of the
Advent, at the corner of Mount Vernon and Brimmer Streets. As
St. Margaret's Convent in Louisburg Square and the Church of
St. John the Evangelist in Bowdoin Street were occasional, although
less regular, ports of call, I thus came at an early age to know the
streets of Beacon Hill as a kind of fringe benefit of Anglican piety.
During a couple of years at the Boston Latin School I got to appreciate the difference between regions from a daily walk from the
subway along Dartmouth Street from Copley Square to the gloomy
great school in Warren Avenue. The railway tracks at Back Bay
station formed a sharp line of demarcation between two worlds.
Elsewhere buildings on the "wrong side of the tracks" were usually
of wood and in a tumble-down condition, but in Boston the blocks
around the Latin School were of red brick or brown stone, sym-
metrically and even handsomely designed. There was no doubt,
even to a school boy, that the South End *was* the wrong side, although schoolboys and undergraduates — who, like dogs, simply
sense class distinctions — waste little time wondering why their
surroundings are what they are. Indeed for twenty-five years I
took New England in general, and Boston and Cambridge in particular, for granted, without strong emotion for or against. It was
only in 1935, when I returned from five unbroken years in Europe,
that I looked at them with the slightest interest. During those five
years I had been studying and photographing Romanesque architecture in Spain. In that relatively thinly populated and unindus-
trialized country, which I loved, I had come to see something of the
influence of geography and topography upon the settlement, planning and growth of towns and cities. With a small Spanish town,
free of sprawling suburbs, it is easy to see the relation between
sites and buildings and the importance of rivers — in short to
begin to understand why someone first considered a given spot
useful for settlement, and how, from that beginning, churches,
mills, markets, and houses had been placed where they were. As
I looked at New England with eyes fresh from a long absence, I
found a wholly new amusement in trying to fathom the archæo-

logical and topographical reasons why my childhood surroundings had become what they were rather than something else. In the end I became so absorbed in this, and related games, that New England history has become my chief interest.

During half a dozen years at the Peabody Museum of Salem I greatly enjoyed the opportunity to explore the maritime history of New England. Coming to the Boston Athenæum at the end of World War II, I found myself equally fascinated by the file drawers of photographs of Boston buildings, accumulated by my predecessors. To these was soon added on deposit the important collection of five hundred prints and drawings of local architectural and topographical subjects, assembled by Charles E. Mason, Jr., for the New England Historical Art Society. Mr. Mason's especial field of interest had been the work of the nineteenth-century New England lithographers. In the years since 1948, when the Society voted to give its collection and funds to the Athenæum, Mr. Mason has continued to add further lithographs in generous quantity, while the Athenæum has purchased from its own funds various eighteenth-century prints and maps that illustrate the appearance of colonial Boston, as well as documentary photographs of modern times by Samuel Chamberlain, Berenice Abbott and George M. Cushing, Jr. Some day this collection will, I trust, become the basis for an iconography of Boston, as useful and detailed as that prepared for New York by I. N. Phelps Stokes.

The Lowell Institute has served many useful purposes during the past one hundred and twenty years, not the least of which is in stimulating some of its lecturers to assemble their thoughts more promptly than would otherwise have been the case. When I was asked to give a series of eight lectures in the spring of 1958 upon any subject that seemed good to me, I took the opportunity to try to organize into some order my random observations upon the topographical evolution of Boston, based largely upon constant walks and the Boston Athenæum's print and photograph collections. Thus on Wednesday evenings from 19 March to 7 May 1958 I gave, in the auditorium of the Museum of Fine Arts, the Lowell Lectures that are here printed, almost without change. I am deeply grateful to the Trustee of the Lowell Institute, Ralph Lowell, and its Curator, Richard M. Gummere, for this opportunity, and to the stimulating audience that came to share my interest in this subject.

These eight lectures only skim the surface of a large subject, yet as the information that they contain had to be assembled from a wide variety of sources, it seems worth while to print them as delivered. Boston, like all American cities, is changing so rapidly that it is desirable that as many of her responsible residents as possible should know something of her evolution during the past three hundred and thirty years. Moreover, the illustrations — skilfully reproduced by the Meriden Gravure Company through the constant helpfulness of E. Harold Hugo — will serve as the beginning of a pictorial record of the Boston Athenæum collection that I hope may be amplified in the future.

The staff of the Boston Athenæum, particularly David McKibbin and Miss Margaret Hackett, have been most helpful in ferreting out useful scraps of information. I am grateful to George M. Cushing, Jr., to Vice Admiral John L. McCrea of the John Hancock Mutual Life Insurance Company and to Miss Margaret Murphy of the Prudential Insurance Company of America for several of the illustrations in the final chapter.

David McCord, whose *About Boston* offers a subtle distillation of the "sight, sound, flavor and inflection" of the contemporary city, has said some things so succinctly and finally that they have to be quoted. Similarly Francis W. Hatch's verses "Beef before baubles" are indispensable in any reference to Faneuil Hall. I am grateful to these two fellow enthusiasts, not only for permission to quote from their works, but for much cheerful encouragement during the preparation of these lectures. Their publication has been the pleasanter for the intuitive and helpful interest of the members of the staff of Harvard University Press.

WALTER MUIR WHITEHILL

Boston Athenæum
25 March 1959

Preface to the Second Edition

WHEN I GAVE THESE LECTURES at the Lowell Institute in 1958, "urban history" had not yet become a fashionable academic subject. The subsequent decade having been one of extraordinary change in Boston, far more readers than I had anticipated were attracted by a book that tried to outline some of the transformations of the previous three and a third centuries. As those who were rebuilding the city and those who were simply observing the process found the book of interest, it was reprinted in 1963. That printing now being exhausted, the Harvard University Press has suggested a new edition, with a ninth chapter describing the decade of renewal that has passed since the lectures were given. This is largely concerned with the activities of the Boston Redevelopment Authority from the fortunate day in 1960 when Mayor Collins chose Edward J. Logue as its administrator, and with the simultaneous efforts in new private construction and historic preservation that have evolved alongside this official pump-priming. It is a chapter that needs to be added, for the work of this decade has brought about conspicuous changes in the city, many of which are for the better. The first eight chapters are reprinted with only very minor changes; the ninth attempts to describe what has occurred between 1958 and the summer of 1968.

This book has been the record of constant topographical change, brought about by changes in numbers and habits of the people.

Although a historian by trade and a historic preservationist by temperament, I am delighted by many of the changes summarized in this new chapter, for they represent a remarkable blending of public and private effort, guided by a higher concept of urban design and a keener awareness of historical continuity than is normal in American cities in the third quarter of the twentieth century. Indeed I find Boston a more agreeable and exciting place to live in each year. When the University of Oklahoma Press a few years ago asked me to do a volume on Boston for their Centers of Civilization series I made it clear that I had no desire to rewarm any supposed "Golden Age" of the past, for I felt that present-day Boston then possessed more of the elements that make a city a center of civilization than it had at any earlier time. Thus I wrote *Boston in the Age of John Fitzgerald Kennedy*, published in 1966, which contains a brief historical sketch of the city and an account of some of the institutions that make it a center of civilization. Chapter IX of this new edition of *Boston: A Topographical History* attempts to show how this city has recently dealt, in civilized manner, with large problems of urban design and architecture.

The 1958 preface is unchanged, for most of what it says about Boston is still substantially true. The view from the Mystic River Bridge is as fine as ever, although the Legislature has officially renamed the bridge to honor the memory of Maurice J. Tobin, sometime Mayor of Boston, Governor of Massachusetts, and Secretary of Labor. But most people still call it the Mystic River Bridge, for familiar names have a way of outliving official change everywhere. Indeed in Spain one sometimes sees, for popular convenience, the old name posted below the new one, as in the case of a street where, during the Republic, Karl Marx supplanted the Emperor Charles V, producing the euphonious sign: CALLE CARLOS MARX, ANTES CARLOS QUINTO. The illusion of a miniature Manhattan, seen from the bridge, is today enhanced by the increased number of tall buildings that have sprung up, not only in the region of State Street but in the West End and at the Prudential Center beyond Copley Square.

In this decade the railroads have redoubled their efforts to discourage passenger traffic. There is in 1968 but one passenger train a day from Andover, arriving at the unseemly hour of eight ten. Moreover, the Boston and Maine Railroad has transformed much of the area behind the North Station into a parking lot for automobiles, eliminating a number of tracks and ending halfway to the Charles River those that remain. In 1958 the North Station of an evening seemed a veritable gateway to the north and east, with somber trains of sleeping cars on adjacent tracks, awaiting passengers bound for Montreal, St. John, New Brunswick, and Halifax. Today there is no passenger service to Maine, New Hampshire, or Vermont, let alone the province of Quebec and the Maritimes. As a destination, Reading is an inadequate substitute. All that the station now offers is un-shiny aluminum Budd cars that continue to bring commuters in from certain Massachusetts towns. These continue only because of subsidies from the Massachusetts Bay Transit Authority, which, to keep needless automobiles out of the city, is making valiant efforts to improve public rapid transit. But because of the MBTA subsidies, many people still make their normal daily entry into Boston from the North Station in the manner that I described a decade ago.

In the late fifties and early sixties, walkers from the North Station frequently had to chart new courses from week to week. So many buildings were being demolished that for a time it was difficult to find a route free from the danger of falling bricks. That perilous moment has passed. Although some beloved (though smelly) alleyways have disappeared forever, there is now the daily excitement of watching the evolution of the new Government Center. Eventually, when projects now under way are completed, walkers will have greater freedom and pleasanter routes than formerly.

Destinations have changed relatively little in the past ten years, although sometimes, because of new construction, long-established firms are found in quite unfamiliar settings, with a startling change of decor. Shortly before the law firm of Ropes & Gray moved to such glittering quarters in the State Street Bank Building, Charles A. Coolidge, a partner in the firm, was told by a New York friend of the following exchange between two New York lawyers. "I hear Ropes & Gray are expanding." "No, they're not. They can't." "Why can't they?" "Because there's no more secondhand office furniture left in Boston." Nevertheless, Ropes & Gray, and other Boston firms, today have both new quarters and new furniture, without having mislaid any of their essential qualities during the change. Moreover, constant association with the views from some of these new tall buildings has given a sense of the sea and an awareness of the shape of the city to many who would never have dreamed of climbing Bunker Hill Monument or going up the Custom House Tower.

I have been able to follow some of the projects of the Boston Redevelopment Authority since 1960 through the kindness of the Right Reverend Monsignor Francis J. Lally, Chairman, Edward J. Logue, Development Administrator (1960–1967), John P. McMorrow, Director of Administrative Services, and other ever helpful members of its staff. Arnold Savrann, project architect for Government Center, greatly assisted me by furnishing several of the illustrations needed for Chapter IX. Other photographs I owe to the kindness of Dr. Walter Gropius of The Architects Collaborative, Inc.; Daniel G. Becker of the Prudential Insurance Company; Erwin D. Canham and Carl B. Rechner of The First Church of Christ, Scientist, in Boston; Professor Robert E. Moody of Boston University; Philip J. McNiff, Director of the Boston Public Library; Philip A. Stack of *The Pilot*; and my old friend and ally, George M. Cushing, Jr. Individual acknowledgments are given in the list of illustrations, but I wish here to express my collective thanks for permission to reproduce the illustrations that are so essential to any understanding of the complicated changes described.

To the acknowledgments of the first edition, I must add my gratitude to William Bradford Osgood of the State Street Bank and Trust Company, who has been of unfailing help in many matters of Boston history and preservation over the past decade, and reiterate my thanks to the staffs of the Boston Athenæum, especially the late Susan Parsons (1933–1967) and Miss Jane A. Ramsay, and of the Harvard University Press.

On several occasions in the last decade I have published elsewhere prints and photographs of early Boston buildings that supplement those that illustrate the text of this book. In *Destroyed Boston Buildings,* a Massachusetts Historical Society Picture Book that I prepared in 1965 from material in that institution's collection, views are reproduced of many structures that have disappeared. In a Bostonian Society picture book of 1967, *Back Bay Churches and Public Buildings*, Mrs. Ropes Cabot and I published early photographs of seventeen buildings, thirteen of which still grace the Back Bay. Mrs. Cabot had in 1966 prepared an earlier picture book entitled *Vanished Boston: An Album of Nineteenth-Century Photographs from the Collections of the Bostonian Society* in which old photographs of destroyed Boston buildings were matched by contemporary views of the sites taken especially for the purpose by Henry D. Childs. This melancholy commentary on the decline of architectural taste fully warranted the query "Who can claim that change is improvement?," which she placed on the title page. I included other illustrations of topographical and architectural interest in my *The Provident Institution for Savings in the Town of Boston, 1816–1966, a Historical Sketch,* that that bank published to commemorate its hundred and fiftieth anniversary.

The greatest treasure of supplementary illustrations is to be found in Professor Bainbridge Bunting's *Houses of Boston's Back Bay: An Architectural History, 1840–1917,* published by the Belknap Press of Harvard University Press in 1967. Professor Bunting rightly observes (page 6) that, because of the nature of the Back Bay filling and construction, "a pedestrian starting at the Public Garden and walking westward can review American architectural development of half a century within the confines of a single street. Nowhere else in America is this possible on so impressive a scale." If one cannot walk the length of Commonwealth Avenue, the illustrations of *Houses of Boston's Back Bay* furnish an excellent substitute. Two maps by Samuel H. Bryant that are used as Figs. 3–4 in this book are especially helpful. The former, representing Boston and vicinity, 1790–1820, shows the relation

of the town to the harbor and adjacent countryside; the latter re-
duces to a single drawing the relation of present-day Boston to the
original shoreline.

The Joint Center for Urban Studies, a cooperative venture of
the Massachusetts Institute of Technology and Harvard University, since its establishment in 1959, has published a number of
books and monographs that illuminate the history of Boston. Sam
B. Warner, Jr., *Streetcar Suburbs: The Process of Growth in Boston, 1870–1900* (Cambridge: Harvard University Press, 1962)
can be read with particular profit in conjunction with this book,
for it shows how through the introduction of horse-drawn and electric streetcars large elements of the population of Boston sprayed
out of the original city and inundated the once rural Dorchester,
Roxbury, West Roxbury and Brighton, which are now submerged
in inelegant urban sprawl. Such centrifugal expansion of population eventually led to the extension of city boundaries far beyond
the limits of the Boston peninsula, and to many of the problems
of the city today. A more recent publication of the Joint Center,
Boston: the job ahead (Cambridge: Harvard University Press,
1966), by Martin Meyerson, its former director, and Edward C.
Banfield, Henry Lee Shattuck Professor of Urban Government at
Harvard, discusses the present scene without uttering shrill cries
of an "urban crisis." Its final chaper, "Beauty in the City," is
particularly relevant to the new final chapter of this book.

WALTER MUIR WHITEHILL

Boston Athenæum
15 July 1968

Contents

Illustrations

lished by Imp. Lithog. de Henry Gaugain, owned by the
Boston Athenæum.

shore near M.I.T., showing the change in the skyline of
the Back Bay in the decade since Fig. 107 was taken.

Photograph of poster-color painting by Robert E. Schwartz for I. M. Pei and Associates, showing the addition of the proposed Hancock tower to the 1967 skyline, furnished by the John Hancock Mutual Life Insurance Company, through the kindness of H. H. Sharpe. This is offered as a possible 1971 counterpart to the photographs of the Back Bay from the State House in 1858 (Fig. 76), 1900 (Fig. 106), and 1958 (Fig. 115).

Boston

A Topographical History

Supra montem posita

CHAPTER I

"Fittest for such as can trade into England"

Boston, which now appears to the casual visitor to be built upon a solid segment of the Massachusetts coast, was in the early seventeenth century a hilly peninsula, almost completely surrounded by water. To the geologist, whose sense of time is more spacious than that of the historian, the site of Boston has worn more aspects than can even be hinted at here. To attempt to relate a volcano in West Roxbury to the Merrimac River crossing Washington Street and that, in turn, to a glacial lake whose waters at the end of the Ice Age completely covered Boston, would be an enterprise in itself.[1] At various times in geological history the relation between sea and shore has changed startlingly, for the New England coast, with its deep bays, islands and peninsula, is a shore line of submergence formed by what is, in effect, the encroachment of the sea upon land topography. Public attention has been focused upon this geological process of submergence in recent years by the discovery, in 1913, when excavation for the Boylston Street subway was being carried out, of the remains of an Indian fish weir which could only have caught fish when sea level was markedly lower than in our time.[2] During the construction of the New England Mutual and the John Hancock Mutual

Life Insurance Companies' buildings, the Robert S. Peabody Foundation for Archæology of Phillips Academy, Andover, excavated further portions of this fish weir. Frederick Johnson's admirable reports of these digs [3] and the exhibitions in the museum at Andover carry the history and topography of Boston back to the period of 1700 B.C. This book is only concerned, however, with the topographical changes that have occurred in the relatively brief period since Englishmen first came to the Massachusetts Bay.

In these centuries the hills of the Boston peninsula have all but vanished, and so has much of the water. Long before the invention of bulldozers and steam shovels, Bostonians had begun to modify their landscape in the attempt to accommodate an expanding population on the limited site that had been chosen for a wilderness village. Here the tops of the hills have literally been taken off to fill the valleys and coves.

Boston has inspired a vast amount of antiquarian research and historical writing — so much, in fact, that the casual inquirer is frequently in danger of becoming lost in the intricate by-ways of available material. In attempting to discover what has become of Boston's hills and coves one has constant cause, therefore, to bless the memory of four devoted and formidably industrious scholars of the last century:

NATHANIEL INGERSOLL BOWDITCH, a conveyancer, whose articles contributed to the *Transcript* of 1855 under the pen name of "Gleaner" [4] are but an indication of the wealth of notes on Boston land titles that he bequeathed to the Massachusetts Historical Society;

WILLIAM H. WHITMORE, who as Record Commissioner of the City of Boston published an immense quantity of official town records; [5]

NATHANIEL BRADSTREET SHURTLEFF, sometime Mayor of Boston, editor of the records of the Massachusetts Bay Company and author of *A Topographical and Historical Description of Boston*; [6] and

JUSTIN WINSOR, successively Librarian of the Boston Public Library and of Harvard College, whose *Memorial History of Bos-*

ton [7] remains, after eighty-five years, the best of guides. Nor should one forget, in the present century,

MISS ANNIE HAVEN THWING, whose published work *The Crooked and Narrow Streets of Boston* [8] is like Bowditch's "Gleaner" articles, only a shadow of the more extensive material that she placed in the Massachusetts Historical Society. Without their detailed investigations of deeds, land titles and public records, it would be impossible to attempt a simplified and intelligible narrative of what has happened to the topography of Boston in historic times.

William Wood in his tract *New England Prospects,* published in London in 1634 in the hope of luring settlers to the region, described the situation of Boston as "very pleasant, hem'd in on the South-side with the Bay of Roxberry, on the North-side with Charles-river, the Marshes on the backe-side, being not halfe a quarter of a mile over; so that a little fencing will secure their Cattle from the Woolves." Having pointed out that the site of Boston, "being a necke and bare of wood," was free from "the three great annoyances of Woolves, Rattle-snakes and Musketoes," Wood went on to describe it as "having on the South-side at one corner, a great broad hill, whereon is planted a Fort, which can command any ship as shee sayles into any Harbour within the still Bay. On the North-side is another Hill equal in bignesse, whereon stands a Winde-mill. To the North-west is a high Mountaine with three little rising Hills on the top of it, wherefore it is called the Tramount. From the top of this Mountaine a man may over-looke all the ilands which lie before the Bay, and discry such ships as are upon the Sea-coast." [9]

The first English settler on the hilly peninsula, which local Indians called Shawmut, was the Reverend William Blaxton. This Anglican clergyman, a Master of Arts of Cambridge University, had come to New England as a chaplain in the pretentious but abortive attempt at colonization led by Robert Gorges, which had landed at Wessagusset (now Weymouth, Massachusetts) in the summer of 1623. When Gorges's plantation broke up, Blaxton — a bachelor with a taste for his own company —

wandered north to the Shawmut peninsula, where in 1625 he settled near an excellent spring on the western slope of what is now called Beacon Hill. There, in the vicinity of Beacon and Spruce Streets, he built a house, planted an orchard, and lived in solitary peace with his vegetables, flowers and books, until the autumn of 1630 when his quiet was rudely interrupted by the arrival of settlers of the Massachusetts Bay Company.[10] These Puritan Englishmen, led by Governor John Winthrop, who had left England in April 1630, settled first at Charlestown, on the mainland. Owing to lack of fresh water there, they soon moved across the Charles River to Blaxton's peninsula of Shawmut or Trimountain, which on 7 September 1630 they renamed Boston.

To visualize the limits of Boston in 1630, one must imagine away considerably more than half the land that appears on a modern map. This is most easily done by reference to the frontis-

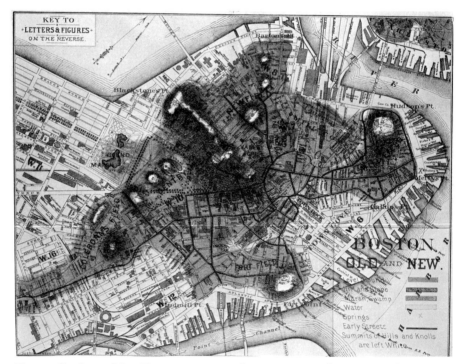

Fig. 1. Outline of the Shawmut peninsula superimposed upon a modern map

piece of Volume I of Winsor's *Memorial History*, where the outline of the peninsula is superimposed upon a more modern map (Fig. 1). To begin with, the Shawmut peninsula was connected on the south with the Roxbury mainland by a narrow neck (along the line of Washington Street), that only just prevented Boston from being an island. To the west of the neck were the great reaches of mudflats and salt marshes, which were covered by the tides at high water, known as the Back Bay; and beyond this the Charles River flowed down to the peninsula, dividing it from the mainland on the north and east as it approached Boston Harbor. Following this original shore line northward from the Neck, one finds that it runs to Park Square, along the line of Charles Street inside the Common, and continues toward Cambridge Street — still to the east of the present Charles Street — to Blackstone's Point. There a cove runs in to about the line of North Russell Street and continues out to Barton's Point, near the foot of Leverett Street. From Barton's Point the shore line turns sharply to the southeast and runs almost to Hanover Street before swinging northwest to Hudson's Point in the North End, thus enclosing a large marshy north cove which corresponds to the present Causeway-Merrimac-Washington Street triangle. An island of relatively solid ground, not far from Causeway Street, which almost separated this marshy area from the Charles River, made it easy at an early date to dam the cove into a Mill Pond. On the east the peninsula fronted on the harbor, with a shore line that receded into marshes as it approached the Neck on the south. Dock Square, now well inland, very reasonably derived its name from the town dock that was at the head of Town Cove, which, jutting in from the harbor, divided Boston into North and South Ends. The most conspicuous feature of the North End was Windmill Hill, later Snow Hill, now Copp's Hill, while Fort Hill (now leveled, approximately at the angle in High Street as it approaches Atlantic Avenue) dominated the South End.

On the main part of the peninsula rose the Trimountain, of which Beacon Hill is the sole, and greatly mutilated, remnant. While the hills of the North and South Ends were simple single elevations standing alone, the Trimountain — which was the characteristic landmark of the place — was, in the natural state, a high ridge extending through the center of the peninsula. So radically was this area altered in the early nineteenth century that one must turn to early views to get any notion of the triple peaks. An *Atlantic Neptune* view of Boston from Willis' Creek, published in London by J. F. W. Des Barres in 1776 [11] (Fig. 2), shows the rugged mass of the Trimountain as seen from the Cambridge shore of the Charles River.[12] The separation of the peaks, as seen from Charlestown, is depicted more clearly in one of Abel Bowen's wood cuts for Dr. Caleb H. Snow's *A History of Boston* [13] (Fig. 3), which was used in 1830 as the emblem on the badge for the bicentennial celebration of the settlement.[14] A revised cut in *Bowen's Picture of Boston* [15] (Fig. 4), first issued in 1829, designates the three hills as Pemberton, Beacon and Mount Vernon.

Pemberton, the eastern peak, which was more generally called Cotton Hill from the circumstance of the Reverend John Cotton having lived on its slope,[16] rose some eighty feet above the present level of Pemberton Square. The high central peak, with an eleva-

Fig. 2. The Trimountain as seen from Cambridge

THE TRAMOUNT.

Fig. 3. The Trimountain

tion of about one hundred and thirty-eight feet above sea level, which was originally known as Sentry Hill, derived its permanent name from an order of the General Court of 4 March 1634/5 [17] that "there shalbe forthwith a beacon sett on the sentry hill att Boston, to give notice to the country of any danger." To the west of Beacon Hill, the ridge continued toward the Charles River, with another summit at a point that we would describe today as between Mount Vernon and Pinckney Streets, just above Louisburg Square. Bowen designated this as Mount Vernon, but there was always a certain veiled sniggering among local antiquaries about the name of this peak, which appeared quite unequivocally on Lieutenant Page's 1776 map as Mount Whoredom.[18] The same

Fig. 4. The Trimountain

Pemberton.   Beacon.   Mt. Vernon.

name appears on the panoramic view of Boston in 1775, made by officers of the Royal Welsh Fusiliers, which is owned by the Massachusetts Historical Society,[19] while N. I. Bowditch recalled in 1855 having seen "a very large and accurate plan in the possession of the Mt. Vernon proprietors, made 60 or 70 years ago, which was entitled by the surveyor in large and elaborate letters, a plan of 'Mount Hoardam'." [20] Bowditch remarked upon this "very ingenious and modest way of conforming to the then popular nomenclature of the spot, without giving offence 'to ears polite'." That the hill was so designated for cause is indicated by Lieutenant Williams of His Majesty's Twenty-Third Regiment, who, arriving in Boston in June 1775, noted in his journal: "No such thing as a play house, they were too puritanical a set to admit of such lewd

Diversions, tho' ther's perhaps no town of its size cou'd turn out more whores than this cou'd. They have left us an ample sample of them." [21] The western ridge of the Trimountain terminated in a high bluff near the water, sometimes called West Hill.

For the first century and a half of Boston, the Trimountain remained chiefly as a hilly background against which the town nestled, for it was in the plain between the harbor and the Trimountain that the Massachusetts Bay Company colonists settled. In the autumn of 1630 the level portions of the Shawmut peninsula, being treeless, must have resembled a vast rough field, in which the settlers accommodated themselves for the winter as best they could, in the sites most appropriate to each man's individual needs. John Winthrop speaks of "the poorer sort of people who lay long in tents" [22] and mentions English "wigwams," [23] but at the earliest possible moment houses, inspired by recognizable English models, were built. Deputy Governor Dudley, writing to the Countess of Lincoln in March 1631, explained that for the prevention of fire "we have ordered that no man shall build his chimney with wood, nor cover his house with thatch; which was readily assented unto, for that divers other houses have burned since our arrival, (the fire always beginning in the wooden chimneys,) and some English wigwams, which have taken fire in the roofs covered with thatch and boughs." [24] Frame houses covered with weather-boarding, or with clapboards, in the manner of Essex County,[25] were soon built. Much of the available evidence is summarized in George Francis Dow's *Every Day Life in the Massachusetts Bay Colony* [26] for those who cannot conveniently visit the Pioneer Village, built at Salem in 1930 upon the basis of Mr. Dow's investigations, which gives a reasonable notion of what Boston must have looked like in the earliest years of the settlement.

Cows are popularly though erroneously blamed for the pattern of Boston streets. Actually the oldest streets of Boston are perfectly decently laid out on the basis of English precedent. Public life was centered at the spot now occupied by the Old State House, where the Great Street (later King, now State Street) leading from the harbor joined what is today Washington Street, which was the road leading to the Neck and the mainland. At this point the Great Street was 113 feet wide. Within this area was an open air market place where farmers, sailors, townspeople and visiting Indians jostled each other for decades. The first meeting house fronted on the market place; the governor's house was nearby, and here in 1657 was built a Town House which served as the seat of government until its destruction by fire in 1711. Nearby to the east was the town dock, which has left its name in Dock Square.

The General Court on 1 April 1634 [27] ordered every town to make up a book recording the ownership and transfer of properties. Actually Boston seems to have been dilatory in complying, for the *Book of Possessions*, which is the earliest thorough survey of land-holdings, seems to have been compiled about 1643.[28] This volume, which was published in the *Second Report of the Record Commissioners of the City of Boston* through the energy of that indefatigable archivist and antiquary William H. Whitmore, has furnished

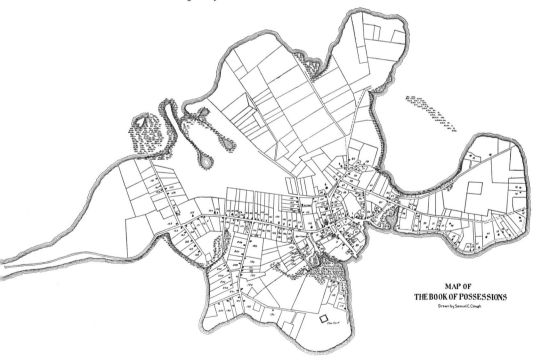

MAP OF
THE BOOK OF POSSESSIONS
Drawn by Samuel C. Clough

Fig. 5. Boston in the 1640's

the evidence for several reconstruction maps of Boston in the mid-seventeenth century.

While Captain John Bonner's map of 1722 is the first detailed contemporary map of the town, one can get a fair notion of the distribution of population from the modern map (Fig. 5) that Samuel C. Clough prepared in 1927 for the Colonial Society of Massachusetts from the data contained in the *Book of Possessions*. There one notes the considerable amount of marshy ground along the shore front; the absence of any settlement on Fort Hill, Copp's Hill or the Trimountain; the rather heavy concentration around the market place and the road to the Neck, and the number of householders who had established themselves along the shore in the North End. William Wood in 1634 described Boston as "fittest for such as can Trade into England, for such commodities

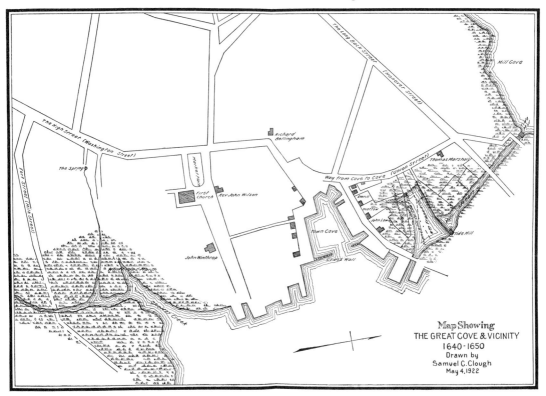

Fig. 6. The center of Boston in the 1640's

as the Countrey wants, being the chiefe place for shipping and Merchandize." From the early years of the settlement merchant owners of waterfront property were constantly building wharves into the harbor, and thus began the inexorable encroachment of land upon water that has marked the history of Boston. From Mr. Clough's reconstruction map of the Great Cove and vicinity between 1640 and 1650 [29] (Fig. 6), one readily sees that very little of the shore front between the present Milk and Hanover Streets was free of marshy ground. Moreover, the several creeks and coves made it extraordinarily irregular. The need of more wharf space led to early tampering with the shore line. On 29 November 1641 the town granted to Valentine Hill, merchant, and his associates, all the waste land in Bendalls Cove, now Faneuil Hall Square,[30] for the purpose of building wharves and warehouses, with the right to take tonnage for such vessels as might land there, and wharfage on goods. The result was the development of a convenient and orderly Town Cove. A year and a half later Governor Winthrop, Valentine Hill and others attacked the project of digging out Shelter Cove [31] (between the present State and Milk Streets) to make provision for wharfing there.

Two months later, on 31 July 1643, Henry Symons, George Burden, John Button, John Hill and their partners received the grant of the north cove facing Charlestown, with adjoining marsh land, on condition that within three years they "erect and make upon or neere some part of the premises, one or more corne mills, and maynteyne the same for ever." [32] They were to make a flood gate ten feet wide for the passage of boats into the cove, and were to have the right of cutting through the marsh from the cove to a creek on the line of the present Blackstone Street, and to dig trenches in the highways or waste grounds provided they "make and mainteyne sufficient, passable and safe wayes over the same for horse and Cart."

This cove was, as we have seen, a marsh partially separated from the Charles River by a long narrow island of solid ground. There was seemingly an Indian track, transitable at low tide, across the marshy stretches that separated this island from the peninsula,

along the line of the present Causeway Street. This the mill proprietors reinforced into a dam, thus converting the north cove
into a mill pond, which maintained a grist mill, a saw mill and,
later, a chocolate mill. They further exercised their right to dig
through from their mill pond to the harbor, thereby creating Mill
Creek, which furnished tidal water for the operations of their
mills. Mill Creek, which practically converted the North End
into an island, dividing Boston in two, was spanned by draw-
bridges at North and Hanover Streets. This only accelerated a
natural process, for at high tide waves would carry across the low
land between Copp's Hill and the Trimountain.[33] The water in
the Mill Creek was obviously swift flowing, for in 1656 the draw-
bridge at North Street was designated as the only place from
which butchers might case "their beasts entralls and garbidg" without penalty of a fine.[34]

The frequent appearance of such sanitary problems in the town
records indicates the urban character of Boston in the second
decade of settlement. On 31 October 1642 it was "ordered that the
Constable shall give speedy notice to Robt. Nash, Butcher, that
with all speed he remove the Stinking garbage out of his yard, nere
the street, and provide some other remote place for slaughter of
Beasts, that such loathsome smells might be avoyded, which are
of great annoyance unto the neighbors, and to strangers." [35] Similar admonitions are given about the unrestrained movement of
goats and hogs,[36] the digging of clay in the highway [37] and other
public nuisances. For Boston was, as Professor Carl Bridenbaugh
points out, not a frontier town but a "city in the wilderness." His
books *Cities in the Wilderness* and *Cities in Revolt* [38] contain much
that is fascinating about the urban development of Boston, Newport, New York, Philadelphia and Charleston from their settle-
ments to the Revolution, and summarize much about the life of
Boston that bears upon the background of the subject of these
lectures. Professor Bernard Bailyn in his *The New England Merchants in the Seventeenth Century* justly points out the effect
upon Boston of the migration of Puritan tradesmen from the City
of London. "Once in America," he writes, "they sought to recreate

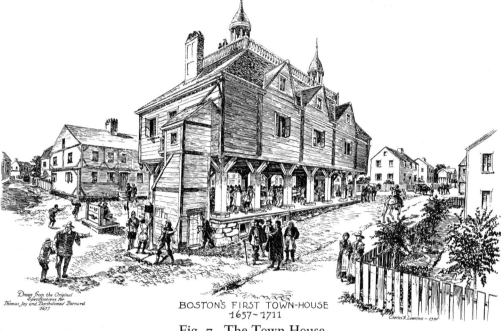

Drawn from the Original
Specifications for
Thomas Joy and Bartholomew Barnard
1657

BOSTON'S FIRST TOWN-HOUSE
1657~1711

Charles A. Lawrence - 1930

Fig. 7. The Town House

the life they had known at home. Congregating in the towns around Boston Bay, in Salem, and in New Haven, they saw many of the same people with whom they had pushed through the crowds of Cheapside a few years earlier. From the first they called the main thoroughfare of Boston Cornhill, and along it and the intersecting King Street, which led to the wharf, many established their residences. The list of property owners on Cornhill between Milk and Dock Streets during the first decade reads like the roster of expatriated tradesmen and shopkeepers of the old business district . . . The settling together of friends and the use of old street names were fragments of the settlers' never-ending attempts to make the wilderness of America familiarly English." [39]

It was one of the transplanted London tradesmen, Robert Keayne, a merchant tailor, who, arriving in 1635 and establishing a house and shop facing the market square, left on his death in 1656 the bequest that led to the building of the first Town House (Fig. 7) the following year. This structure was, as Professor Bailyn points out, "the true center of the business life of Boston and, indeed, of the whole of New England." He continues:

This two-storied structure lay at the main intersection of the town, in the center of the market and meetinghouse square. Keayne's desire that the townhouse combine a shelter "for the country people that come with theire provisions . . . to sitt dry in and warme both in colde raine and durty weather" with a "convenient room or too for the Courts to meete in" and a "roome for a Library and a gallery or some other handsome roome for the Elders to meete in and conferr together," as well as an armory for the Artillery Company — all built on pillars so that "the open roome between the pillars may serve for Merchants, Mr of Shipps and Strangers as well as the towne . . . to meete in" — had been fully realized. Under the chambers of the court and library the merchants congregated daily. From this townhouse exchange radiated a large part of the commercial cords that laced New England to the other coastal ports, to the West Indies, the Wine Islands, Spain, and especially to England. Since, by 1660, almost all importations from England were handled by Boston merchants, their meeting place in the townhouse exchange was economically closer to the "New England walke" on the London exchange than it was to some of the market places of the surrounding towns. It was the exact pivot point of the primary orbit of Atlantic trade in New England.[40]

Detailed descriptions of seventeenth-century Boston are scarce and meager. John Josselyn made two voyages to New England. On his first, in 1638–1639, he cavalierly dismissed Boston as a village of "not above Twenty or thirty houses," which throws some doubt upon his ability to count, but devoted considerable space to describing a rattlesnake that he met in Charlestown.[41] Returning to New England in 1663 for a stay of eight years, he did rather better in recording the appearance of Boston, which he described as "the Metropolis of this Colony, or rather of the whole Countrey, situated upon a Peninsula, about four miles in compass, almost square, and invironed with the Sea, having one small Isthmus which gives access to other Towns by land on the South-side."

The Town [continued Josselyn] hath two hills of equal height on the frontire part thereof next the Sea, the one well fortified on the superfices with some Artillery mounted, commanding any Ship as she sails into the Harbour within the still Bay; the other hill hath a very strong battery built of whole Timber and fill'd with earth, at the descent of the hill in the extreamest part thereof, betwixt these two strong Arms, lyes a large Cove or Bay, on which the chiefest part of the Town is built, to the North-west is a high mountain that out-tops all, with its three little rising hills on the summit called Tramount, this is furnished with a Beacon and great Guns, from hence you may overlook all the Islands in the Bay, and descry such ships as are upon the Coast: the houses are for the most part raised on the Sea-banks and wharfed out with great industry and cost, many of them standing upon piles, close together on each side of the streets as in London, and furnished with many fair shops, their materials are Brick, Stone, Lime, handsomely contrived, with three meeting Houses or Churches, and a Town-house built upon pillars where the Merchants may confer, in the Chambers above they keep their monethly Courts. Their streets are many and large, paved with pebble stone, and the South-side adorned with Gardens and Orchards. The town is rich and very populous, much frequented by strangers, here is the dwelling of their Governour. On the North-west and North-east two constant Fairs are kept for daily Traffick thereunto. On the South there is a small, but pleasant Common where the Gallants a little before Sun-set walk with their Marmalet-Madams, as we do in Morefields, &c till the nine a clock Bell rings them home to their respective habitations, when presently the Constables walk their rounds to see good orders kept, and to take up loose people.[42]

Of the town described by Josselyn, the Common is the only recognizable trace. The hills have all but disappeared. The "Sea-banks" continued to be "wharfed out with great industry and cost" until the original shore lines were far inland, and a series of fires [43] practically obliterated the earliest buildings. The Paul Revere House (Fig. 8) at 19 North Square, which was probably built about 1680 on the site of the Reverend Increase Mather's house — which was destroyed in the great fire of 1676 — is all that remains standing to give one a suggestion of the seventeenth-century North End of Boston. This low-studded wooden house, with its leaded casement windows and overhanging second story was, however, extensively rebuilt in the mid-eighteenth century, and restored to its present appearance in 1907–1908.[44] A few buildings of the last quarter of the seventeenth century survived long enough to be engraved, or even photographed, as objects of antiquarian interest. One knows the form of a very modest wooden house (Fig. 9) in Milk Street, opposite the Old South Meeting House, solely

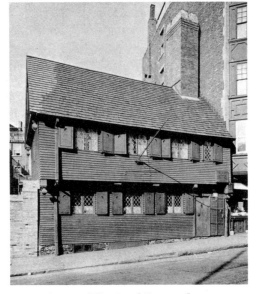

Fig. 8. The Paul Revere house

because its owner, Nathaniel Reynolds, a shoemaker, chanced to rent it in 1685 to Josiah Franklin, whose son Benjamin was born there in 1706. Although this narrow structure of two stories and attic, with a pointed gable toward the street, burned in 1810, its repute as Benjamin Franklin's birthplace caused Abel Bowen to engrave a view of it.[45]

More ambitious two story and attic houses of the last third of the seventeenth century were graced with a picturesque multiplicity of gables. In 1670 Deacon Henry Bridgman, a leather dresser, built such a house (Fig. 10) off Milk Street, near a creek in which he and earlier tanners watered their leather. Occupied in the eighteenth century by the Borland family, this building was bought in 1794 by Jean Baptiste Gilbert Payplat, called Julien, a French cook,[46] who maintained it until his death in 1805 as a well-known place of public entertainment, somewhat illiterately called Julien's Restorator. Although destroyed in 1824, the house was engraved by both Nathaniel Dearborn [47] and Abel Bowen.[48]

The Old Feather Store (Fig. 24) in Dock Square, a wooden building covered with stucco, built in 1680 as a two-tenement

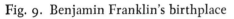

Fig. 9. Benjamin Franklin's birthplace   Fig. 10. Bridgman house

house, with overhanging stories and picturesque gables, survived until July 1860, and so came within the era of both lithography and photography.[49] Nearby, on the narrow point of low land between the town dock and mill creek, stood from about 1680 to 1824 a curious two-story brick structure with a high, pyramidal slate roof, built by Richard Wharton after the great fire of 1679 and known, from its conformation to its site, as the Triangular Warehouse (Fig. 11). At each corner were three-story hexagonal towers, surmounted by pyramids, topped by stone balls. Before this characteristic landmark was removed in 1824, in preparation for the construction of Quincy Market and North Market Street, it was engraved by Nathaniel Dearborn.[50]

On a far more elegant scale than any of the buildings mentioned previously, which had continued the crowded late medieval tradition of the City of London, was the great three-story, free standing house built by Peter Sargeant in 1679, which in 1716 became the residence of the governors of the province of the Massachusetts Bay. The Province House (Fig. 12), which (before its destruction by fire in 1864) inspired four of Hawthorne's *Twice-Told Tales,* stood in spacious grounds some seventy feet west of Washington (then Marlborough) Street nearly opposite the head of Milk Street. It was a high-shouldered building of brick, laid in English bond, with a high attic lighted by dormers, and an octagonal cupola surmounted by Shem Drowne's Indian archer weathervane, which is now, like the royal arms that hung over the front entrance, in the Museum of the Massachusetts Historical Society.[51]

Such a building as the Province House, coming only half a century after the first settlement of Boston, indicates the prosperity of trade which in its turn led to constant tinkerings with the coast line. The seventeenth-century town records abound in liberties granted to one captain and another "to wharfe before his owne ground adjoyninge to his dwellinge house."[52] With the waterfront improvements for berthing vessels and warehousing goods went a preoccupation with harbor defense. About 1646 a North Battery (Fig. 13) of timber filled with earth, had been built at Merry's Point in the North End to command the harbor and river entrance. Twenty years later in 1666 Major General John Leverett (subsequently Governor of the colony) built on the site of Rowe's

Fig. 11. The triangular warehouse

Fig. 12. The Province House

Fig. 13. The North Battery

Wharf, under the shadow of Fort Hill, the Boston Sconce, or South Battery (Fig. 14), for which the General Court gave him a vote of thanks and a gratuity of one hundred pounds.[53] A special town meeting on 5 September 1673, called to consider a recommendation of the Colony Council for "the erecting of a wall or wharfe upon the flatts before the towne from the sconce to Capt Samuell Skarlets wharfe" as a defense precaution, declined to undertake such a work at town expense,[54] but within the week seven citizens turned up with a plan for building such a barrier as a private enterprise.[55] They proposed that "a wall or wharfe of wood and stone be erected from the said sconce to Capt. Skarlets wharfe which is in length about two thousand and two hundred

Fig. 14. The South Battery

foote, that it be made in breadth 22 foote at the bottom and to be raised 6 foote high at the least with all expedition and afterwards (as soone as may be) to ad thereto in height as shall be judged convenient for a brest worke to play Guns on which is supposed to be about 14 or 15 foote high in all and soe carryed up to be 20 foote broad at the topp." All this was to be built at the expense of private citizens who would have in return the right to build wharves and warehouses between the wall and the shore. This proposal having been approved by the Council on 11 November 1673 [56] over forty subscribers undertook to build from 20 to 150 feet each, thus obtaining proportionate rights in the use of the cove flats enclosed by the new wall.[57] On 11 May 1681 when the Sea Wall, Barricado, or Out Wharves, as it was variously called,[58] had been "almost finished," the General Court passed an act incorporating the "undertakers" of the work.[59] As no enemy appeared to send fireships in among the wharves, this fortified breakwater never fulfilled its intended purpose. The openings necessary to permit the entrance of vessels into the cove made the central section of the Barricado inaccessible. Outward bound vessels would help themselves to stones from the wall for ballast. Serving no necessary mercantile purpose, it was soon allowed to fall into decay. It appears on Bonner's map of 1722 (Fig. 16) in vague and somewhat fragmentary fashion as "Old Wharfe." Nevertheless, parts of the Barricado remained for well over a century, as Henry Pelham's map of 1776 [60] shows five of these "Island Wharfs." One last survival was incorporated into Central Wharf in 1816.

Of more permanent value to the town was another private enterprise — the building of Long Wharf at the foot of King (now State) Street, which was undertaken in 1710 by Captain Oliver Noyes and his associates.[61] This significant venture amounted to extending King Street through the Cove and well out into the harbor, for the new wharf crossed the central part of the Barricado, one section of which formed the original T of T Wharf, and went well beyond it. Long Wharf was early lined with continuous rows of shops and warehouses (Fig. 15). It permitted the direct loading and unloading of the largest ships of the time without the use of boats or lighters. Moreover it amounted to a dramatic road from Boston to the sea. Starting at the Town House, the old Cornhill, and Marlborough, Newbury and Orange Streets meandered a mile and a quarter southwest toward the Neck and Roxbury. To the eastward King Street ran straight and wide onto the Long Wharf, where lay the ships that were the source of the town's prosperity. This broad half mile was the obvious avenue to Boston from the part of the world that really mattered.

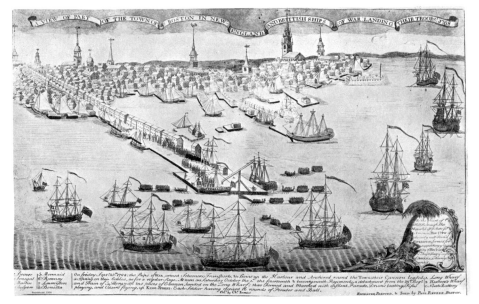

Fig. 15. The Long Wharf in 1768

CHAPTER II

The Eighteenth Century

ONE KNOWS SEVENTEENTH-CENTURY Boston chiefly from pieces and scraps, diligently sifted by nineteenth-century antiquarians. The eighteenth century is quite another matter. For one thing the selectmen got around to naming the streets. In reading seventeenth-century town records one has to cope with such mystifications as Peter Oliver being allotted fifteen pounds per annum for seven years "to maintain the High wayes from Jacob Eliots Barne to the fardest gate bye Roxsbery Towns end." [1] In 1701 the selectmen were empowered to assign and fix names; by 1708 the job was done, the results entered in the Town Book and Bartholomew Green had printed a handsome broadside that, for threepence at any bookseller's, would provide the information. [2] Thus one would find the highway that Peter Oliver was maintaining in 1650 described as:

1. The broad Street or Way from the Old Fortification on the Neck, leading into the Town as far as the late Deacon *Eliot's* corner.

   ORANGE STREET

Of the names of the 110 streets, lanes and alleys, many are familiar even today. Essex, Summer, Milk, Oliver, Beacon, Water, Union, Brattle, Salem, and Hull are trusted friends. But without Bartholomew Green's broadside and the succeeding volumes

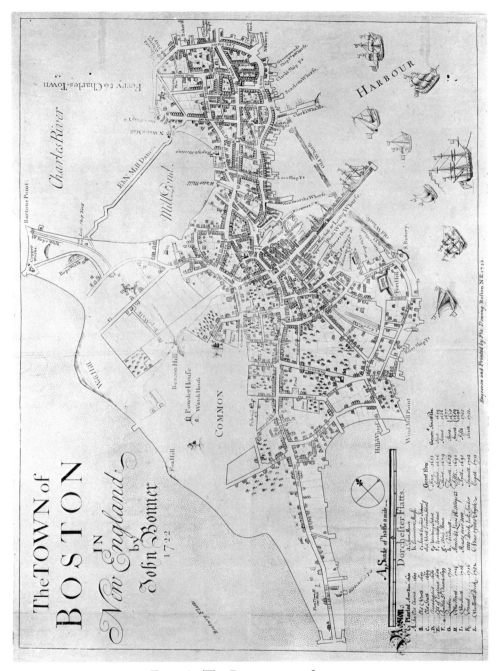

Fig. 16. The Bonner map of 1722

published by the City, how would we find our way to Cow Lane, Flownder Lane, Turn again Alley, Half-square Court, Mackeril Lane, Paddey's Alley, Sliding Alley and Crooked Lane?

Moreover, beginning in the third decade of the eighteenth century, the plan of the streets and the appearance of the town were recorded in a series of maps and views. The first of these is Captain John Bonner's map of 1722 [3] (Fig. 16), engraved and printed in Boston by Francis Dewing [4] and sold by Bonner and William Price, who dealt in prints, frames, looking-glasses and toys "at the King's Head & Looking Glass" in Cornhill, near the Town House. In the same year, Price invited subscriptions for a view of Boston from Noddles Island, drawn by William Burgis, that was to be engraved in England if sufficient interest were shown.[5] As this "North East Prospect" met with few takers, Burgis tried again from another angle and produced "A South East View of ye Great Town of Boston in New England in America," which Price was advertising for sale in the summer of 1725.[6] This earliest form of the Burgis-Price view survives only in a copy in the British Museum, but several Massachusetts institutions have a later edition that Price issued in 1743 to commemorate the building of Faneuil Hall.[7] The Essex Institute owns a unique copy of a much smaller engraving entitled "A North East View of the Great Town of Boston." Although this print lacks a date, or any clue to its designer or engraver, John W. Farwell suggested with reasonable ground that it was probably derived from Burgis's first view, taken from Noddles Island.[8]

Burgis in 1728 produced a second map of Boston (Fig. 17), engraved by Thomas Johnston and dedicated to Governor William Burnett.[9] Although on a scale of one half that of Bonner's map, it includes more of the Neck and first shows the division of the town into wards or companies. Burgis's map appeared only in this one edition, but Bonner's was subsequently reissued by Price with various additions and corrections in 1729, 1733, 1739, 1743 and 1769.[10] This fortunate sequence of revisions makes it possible to follow with ease the growth of various parts of Boston in the half century preceding the Revolution.

Fig. 17. The Burgis map of 1728

With Bonner's 1722 map as a guide, let us wander through Boston and try to see what it looks like. Coming from the Roxbury mainland we would cross the narrow neck, a mangy kind of natural causeway, soggy at high tide and sprayblown in a storm, that leads to a fortified gate at what is now Washington and Dover Streets. This is the only means of approaching by foot or horse. All other routes require boats. As it is made no more exhilarating by the presence of a gallows just outside the town gate, and as it leads through the least settled portion of the town, we will gain a more favorable impression by choosing to approach Boston from the sea.

Landing on the Long Wharf one walks a good distance past warehouses, admiring the numerous wharves and docks that crowd along the banks of Town Cove, before reaching the actual shore line, which was then at the level of Mackrell Lane (now Kilby Street) and Merchants Row. The first building that one meets on land is the Bunch-of-Grapes Tavern [11] at the corner of King Street and Mackrell Lane. This source of good punch, much frequented by merchants and masters of vessels, offers a more inviting aspect of the town than the gallows that would greet the traveler by land. Opposite, on the corner of Merchants Row, the Huguenot merchant Andrew Faneuil had his warehouse.[12] Continuing up King Street one reaches the Town House at the intersection with Cornhill (now Washington Street) which leads to the Neck. In this central heart of the town the buildings are new and elegant. A disastrous fire in the evening of 2 October 1711 — the eighth of some magnitude since 1653 — occasioned by the carelessness of "a poor Sottish Woman" burning rubbish in a tenement yard,[13] burned everything along Cornhill from School Street to Dock Square, including the Town House and First Church, as well as the upper part of King Street.

When the wooden Town House (Fig. 7), built with Robert Keayne's legacy, was swept away in the fire of 1711, the town replaced it with a brick structure which housed the town and provincial governments, the courts and the merchant's exchange. Although the interior of this new building was completely burned out in a fire of 9 December 1747, the exterior walls survive in today's Old State House.[14]

The First Church, which had its first meeting house on the south side of King Street, moved in 1640 to its second in Cornhill Square, opening on Cornhill west of the Town House, where the Ehrlichs until 1967 sold pipes and tobacco. Within ten days after the fire of 1711, the First Church determined that its third meeting house should be of brick. The cornerstone was laid on 25 June 1712, and on 3 May 1713 this fine three-story New Brick meeting house was occupied for the first time.[15] The term "new," like "modern," is strictly relative. By 1721 there was a newer "New Brick" in the North End,[16] and this meeting house of 1712–1713 thereupon became the Old Brick, a designation that it retained until its demolition in 1808, when the First Church moved to Chauncy Place, off Summer Street.

From the Town House Cornhill leads both north and south into different ends of the town. We will turn north, and shortly reach Dock Square, which takes its name from the Town Dock. From this point Ann Street and Union Street (running, as today, into Hanover) lead, via bridges across the Mill Creek, into the North End.

This section, isolated by the creek, is the most populous of the town and the most salty. Here merchants have "wharfed-out" before their houses until the shore line has become a strip of wharves and ship yards. The North End has three main thoroughfares: near the water Ann Street (which becomes, appropriately, Fish and Ship Streets); in the center Middle Street, running out of Hanover and becoming North Street; near the Mill Pond, Back Street which, at Prince, turns into Salem Street.

From Fish Street one reaches Clark's Square (today's North Square), the site of the two greatest Boston houses of the time. William Clark, merchant, bought land there in 1711, and soon after built a high three-story brick house with twenty-six richly decorated rooms, which was the most sumptuous private house of the period.[17] Clark died in 1742, and in 1756 his heirs sold the house to Sir Charles Henry Frankland. This gentleman had recently married his Marblehead mistress Agnes Surriage (the subject of Holmes's poem) in gratitude for their escape from the Lisbon earthquake of 1755. Hard by stood the only slightly less handsome house built by John Foster at the end of the seventeenth century. Inherited by Mr. Foster's nephew Colonel Thomas Hutchinson in 1711, it remained the home of his son, the governor, until the Revolution. This great house, fronting on Garden Court, with gardens running through to Fleet and Hanover Streets, although wrecked by the 1765 mob that scattered Governor Hutchinson's historical papers, was repaired and survived into the thirties of the last century [18] as did the neighboring Clark-Frankland house.

A more modest neighbor, the small three-story brick house built by Moses Pierce, glazier, about 1711, and later owned by Nathaniel Hichborn, has not only survived to the present but has recently been restored, furnished and preserved by Carleton R. Richmond. This fine example of an early eighteenth-century small town house is separated by a walled garden from the Paul Revere house, which is the only surviving example in Boston of seventeenth-century architecture in wood.

Returning to 1722, the principal church of the North End, the Second, or Old North — the church of the Mathers — founded in 1650, stands on Clark's Square, but a wooden New North, constituted in 1714, and a New North Brick, that seceded noisily from the New North in 1721, have their meeting houses nearby in North and Middle Streets respectively. The unwelcome Baptists, who organized themselves at Charlestown in 1665, had built themselves a meeting house in Back Street on the edge of the mill pond in 1679. Save for the slopes of Copp's Hill, surmounted by a burying ground and a windmill, the North End is heavily populated, chiefly by merchants who have their dwellings, warehouses and wharves in close proximity, and by shipbuilders who similarly enjoy the convenience of living close to their yards. The largest of the North End wharves — Clark's — is only a few steps from Clark's Square.

The ferry to Charlestown — an early perquisite of Harvard College's — ran from the Ferry Way at the end of Prince Street, beside Gee's shipyard, so even though the North End was a compact and tight little region, completely surrounded by water (the Mill Creek, the harbor, the Charles River and the Mill Pond), persons from other parts of town wishing to go to Charlestown, Cambridge, or the north, traveled its crowded streets on the way to the ferry.

Nevertheless, Boston was sharply divided into separate regions, as one sees from the beginning of the revolt against Sir Edmund Andros, when, on the morning of 18 April 1689, young men ran through the South End shouting that the Northenders had risen in arms while the same news was being cried in reverse through the streets of the North End.[19] The observance of November fifth as "Pope Day" gave seventeenth- and eighteenth-century Bostonians an excuse for boisterous celebrations in gratitude for the foiling of the "gunpowder treason plot." On the eve of the Revolution, North and South Ends would organize rival processions, each with its effigies of the Pope, the Devil and the Pretender. When they met a free-for-all ensued, with broken heads and bloody noses. A North End triumph meant the burning of the Southenders' effigies on Copp's Hill. A southern success led to the burning of the Northenders' Pope, Devil and Pretender on the Common.[20] These regional brawls were by no means confined to one day of the year. Boys were always ready to do battle with anyone from the other end of town. Dr. Edward Reynolds (1793–1881) — great-great-grandson of Josiah Franklin's landlord in Milk Street — observed that in 1800 the "old feud between the Southenders and Northenders, as old as the town itself . . . was the occasion of a regular battle every Thursday and Saturday afternoon" which was "not unfrequently the occasion of very serious injury to wind and limb." [21]

Looking across the Mill Pond to Barton's Point in 1722 there was little to see beyond Lee's shipyard, a copper works, three rope-walks, a windmill and a handful of houses, for the region between the northern slope of the Trimountain and the banks of the Charles River was an inaccessible, sparsely settled quarter.

Fig. 18. The Bulfinch house in Bowdoin Square

Returning from the North End by way of Middle and Hanover Streets one passes, at the corner of Union and Hanover, the Blue Ball. This was the tradesman's sign that Josiah Franklin, tallow chandler, had removed to that location in 1712 when the rented house in Milk Street that had been the birthplace of his son Benjamin was sold.[22] A few doors down Union Street stands the low studded, three-story brick house where the Capen family sell dry goods. This building, with a gambrel roof with the short upper slope so characteristic of eighteenth-century Boston architecture, survives today as the Union Oyster House.[23]

Continuing up Hanover Street, one passes near Brattle Street, where a new and liberal "manifesto church" had been established in 1699, near the site of the first Quaker meeting. At the head of Hanover Street, Sudbury Street curves off to the right toward the Mill Pond. Cambridge Street, leading out of Sudbury in the direction of Barton's Point and what came to be known as the West End, was built up only in its first blocks, for in the region of the future Bowdoin Square a bowling green appears on Bonner's first map. The region was soon to develop into one of spacious houses and gardens. Dr. Thomas Bulfinch, who returned to Boston in 1722 from studying medicine in Paris, married in 1724 a daughter of John Colman. This merchant gave Bulfinch and his other son-in-law, Peter Chardon, land in the region of Bowdoin Square, where they built themselves houses. Something of the appearance of Dr. Bulfinch's three-story wooden house (Fig. 18), which was the birthplace in 1763 of his architect grandson Charles, is known through a copy of a painting and a description by his granddaughter, Mrs. Joseph Lyman.[24]

Turning left at the head of Hanover Street one has a choice of directions, for a single line of houses occupies the centre of the inelegant area long known as Scollay Square. To the east of these buildings, Queen Street takes one (along the line of the present Court Street) back to the Town House. To the west, Treamount Street skirts the base of Cotton Hill, leading to the Common. Let us choose Queen Street and return to the Town House in order to inspect the South End, before going to the completely rural Common and Trimountain.

The South End has but one main thoroughfare, the road to the Neck, now our familiar Washington Street. It leaves the Town House under the guise of Cornhill; at School Street it turns into Marlborough Street; at Summer Street its name changes to Newbury Street, and finally, at Beach Street, it becomes Orange Street, the designation under which it continues to the gate at the Neck.

The buildings along Cornhill, in consequence of the 1711 fire, are recent. At the corner of School Street, so named from the presence of the South Grammar School (on the site of the former City Hall), is a new two-story red brick house (Fig. 19) with a double pitch roof, built soon after the fire by Thomas Crease, an apothecary, on the site of land owned by Anne Hutchinson's husband William in the earliest days of the town. Occupied as a dwelling house for more than a hundred years, it acquired literary connotations during the nineteenth century as the Old Corner Book Store, and as the place of business of the publishers Ticknor and Fields.[25] It still survives as a unique example of early eighteenth-century domestic architecture in this area, restored by Historic Boston Incorporated, which rescued it from demolition in 1960.

Continuing, past School Street, into Marlborough Street, it is only a few steps to the corner of Milk Street, where in 1669 the Third Church — or Old South — built its meetinghouse. The order of the establishment of the churches is an indication of the relative growth of and density of population in the various parts of the Boston peninsula. The First Church (1630) is in the center; the Second Church (1650) is in the North End; and the Third Church (1669) is in the South End. Nearly opposite the Old South is the Province House (Fig. 12), for in spite of the elegance of Clark's Square the North End had no monopoly upon the great houses of the period.

Between King Street and Milk Street the area leading to Town Cove is as thickly settled as the North End. Beyond Milk Street, the South End is a relatively open area of fields, pastures, gardens and ropewalks. Milk Street leads east to the waterfront and the unsettled region of Fort Hill, below whose eastern slope stands the South Battery (Fig. 14). The shore line is turned to good

ANTIQUE BUILDING, CORNER OF SCHOOL AND WASHINGTON STREETS, BOSTON.

Fig. 19. The Old Corner Book Store

purpose, for between the South Battery and Wind Mill Point Bonner indicates seven wharves, as well as Edes's shipyard. Past Wind Mill Point, Hill's Wharf projects into the South Cove. Behind the wharves is ample space even for ropewalks, which are cumbersome things at best. A maritime community needs cordage; indeed John Harrison, a ropemaker, was plying his trade in the South End at the foot of Summer Street as early as 1642.[26] Bonner's map shows three ropewalks west of Fort Hill, in the area that would now be between Congress and Pearl Streets, with others on the unsettled land behind the Trimountain.

From the ropewalks, Cow Lane (now High Street) leads southwest into Summer Street a little below Church Green, where at the junction of Blind Lane (now part of Bedford Street) a New South meeting house [27] had been built in 1716. Summer Street, between Church Green and Marlborough Street, long remained a pleasant and uncrowded place to live. The area now occupied by the newest building of Jordan Marsh, for example, was recorded in the Book of Possessions of the 1640's as the garden of Gamaliel Waite, which was noted for the superior excellence of its fruits. Leonard Vassall, who bought the property in 1727, appears to have built the spacious gambrel-roofed wooden house (Fig. 20) that, after passing out of his family, was occupied in turn by Thomas Hubbard, Treasurer of Harvard College,[28] by the stylish Tory Frederick W. Geyer, and (after 1803) by the merchant Samuel Pickering Gardner upon his permanent migration from Salem to Boston.[29] As this house survived until 1854, when Samuel Pickering Gardner's son George built on the site a block long occupied by C. F. Hovey and Company, its appearance was recorded both in photographs and in a detailed description by Thomas C. Amory.[30] A carriage gate in a ten-foot-high fence, extending seventy feet along Summer Street, led into a paved courtyard. The house, which stood endwise to the street, had a main front of more than one hundred feet on the court, with nine windows and two doors on the first floor and eleven windows above. A drawing room occupied the Summer Street end of the house; then came the main staircase; beyond it a thirty-foot family

parlor, a secondary stair hall and two kitchens. Beyond the courtyard, which was of fifty by one hundred feet, came stables, sheds
and fruit rooms in which the pears from the extensive garden
were put to ripen. In addition to four large square beds edged
with box, to roses, syringa, honeysuckle and trellises of grapes, the
garden contained no less than forty-four fruit trees.

This South End of Boston was through the eighteenth century,
and even into the nineteenth, an area of fields, gardens and large
houses. Pond Street (now Bedford), the next beyond Summer,
derived its name from a pond which served as the town watering
place for cattle. Directly opposite the pond, Bonner's map shows
a sizable area with trees, designated as "Coal's Garden."

Fig. 20. The Vassall-Gardner house in Summer Street

While Marlborough and Newbury Streets are continuously built up, as befits the main highway, when their extension becomes Orange Street there are hardly more than two dozen houses in the entire remaining length. Thus, as one would only look across open fields to the Back Bay in the west, and to the harbor in the east, there is little to be gained by following Orange Street to the Neck. Instead we will turn west from Newbury Street into Frog Lane (now Boylston Street), which leads to the Common, with the unspoiled summits of the Trimountain towering beyond it.

The forty-five acres of the Common, purchased by the town from the Reverend William Blaxton in 1634, were by 1722 a versatile community resource useful for pasturing cattle, training military companies, and hanging unwelcome Quakers, as well as for the promenades described by John Josselyn. Here was open country running down to the waters of the Back Bay, or, as Bonner named them, the "Roxbury Flatts." At the northeastern end of the Common, along the present Park Street, are the Alms House and Bridewell. Beyond them lies the third, or South, Burying Ground, which had been set apart from the Common in 1660.

At the corner of Treamount and School Streets stood the wooden King's Chapel, the first Anglican church in Boston, built in the autumn of 1688 on a corner of the town burying ground — seemingly appropriated for the purpose by Governor Andros,[31] in what N. I. Bowditch described as "a barefaced *squat*." [32] Opposite King's Chapel on the hillside, set well back from the street, was the large house (Fig. 21) of Peter Faneuil, a French Huguenot merchant from La Rochelle who was settled in Boston by 1691. This handsome property, with gardens extending behind it up the hill, was inherited in 1738 by Andrew's nephew Peter Faneuil.[33]

Beacon Street, which ran up the hill beyond the Faneuil property, led to the Beacon past a handful of country houses and gardens. The most remarkable of these, both as to its considerable size and fine view, was the three-story house (Fig. 22) built in 1722 by Edward Bromfield, behind which successive terraces, filled with flowers and fruit trees, led to a summer house which commanded a panoramic view of the harbor.[34]

Fig. 21. The Faneuil house in Tremont Street

Fig. 22. The Bromfield house in Beacon Street

Retracing our steps to King's Chapel, we follow northeast on Treamount Street, skirting the base of Cotton Hill, and turn east into Queen Street to return to the Town House and the straight course back to the Long Wharf.

Thus we have completed a casual circuit of the town that Captain Bonner described in 1722, on the first issue of his map, as having 42 streets, 36 lanes, 22 alleys, and "Houses near 3000, 1000 Brick, rest Timber." The pattern of growth over the first ninety-two years is clear enough. Substituting the modern place names, the heart is the intersection of Washington and State Streets, at the First Church and the Town House, with the Town Dock hard by; for Washington Street affords the only approach to the town by land, and State Street the principal access from the sea. The churchyard adjoining King's Chapel is the oldest burying ground in the town. In 1650 a second church is established in North Square, and from 1660 the North End has its own burying ground on Copp's Hill. The third church, of 1669, is the Old South at Washington and Milk, while the Granary Burying Ground of 1660 serves the central area and South End. By 1722 the North End has three Congregational meeting houses and one Baptist; the South End two Congregational, and the central area two Congregational, one Quaker and one French Protestant meeting house, as well as the Church of England King's Chapel.

If one had no other documents on colonial Boston, the crowded shore line of Bonner's map alone would testify to the maritime nature of the place, for a town of twelve thousand inhabitants with upwards of forty wharves, more than a dozen shipyards and six ropewalks, could only be a thriving seaport. It was, of course, not only that but the largest town in British North America — a place that it continued to hold until the middle of the eighteenth century, when it fell behind the faster growing ports of Philadelphia and New York. Professor Bridenbaugh's figures in *Cities in Revolt*[35] give Boston 16,382 inhabitants, Philadelphia 13,000 and New York 11,000 in 1743. In 1760 all positions are changed, for Philadelphia had moved into first place with a population of 23,750, New York had advanced to second with 18,000, while

Boston had fallen to third, with 15,631 inhabitants — a decline of 751 over the figure of seventeen years earlier. It was, of course, this sudden slackening of growth in the mid-century that permitted Boston to remain within the confining original limits of the Shawmut peninsula until the early 1800's. Professor Bridenbaugh estimates the population of Boston as 7,000 in 1690, 6,700 in 1700, 9,000 in 1710, 12,000 in 1720, 13,000 in 1730, 16,382 in 1743, 15,631 in 1760 and 16,000 in 1775. Thus with an increase of only one third between the 1722 date of the Bonner map and the outbreak of the Revolution, there was little likelihood of the town bursting its seams. Nevertheless, the various issues of Bonner's map between 1722 and 1769 (Fig. 25) permit us to follow the changes that did occur. William Price was, of course, simply tinkering with Bonner's plate so far as the techniques of copper engraving permitted erasures and new insertions, but the changes that he made, within these restricted limits, indicate the matters that to the eighteenth-century Bostonian were particularly worthy of note.

The four new buildings for which references are added on the 1733 issue of the Bonner map are the Town Granary, "Christ Church Founded 1723," "Irish Meeting House 1731" and "Hollis Street Meeting 1731." The granary in question had been built on the Common in 1729 near the site of the present subterranean public toilets; in 1737 it was moved to the site of Park Street Church and so gave its name to the adjacent burying ground.[36]

The building of Christ Church, Salem Street — the second Anglican parish in Boston — indicates the spreading of the once detested Church of England to the point where the North End required its own accommodations. This brick building of 1723 is now the oldest surviving church in Boston. Its preservation as a historic and architectural monument, through decades when changes in the population of the North End deprived it of a natural congregation as completely as if it were a Wren building in the City of London, is one of the many good things that Boston owes to William Lawrence and to his successors as Bishop of Massachusetts and Vicar of Christ Church. The fortunate circumstance of Paul Revere having hung signal lanterns in its steeple, and of H. W. Longfellow having commemorated that event in verse, have made Christ Church known to millions of Americans. They have also tagged it with the nickname "Old North Church," which, considering the number of "North Churches" there have been in Boston, leads only to confusion.[37]

The "Irish Meeting House" noted on the 1733 map was a barn in Long Lane in the South End, converted to religious uses by a group of North of Ireland Presbyterians. By 1744 they built a new meeting house which became known as the Federal Street Church, but after the death of their pastor John Moorhead — who had served them for forty-four years — their society no longer flourished. In 1780 the church became Congregational and later Unitarian. This was from 1803 to 1842 the church of William Ellery Channing.[38]

Unlike Christ Church and the Federal Street Church, which were built in normally populated areas, the Hollis Street Church represented the opening up of a new locality. Orange Street, from the fortification on the Neck to Frog Lane, had been very sparsely settled on the 1722 map. The 1733 version shows Castle Street crossing the Neck; Hollis Street running west off Orange and connecting with Frog Lane by means of Clough Street, as well as four new wharves and still houses on the South Cove. Jonathan Belcher, Governor of the Province of the Massachusetts Bay from 1730 to 1741, who had a house in Orange Street near the newly opened Hollis Street,[39] in 1732 gave land in Hollis Street for a new Congregational society. C. K. Shipton undoubtedly appraised Belcher's motives correctly in suggesting that the real estate he owned in the vicinity "would rise in value if more people could be induced to build there by the establishment of a church which would make unnecessary the long Sunday walk into town." [40] The Old South Church, to which Belcher belonged, was amiably disposed toward the venture, several of its members joining the new group. A wooden meeting house was built, and on 20 December 1732 Mather Byles, a grandson of Increase Mather, was ordained as minister of the new Hollis Street Church.[41] This witty poet and humorist, whose barbed quips are still fondly remembered in the twentieth century, was dismissed from his pastorate in 1776, after forty-four years of service, for his unmistakably Tory sentiments.

The most conspicuous changes in the town to be noted in the 1733 map are new streets laid out in the West End on the western slope of the Trimountain and in the region between Cambridge Street and Barton's Point. Cambridge Street is carried west to the Charles River, and then south along the shore to the Common. The land in the angle formed by the turn in Cambridge Street — known in the seventeenth century as Zachariah Phillips's nine-acre pasture [42] — is divided into lots with Southack and May Streets (today known as Phillips and Revere Streets) running east and west below Cambridge Street. Southack, before reaching the shore, turns south and runs (along the line of the present West Cedar Street) to the Common. However this remote development began, its reputation soon slipped to such an extent that the western peak of the Trimountain, on whose slopes it nestled, was dubbed Mount Whoredom.

The 1733 Bonner map shows not only Cambridge and Southack Streets leading from the Common to the undesirable western slopes of Mount Whoredom, but a new street, crossing the Trimountain from the Common to the original portion of Cambridge Street between Mount Whoredom and Beacon Hill. This road, known as George Street, ran north from Beacon Street on the present line of Joy Street, jogged east a bit along what was later to become part of Mount Vernon Street, and turned north, running downhill to Cambridge Street along the present line of Hancock Street.

North of Cambridge Street the pastures of Simon and Samuel Lynde, John Staniford and Charles Chambers were laid out into streets that still bear their names,[43] leading to Leverett Street and other new developments on the way to Barton's Point.

On the 1743 Bonner map one observes a reference to the Lynde Street Meeting House. This new Congregational church — the first in the West End — was built in 1737 on the principle of the Hollis Street Church's foundation, as an inducement to the development of a new residential area. Two other new churches and two new public buildings are noted on this revision. Trinity, the third Anglican parish in Boston, was founded in 1733, built in Summer Street, and first used on 15 August 1735. It stood opposite the Vassall House, and Leonard Vassall was, in fact, treasurer of the building committee, of which William Price, the print seller, was a member. The Bennet Street Meeting House of 1742, in the North End, sprang solely from contention, for it was built by seceders from the Second Church who withdrew when the Reverend Samuel Mather was dismissed from the pulpit that his father and grandfather had filled with greater distinction.[44] C. K. Shipton, after quoting some of this unfortunate man's prose, observed: "With this as a sample one is inclined to believe Robert Treat Paine's statement that his dog ran away after hearing Mather preach." [45]

The Workhouse, built in 1738 between the Granary Burying Ground and the Common, for the accommodation at oakum picking of idle persons, vagabonds and tramps, was a two-story brick building one hundred and twenty-five feet long.[46] The final addition made by William Price to the plate of Bonner's map in the 1743 version concerns a very recent gift to the town that merited not just inclusion but words of high praise; thus, symbol T represents "Faneuil Hall & Market house, a ha[n]dsom large brick building Worthy of the Generous Founder Peter Faneuil Esq: who in the Year 1742 Gave it to the Town for the use of a Market." Price's gratitude to the French Huguenot benefactor of the town was so strong that in the same year he published a new issue of Burgis's southeast view of Boston, adding the market and other recent buildings to the plate as best he could and substituting, by erasure, a dedication to Peter Faneuil for the original one to Governor Samuel Shute.

The new market, built near the Town Dock at Faneuil's "own cost and charge," was a two-story brick structure, one hundred feet long and forty feet wide, designed by the painter John Smibert. On the ground floor was the market and above, as in many English buildings, rooms for town offices and a sizable hall, to which the town meeting of 13 September 1742, on motion of Thomas

Fig. 23. Faneuil Hall in 1789

Hutchinson, gave the name of the donor.[47] A fire of 13 January 1761 consumed all but the brick exterior walls of the original hall, but it was soon rebuilt in the form known to us through an engraving in the March 1789 issue of the *Massachusetts Magazine* (Fig. 23).[48] In 1805, when with the growth of Boston more space became necessary both for victuals and town meetings, Charles Bulfinch enlarged Faneuil Hall to its present form by doubling the width of the building and adding a third story (Fig. 24). Smibert's south and east walls were retained; the Tuscan and Doric pilasters of the first and second stories were continued in the new work, and an Ionic order provided for the new third story. Thus a two-story building, nine bays long and three wide, was enlarged to a height of three stories and width of seven bays without change in length.[49] Through these rebuildings and the vicissitudes of two and a quarter centuries, the ground floor of Faneuil Hall has continued to serve its donor's original design, to the delight of those who enjoy honest beef and historical continuity and to the puzzled confusion of certain tourists whose historical experience has been confined to glittering restorations elsewhere, and whose shopping has been limited to the cellophane-wrapped fragments of the modern supermarket. A recent proposal that the markets be removed and the hall prettied up for the tourist trade has aroused vociferous opposition.[50] *The Pilot,* in a witty editorial, characterizes the suggestion — "brought in by gypsies we must imagine" — as "nonsense," and observes that "old things, full of memory, should not be sterilized, polished and wrapped as if to make of the city some precious antiseptic museum." [51] Francis W. Hatch has sprung to pen with a verse — published in *The Boston Globe* [52] and widely distributed, in the Revolutionary tradition, as a handbill, which describes the delights of buying bacon, broiler, tripe and cheese in Faneuil Hall and concludes with the ringing stanzas:

VIEW OF THE OLD BUILDING AT THE CORNER OF ANN ST.
BOSTON, MASS.

Fig. 24. The Old Feather Store, Quincy Market, and Faneuil Hall

Bestir ye!
Peter Faneuil,
Old Frenchman in your grave,
'Twas not for tourist folderol
Your deed of trust you gave.

You planned and gave
A Market Hall
Designed for honest trade,
With quarters up above, where men
Could call a spade a spade.

Here orators
In ages past
Have mounted their attack
Undaunted by proximity
Of sausage on the rack.

Here men have shouted,
Age on age,
With fervor for their cause,
And, going home, bought nourishment
To steel a freeman's jaws.

Let tourists come,
Let tourists go
And carry home belief
That Boston Patriots are backed
By *honest Yankee beef*!

The 1769 revision of Bonner's map (Fig. 25) shows few
changes in the streets beyond the addition of Temple and Mid-
dlecot (now Bowdoin) Streets running from Cambridge Street up
the back of Beacon Hill. Clark's Wharf in the North End has now
assumed the name of Hancock's, and a reference to "Esqr. Hancock
Seat" is added on Beacon Hill for the house built facing the Common by Thomas Hancock about 1737 and later occupied by his
nephew John Hancock.

During the period covered by the revisions of the Bonner map
two religious societies built on their original sites new churches

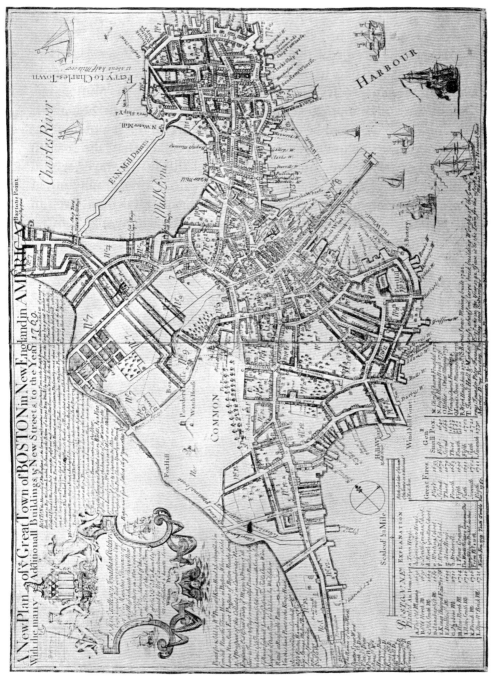

Fig. 25. The Bonner map of 1769

that still stand. The Old South Church in 1729 replaced its wooden building of 1669 with the present Old South Meeting House. The present King's Chapel, designed by Peter Harrison, was begun in 1750 upon the site of the original church of 1688.

The agitated years immediately preceding the Revolution saw political rather than topographical or architectural developments in Boston. There had been no marked change in the population for thirty years. The town was now the third, rather than the first, in size in British North America. Because of this it still stayed within the bounds of the Shawmut peninsula with a comfortable air of space, not only on the Common and the Trimountain, but even in the streets of the South End. It still, after a century and a third, remained isolated from the mainland.

CHAPTER III

The Boston of Bulfinch

IN THE DECADE following the Revolution, Boston remained a pleasant, uncrowded seaport. Although its ships were ranging far afield in new trades — to the Northwest Coast, to China and to Russia — these expanded commercial enterprises hardly affected the appearance of the town. Thomas Pemberton, whose *Topographical and Historical Description of Boston* [1] of 1794, is the first systematic account to have been published, observed that "the town is capable of great increase, as many large spaces of land still remain vacant." [2] He amplified this sense of spaciousness when he wrote: [3]

The dwelling houses in Boston have an advantage above most of the large towns on the continent with respect to garden spots. Few houses are without them, in which vegetables and flowers are raised, in some fruit trees are planted; and what is still more intrinsically good and valuable, the inhabitant is supplied with pure wholesome water from a well in his own yard.

The comfortable air of Boston came, of course, from the circumstance that, while its merchants were making respectable fortunes overseas, the population had increased only very slightly during a half century. The 1790 figure of 18,038 is an extremely modest advance over the 16,382 inhabitants of 1743. Boston continued to be a town in which the artisans and craftsmen were meeting a purely local demand; where shipyards, ropewalks and duck manufactories were building and outfitting local ships, and where carpenters, masons, tailors and butchers were engaged in housing, clothing and feeding their neighbors who owned and manned those ships.[4] Pemberton proudly observed that

Boston, although denominated a commercial town, has a variety of manufactures carried on within its limits; among which are the following: — Soap, candles, rum, loaf sugar, cordage, duck, twine and linen, cards, fish-hooks, combs, stained paper, stone ware, chocolate, glass, &c.

One notes, however, that most of these products are either for or from the sea. Ropewalks had been a familiar feature of the remoter parts of the town almost from the beginning, but in 1789 a duck manufacture for the production of sail cloth was established, with the assistance of the General Court, near the Common in Frog Lane.[5] Distilleries were conspicuously noted in connection with wharves on the various issues of Bonner's map. Pemberton found, however, that the demand for New England rum for export had fallen off; that in 1794 only eighteen out of the twenty-seven distill-houses were at work, and most at half capacity.

The essential homogeneity of late eighteenth-century Boston is shown by the nature of the procession organized in honor of General Washington's visit in October 1789.[6] In the order of march town officials were followed by magistrates, consuls, French naval officers, clergy, physicians, lawyers, merchants and traders, the Marine Society, masters of vessels, revenue officers and strangers. Then came forty-six groups of artisans and tradesmen, arranged alphabetically — bakers, blacksmiths, block-makers, boat-builders, cabinet and chair makers, and so on — followed at the end by seamen.

The location of Boston on a peninsula with but one path of access overland gave the colonial town something of the character of a "tight little island." The first change in this pattern came with the completion of the Charles River Bridge (Fig. 26) in 1786.[7] As early as 27 April 1720 a town meeting had considered a proposal "to promote the building of a Bridge across the Charles River at the place where the Ferry hath been usually kept," [8] but nothing materialized until 1785, when an act passed on 9 March incorporated John Hancock, Thomas Russell and eighty-two others to build a toll bridge there as a private enterprise. It was at the time considered "the greatest that had ever been projected in America," [9] for its total length was 1,503 feet and its cost £15,000. Supported upon 75 piers of oak timber, with a thirty-foot draw near the center, the bridge was forty-two feet wide, with six-foot railed passages for pedestrians on each side and "forty elegant lamps" for night illumination. The last pier was ready to be put down on 31 May 1786, and on 17 June, the eleventh anniversary of the battle, twenty thousand spectators — all of Boston and then some — assembled for the dedication. A procession, consisting — according to Snow — of "almost every respectable character in publick and private life," marched across the bridge, to the pealing of Christ Church bells and the firing of thirteen cannon from Copp's Hill, to Breed's Hill. Here, after further cannon salutes, 800 gentlemen took their seats at a great horseshoe table to spend the day in what is described as "sober festivity." The Charles

A View of the Bridge over Charles River. MASSACHUSETTS.

Fig. 26. The Charles River Bridge

River Bridge, and three others that were to follow it during the next quarter century, radically changed the pattern of life in Boston, for regions that had been remote cul-de-sacs suddenly developed into busy thoroughfares to the surrounding world.

Although Boston was growing but slowly, the frequency of devastating fires kept the building trades busy and changed the face of the town with some regularity. Pemberton recorded fifteen fires between 1702 and 1794 as worthy of note;[10] indeed the destruction by fire became so frequent that finally, in 1803, the town meeting requested the General Court to require by law that all buildings in Boston exceeding ten feet in height be built of stone or brick and be covered with slate, tile, or other noncombustible material. The worst disaster after the close of the Revolution occurred on 24 April 1787 when, from a fire beginning in a malt house on Beach Street, more than one hundred buildings in the area leading toward the Neck were destroyed. Sixty dwellings and the Hollis Street Meeting House were lost in this conflagration.

At the time of the fire, Charles Bulfinch, of the Harvard class of 1781, son of Dr. Thomas Bulfinch, Jr., of Bowdoin Square in the West End, had recently returned from an eighteen-month grand tour. Between graduation and his continental travels, the twenty-four-year-old Bulfinch had been in Joseph Barrell's counting-room where, with the unsettled state of business in the early eighties, he was — in his own words — "at leisure to cultivate a taste for Architecture."[11] In Paris he had come under Thomas Jefferson's wing; at Bordeaux and Nîmes he had seen buildings that were a far cry from the Boston of his youth. On returning home, this young man of taste and property was, as he wrote in an autobiographical sketch, "warmly received by friends, and passed a season of leisure, pursuing no business but giving gratuitous advice in architecture, and looking forward to an establishment in life."[12] The "gratuitous advice" was soon turned to good purpose, for a new Hollis Street Church was built in 1788 from Charles Bulfinch's plans,[13] a square building with a domed interior and a façade with twin cupolas flanking a Tuscan portico, which was Bulfinch's first executed design. No one would claim that it was his happiest, but it introduced an echo of Wren into Boston. It also marked the beginning of a career that, during the next three decades, was to leave a lasting mark upon the buildings and topography of Boston.

While Bulfinch was still abroad, he had heard news of the Charles River Bridge, for he wrote his father from London on 12 December 1786: [14]

I have seen Capt. Cushing, who informs me the Bridge is in great forwardness. I hope it will stand till I return, as I should like much to see it, but I am not sure whether I would venture to pass over it.

It not only stood, but proved so successful that a corporation was formed in the spring of 1792 for building a second toll bridge across the Charles from the west end of Cambridge Street to the opposite shore in Cambridge.[15] This West Boston Bridge was an even greater undertaking, for it was 3,483 feet long, stood on 180 piers and cost about £23,000. From its opening on 23 November

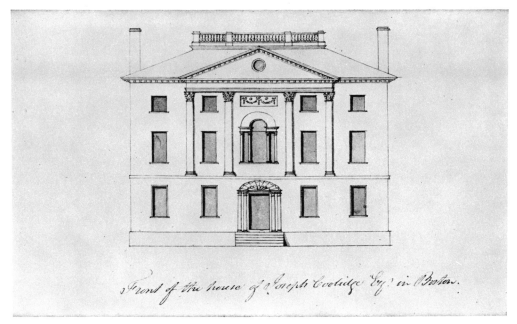

Fig. 27. The Joseph Coolidge house near Bowdoin Square

1793 the West End rapidly developed, for Bowdoin Square and Cambridge Street became part of the most direct road to Cambridge and Harvard College. In 1792 Charles Bulfinch had built, for his kinsman Joseph Coolidge (1747–1829),[16] a three-story brick house (Fig. 27), sixty feet square, with an ell, that stood in large gardens near Bowdoin Square between Temple and Bowdoin Streets.[17] The building of this "noble mansion," as Bulfinch described it,[18] indicated the movement of prosperous merchants to the West End, for Joseph Coolidge had previously lived in the center of town, at 20 Cornhill.[19]

Bulfinch worked extensively in this increasingly handsome West End region of his birth. In 1796 he built for Harrison Gray Otis, at the corner of Cambridge and Lynde Streets, the three-story brick house that is today the headquarters of the Society for the Preservation of New England Antiquities.[20] In 1810 he built a brick market for Samuel Parkman, at the corner of Cambridge and Green Streets, to accommodate the residents of the West End,[21] and in 1815 built for Parkman the fine pair of double houses of Chelmsford granite that long stood at the end of Bowdoin Square between Cambridge and Green Streets.[22]

Bulfinch's most original contribution to the new aspect of Federalist Boston lay not in his West End mansions, but in the development of Franklin Street where, with the Tontine Crescent (Fig. 28) and related buildings, he introduced a wholly unfamiliar aspect of urban elegance to the town. Miss Eliza Susan Morton (later Mrs. Josiah Quincy), visiting Boston for the first time in 1795, noted "the ranges of wooden houses, all situated with one end toward the street," and considered that "at that time, Boston, compared with New York, was a small town." She was struck by the lack of brick sidewalks, save in Cornhill near the Old South, and remarked: [23]

The streets were paved with pebbles; and, except when driven on one side by carts and carriages, everyone walked in the middle of the street, where the pavement was the smoothest.

With such surroundings Bulfinch's proposal of 1793 for a crescent of sixteen connected brick houses, of an elegance reminiscent of the Adam brothers in London, or the dignified symmetries of Bath, was in sharp contrast. The region chosen for this spectacular innovation was an unpromising bit of the South End between Milk and Summer Streets that consisted in part of a quagmire that Joseph Barrell — Bulfinch's former employer, who had a house on Summer Street — had partially drained and converted into a fish pond in his garden.[24] The financing was to follow the Tontine scheme, then popular in Europe, by which a capital stock was, at the end of a stated period, to be divided among surviving subscribers. The graceful curve and unusual width of Franklin Street today below Hawley Street are reflections of the ground plan of this handsome venture. On the south side, sixteen three-story houses, known as Tontine Crescent, extended in a graceful curve 480 feet long. In the center of the block an arch which led through toward Summer Street gave origin and name to Arch

Fig. 28. The Tontine Crescent in Franklin Street

Street. Space in the rooms above the arch was generously offered to the Massachusetts Historical Society, which had been founded in 1791 and was at the time lodged in the northwest corner of the attic of Faneuil Hall. The Society gladly accepted these agreeable quarters and occupied them for close to forty years, while the new Boston Library Society, to whom lower rooms in the arch were similarly given, remained there until the demolition of the building in 1858.[25] On the north side, a straight line of eight houses, in four blocks, were designated as Franklin Place. Between the two lines of houses was a fenced semi-oval grass plot 300 feet long, with trees, in the center of which Bulfinch placed, as a memorial to Franklin, a large urn that he had brought home from his grand tour.

The plan was ambitious. The General Court, disapproving of the smell of Tontine, refused incorporation. Nevertheless Bulfinch, his brother-in-law Charles Vaughan and William Scollay went ahead. Foundations were begun on the south side in August 1793, and the north side seems to have been completed in 1795. Due to bad times, subscriptions came too slowly to meet bills. Although the project was completed, Bulfinch went bankrupt in 1796 and, from a comfortable situation as a gentleman concerned with architecture, turned to a laborious life of architectural practice and public service. He had been elected a Selectman of Boston in 1791 and had been re-elected four times, resigning in 1795 because of pressure of business.[26] In 1799, three years after his bankruptcy, Bulfinch was re-elected Selectman, and served continuously as Chairman of the Board for nineteen years.[27] To permit him to hold this unpaid office he was, on 10 May 1799, appointed Superintendent of Police at an annual salary of six hundred dollars.[28] Although Bulfinch's salary was increased by four hundred dollars in 1810,[29] this was small recompense for the services he rendered the town. That it was utterly inadequate to permit him to meet his obligations is suggested by the fact that, although Chairman of the Selectmen and Superintendent of Police at the time, he spent the month of July 1811 in jail for debt.[30] Such were the unfortunate consequences of his faith in the Tontine Crescent and Franklin Place. Although Charles Bulfinch may have been a poor business man, he was as imaginative an architect as he was a devoted public servant. Boston owes him a unique debt for his skill in transforming an eighteenth-century town into a nineteenth-century city.

While Bulfinch was at work on Franklin Place, one of Boston's periodic fires opened the way for a complete change in an adjoining part of the South End. When the ropewalks between Pearl and Atkinson Streets burned on 30 July 1794, the townspeople (in the words of Dr. Shurtleff [31]) "opened their hearts, though they closed their senses" by granting the marshy flats at the foot of the Common for the erection of buildings to replace those destroyed.[32] This gift, which consisted of part of the area that is today the Public Garden (Fig. 29), was made upon condition that the grantees erect a sea wall to protect the land — thus beginning the encroachment upon the Back Bay — and that no ropewalks be again built on the old sites. Spontaneous emotional generosity in town meeting is dangerous, for it often — as in this case — secures a temporary advantage at the expense of the future. In 1794 the flats at the foot of the Common seemed a remote spot, admirably adapted to ropewalks. Thirty years later, when Boston was beginning to grow toward the west, it cost the townspeople fifty-five thousand dollars to recover the land so cheerfully voted away in 1794. However, the immediate result of the town's generosity was to open for residential use a large tract of land extending from the western slope of Fort Hill toward Bulfinch's new development. Thus Pearl Street became almost over night an area of handsome houses. Josiah Quincy, future Mayor of Boston and President of Harvard College, moved there with his widowed mother, to a large house on the corner of High Street with honeysuckle twined round the porch and damask rose bushes below the windows, set in grounds that sloped uphill toward Oliver Street. Across High Street Jeffrey Richardson, owner of one of the destroyed ropewalks, built himself after the fire a square, three-story house (Fig. 30) that was soon overshadowed, in 1800, by Jonathan Harris's more ambitious house on the opposite corner

Fig. 29. Detail from the J. G. Hales map of 1814 (overleaf)

which long rejoiced in the designation of "Harris's Folly." The China trade merchants James and Thomas Handasyd Perkins were among others who settled in Pearl Street, for the region was singularly pleasant and open. "From the Mall on Fort Hill, there was," as Miss Eliza Susan Morton pointed out, "an uninterrupted view of the town and harbor." [33]

Our present Congress Street is a combination of the earlier Atkinson and Dalton Streets. Although Atkinson Street, like its neighbor, Pearl, was rebuilt after the burning of the ropewalks, a variety of earlier buildings still survived in Dalton Street, as one sees from Lawrence Park's reconstruction drawings of the west side

Fig. 30. Houses in Pearl Street

of that street between Milk and State Streets in 1808 (Figs. 31–33).[34] Julien's restaurant (Fig. 10) still flourished in its seventeenth-century quarters at the corner of Milk Street, on part of the site now occupied by the Post Office. At the Water Street end of the block stood the house built in 1758 by Captain Peter Dalton.[35] Beyond Water came Joy's Buildings, where early in 1807 the Anthology Society opened the reading room that soon was to develop into the Boston Athenæum. The modest Quaker Meeting House on the corner of Salter's Court (now Congress Square) was a startling contrast to the towering Exchange Coffee House, a seven-story wonder completed in 1808 at the cost of half a million dollars,[36] only to burn ten years later. The scale of the building suggests the rapidity of the change that was occurring in Boston during the early years of the Republic.

The state government had already outgrown the old Town House, which had through the eighteenth century accommodated both town and provincial governments, with courts thrown in. As early as 1787, a few months after his return from Europe, Charles Bulfinch had submitted a plan for a new State House.[37] In January 1793, a Boston town meeting approved a report of William Tudor's committee that the Commonwealth grant the town the old State House and the Province House in return for the town providing a new State House.[38] Thus on 13 May 1795, Tudor reported that he and a committee authorized the preceding February had paid John Hancock's heirs four thousand pounds for the late governor's pasture on the slope of Beacon Hill above the Common as a site for the new building.[39] Bulfinch was chosen architect. The cornerstone was laid on the following Fourth of July, and 11 January 1798 the State House (Fig. 37) was occupied for the first time.[40]

Moving the seat of government into the country in this manner brought many changes in its wake. Although the Common had been somewhat tidied up in 1784, with the planting of a new line of trees along the Tremont Street mall,[41] grazing cattle and loads of hay en route to the Hay Scales gave a bucolic air to the region. Drawings of Tremont Street in 1800, made in 1864 from the recollections of Dr. Solomon Davis Townsend,[42] suggest a rural New England village, as do two charming contemporary watercolors in the Boston Public Library.[43] The first of these, painted in 1798, looking south from the corner of Tremont and West Streets, shows the Hay Scales, Hatch's Tavern with Frothingham's carriage-maker's shop in the rear, and the rustic Haymarket Theatre. The second, thought to have been painted by a daughter of General Henry Knox, around 1800, looks north from a similar point past James Swan's garden wall, with King's Chapel in the distance. Moreover Park Street is still given over to Granary, Almshouse, Workhouse and other municipal odds and ends more suitable for the outskirts of town than for the approach to the seat of government. Within fifteen years the whole scene was to change radically, for by a series of building campaigns in which Bulfinch played a major role, first Beacon Hill, then Park Street and finally Tremont Street caught up with the State House in elegance.

The most dramatic change began in 1795 when the Mount Vernon Proprietors bought the property of John Singleton Copley, which comprised the territory bounded today by Beacon Street, Walnut Street, Mount Vernon Street to Louisburg Square, thence by Louisburg Square to Pinckney Street, down Pinckney to the water and along the shoreline to Beacon Street. Copley had lived, until 1774 when he went to England, never to return, in a house on the site of the Somerset Club. The greater part of his land was hilly upland pasture, not particularly valuable until the building of the State House. Harrison Gray Otis, a member of the town committee that had purchased Hancock's pasture, saw the possibilities of developing Copley's adjacent lands. Forming a syndicate with Jonathan Mason and others, Otis induced Gardiner Greene, who had acted as Copley's agent during his twenty years' absence, to agree to sell Copley's entire property at the rate of a thousand dollars an acre. By the time the deed was sent to England for execution Copley had gotten wind of the impending changes on the hill and attempted to disavow the transaction, sending his son, who was afterwards Lord Lyndhurst, to Boston

WEST SIDE OF CONGRESS (OR DALTON) STREET, FROM MILK STREET TO WATER STREET, 1808

Site of the present United States Post Office and Sub Treasury.   The Old South Church is in the Distance

| Milk
Street | Citizen Julien's
Restorator or
Restaurant | Roof of Old South Parsonage
House owned by
R. D. Tucker | Stable | The Dalton Mansion | Water
Street |

Fig. 31

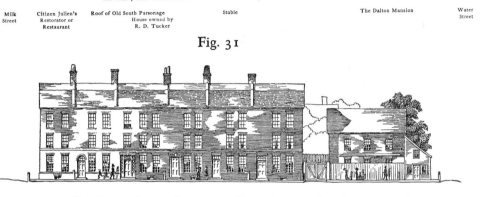

WEST SIDE OF CONGRESS STREET, FROM WATER STREET TO SALTER'S COURT, 1808

| Water Street | Joy's Buildings, where during the early part of 1807
the Anthology Society had its Reading Room.
Site of the National Shawmut Bank Building | Quaker Meeting House.
Site of the Monks Building,
Nos. 35 and 33 Congress Street | Salter's Court,
now
Congress Square |

Fig. 32

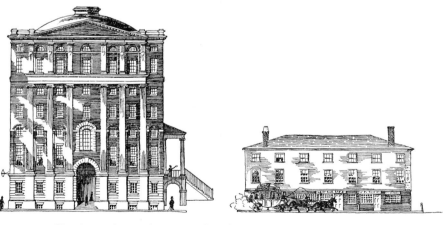

WEST SIDE OF CONGRESS STREET, FROM SALTER'S COURT TO STATE STREET, 1808

| Salter's Court,
formerly Rea's Court,
now Congress Square | The Exchange Coffee House, burned
Nov. 3, 1818. Site of Nos. 19, 15,
and 13 Congress Street | Half Square Court,
now Congress Square | The Rogers Buildings.
Site of the Worthington Building | State
Street |

Drawn by Lawrence Park from studies by C. K. Bolton and Alexander Corbett, 1910

Fig. 33

to break the agent's commitments. Alas for Copley, as S. E. Morison observed, "the future Lord Chancellor of England found that young Mr. Otis had taken care of all the technicalities. The contract was binding, and Copley was forced to convey the property to Otis *et al* for the stipulated sum of $18,450." [44]

This venture of the Mount Vernon Proprietors was the largest land transaction ever to have been undertaken in Boston at that time, for it involved a sudden change in the character of an entire region. The population was beginning to increase notably, for the first time in half a century, and new maritime trades were creating new fortunes. Hence there was room for a new and handsome residential area in spite of the recent developments in Pearl Street. The Mount Vernon Proprietors originally thought in terms of free-standing houses, with ample room for gardens and stables, as was the practice in the South and West Ends. The separate plans made by Bulfinch and by their surveyor, Mather Withington, both called for large lots, ranging from 66 by 160 feet to 100 by 200 feet.[45] Withington proposed the laying out of Walnut, Chestnut, Mount Vernon and Pinckney Streets in substantially their present form. Bulfinch envisioned a more dramatic scheme that converted the ridge-like crest of Mount Vernon into a great square, 460 feet long and 190 feet wide. Broad streets ran out of this square east and west, and from the center of the southern side a street ran straight to Beacon Street, crossed by another that would have been about 30 feet south of Chestnut. Withington's plan was followed, however, when the actual work of cutting the streets was begun in the summer of 1799, and Mount Vernon, the western peak of the Trimountain, was shorn of fifty or sixty feet in consequence. One Silas Whitney set up a gravity railroad — claimed by N. I. Bowditch to be the first one ever used in this country [46] — on which cars of dirt slid down an inclined plane, emptying their loads of Mount Vernon into the water and thus filling in Charles Street to make more land for the Proprietors. This first instance of dumping the tops of hills into coves was said by Otis "to have excited as much attention as Bonaparte's road over the Alps." [47]

The early houses on the land of the Mount Vernon Proprietors were of generous dimensions. Harrison Gray Otis naturally enough abandoned his almost new house in the West End, and in 1800 had Bulfinch build him 85 Mount Vernon Street[48] (Fig. 34), which is more than a century and a half later still the handsomest house in Boston. Otis's chief assistant, Jonathan Mason, settled himself in another Bulfinch house in Mount Vernon Street, opposite the end of Walnut, which was, however, demolished in 1839.[49] Bulfinch in 1805 bought the lot west of Otis, hoping perhaps to settle there himself, but the following year divided it into two lots on which he built houses that he sold to Stephen Higginson, Jr., and David Humphreys.[50] These houses shared a common driveway. Although the Humphreys house has been replaced, Stephen Higginson's house — number 87 — remains as the home of the Colonial Society of Massachusetts.

Harrison Gray Otis moved again in 1806 to an even larger house that he built at 45 Beacon Street[51] facing the Common. There he remained until his death in 1848, living in the generous manner of a prosperous Federalist, with a full ten-gallon Lowestoft punch bowl on the stair landing to assist the weary in their ascent to the drawing room.[52] Just above Otis, on the site of the Copley house, David Sears built in 1819 a two-story granite house, designed by Alexander Parris, that exists today, much altered and enlarged, as the Somerset Club.[53]

This "mansion house" pattern soon proved too expansive, and the majority of the houses built on the lands of the Mount Vernon Proprietors were, although substantial, in blocks. Indeed Otis and Sears eventually built other houses in their own gardens, thus transforming their mansions into elements of a block. The more elevated sites naturally were in the greatest demand, but so much land was involved that thirty years passed before the Proprietors laid out the area west of the Humphreys house at 89 Mount Vernon Street. In 1826 a plan was drawn for Louisburg Square which gradually built up in the decade following 1834 (Fig. 35). Time does not permit any further account of the development of this area, but so many of the houses survive that with Allen Chamber-

Fig. 34. 85 Mount Vernon Street

lain's admirably detailed *Beacon Hill Its Ancient Pastures and Early Mansions* in hand, the inquiring visitor can easily enjoy the sport of determining for himself how Copley's upland pasture reached its present form.

As early as 1790 a town committee was complaining that the Almshouse in Park Street was too near the center of the town and too small.[54] With the building of the new State House it became increasingly desirable to shift the location of the town buildings that straggled up toward it. In May 1795 a town meeting approved the idea of building more suitable replacements in the still remote Barton's Point region, and financing the change by selling the old site as well as town lands facing the Mall.[55] Thus when the new Almshouse in Leverett Street, designed by Bulfinch, was completed in 1801,[56] the Park Street land became available for private houses.[57]

In 1804 Thomas Amory built there the great square brick house at the corner of Park and Beacon Streets (Fig. 36), later divided in two and occupied in part by George Ticknor, that survives in a sadly altered state.[58] The following year a handsome row of four-story brick houses was begun lower down the street (Fig. 37).

Bulfinch's design for the first four shows them to have been very similar to the Colonial Society's house at 87 Mount Vernon Street.[59] The vast Granary at the lower end of Park Street was removed in 1809 and the present Park Street Church built immediately afterward upon its site, from designs by Peter Banner, an English architect. Banner's graceful steeple still remains one of the delights of Boston, although sixty-five years ago it escaped, by the narrowest margin, demolition through the connivance of rapacious real estate developers and greedy deacons.[60]

The sale of town lands opposite the Mall, originally part of the Common, agreed upon in 1795 to finance the new Almshouse, provided the site for another of Bulfinch's handsome developments. Colonnade Row (Fig. 38), built in 1810, was a series of

Fig. 35. Louisburg Square

nineteen houses extending along Tremont Street from West Street to Mason Street.[61] This row for several decades remained one of the most agreeable places to live in Boston, for from its windows occupants looked out across the Common to distant water, hills and the sunsets of a western sky. From the balcony of Mrs. Lowell's house, at the corner of Mason Street, Eliza Susan Quincy viewed, on Washington's Birthday 1815, the procession celebrating the news of peace. Her description [62] suggests that the social climate of Boston had not changed markedly in the quarter century since the great Washington himself had been received with a parade of merchants, artisans and seamen. The peace procession was headed by her father, Josiah Quincy,

as President of the Washington Benevolent Society, followed by the numerous members, and representatives of all the Trades drawn on sleds with appropriate standards, and carrying their tools. The bricklayers were building a house, they broke their bricks and worked busily. The carpenters were erecting a temple of Peace. The printers worked a small press, struck off handbills, announcing peace, and threw them among the crowd. The bakers, hatters, paper-makers, blockmakers, etc., etc. had each their appropriate insignia. They went from the State House to the South end, then to the North and were dismissed in State Street.

This is still an uncrowded, small town celebration, in which all classes mingle cheerfully. But thanks to Bulfinch the externals of the town had, since 1789, taken on a new elegance. Not only had he designed the State House and completely transformed the surroundings of the Common, but he had also made conspicuous improvements in all parts of the town.

The theatre that was opened in Federal Street on 3 February 1794 represented a major advance over the Concert Hall in Hanover Street built by the musician Stephen Deblois in 1756.[63] For Bulfinch's services as architect and trustee the Proprietors of the Boston Theatre awarded him a medal, entitling him to a seat for life, "for his unremitted and liberal Attention in the Plan and Execution of That Building, The Elegance of which is the best Evidence of his Taste and Talents."

When Father Cheverus, the beloved French priest who became

Fig. 36. Looking down Park Street

Fig. 37. Looking up Park Street

Fig. 38. Colonnade Row in Tremont Street

the first Catholic Bishop of Boston, undertook in 1799 to build a church, Bulfinch generously gave the plans. In such esteem was Father Cheverus held that President John Adams headed the subscription list for the building which eventually raised seventeen thousand dollars, a fifth of the total having come from local Protestants — among them John Quincy Adams, James and Thomas Handasyd Perkins, John Lowell, Harrison Gray Otis, Joseph Coolidge and David Sears. The Cathedral of the Holy Cross, in Franklin Street, near Bulfinch's Tontine Crescent, was consecrated on 29 September 1803. In graceful recognition of Bulfinch's help the Catholics of Boston presented him with a handsome silver tea-urn, now in the Museum of Fine Arts.[64] In 1804 he completed a new New North Church of brick in Hanover Street. Although Bulfinch's Holy Cross was abandoned in 1860 [65] when the present cathedral was undertaken, his somewhat similar New North Church houses today St. Stephen's Roman Catholic congregation.[66]

Around the corner from the classical Holy Cross, Bulfinch completed in 1809 a new Federal Street Church,[67] which was his first and only excursion into Gothic, while in 1814 he returned to his natural vein in a new New South Church (Fig. 61), built of Chelmsford granite.[68] In 1810 he built a granite Court House on the site of the former City Hall in School Street.[69]

Although he had enlarged Faneuil Hall in 1805 [70] new markets were needed in expanding parts of town. In 1810 he completed Boylston Hall and Market, at the corner of Boylston and Washington Streets,[71] and a West End market for Samuel Parkman at the corner of Grove and Cambridge Streets.[72] The Handel and Haydn Society's [73] unconcerned use of the hall over Boylston Market for twenty-two years confirms the traditional Boston view that the cutting of meat on a ground floor is no hindrance to what goes on above. Seemingly oratorios, like oratory, can flourish

> Undaunted by proximity
> Of sausage on the rack.

When Charles Bulfinch was once asked if he should train up any of his children in his own profession, he replied that he did not think there would be much left for them to do. "The States and prominent towns," he is reported by his granddaughter [74] to have said, "were already supplied with their chief buildings, and he hardly thought a young man could make a living as an architect." When one recalls that in addition to the entire streets, public buildings and churches already mentioned, he had built in Boston five banks, four insurance offices, two hospitals and three schools,[75] one cannot blame him for wondering what was left for his successors. And in spite of this prodigality of effort he had always had rough going financially, usually from circumstances beyond his control. At the time of his bankruptcy, Bulfinch had retained certain mud flats along the Charles River that were thought to be worthless. When the Mount Vernon Proprietors began moving the top of Mount Vernon into the river, Bulfinch began filling these flats, with the idea of extending Charles Street to the West Boston Bridge. Beginning in 1805, he had just "completed a junction with the bridge and offered a plan of lots for sale" when his prospects were dashed by the "stagnation of business" resulting from Jefferson's Embargo.[76] As he described it later in life,

The Company of Otis & Co., men of large capital, were able to wait for better times for sale of their lands, from which they have since realized immense profit, but no sales could be then made by me, and demands were pressing with accumulated interest, so I was obliged once more to surrender all property, and was even more reduced than before, and we were obliged to leave our neat and commodious home for a humbler and inferior one.

Although the cause of further financial trouble for Bulfinch, these filling operations improved communication between the Common and Cambridge Street and reduced the isolation of the Southack Street settlement that had given Mount Vernon the less flattering name of Mount Whoredom. Through the first quarter of the nineteenth century, this mangy area on the northern slope of the hill — well isolated from the handsome development of the Mount Vernon Proprietors — continued as a source of disorder and subject of complaint. In 1814 the selectmen were noting "disorderly conduct . . . occasioned by a number of Spanish sailors and the sailors from the *Constitution* frigate assembling at West Boston" and requesting Captain Stewart "to order his men on board at sunset every evening." [77]

The following year Bulfinch, who had been momentarily defeated for selectman after fifteen years' service,[78] suggested that he had "incurred the enmity of some whose friendship would have been a disgrace" in his attempts "to roll back the torrent of vice at the Hill at West Boston." [79] The Reverend James Davis, reporting in 1817 to his employers, the Boston Female Society for Missionary Purposes, singled out Southack Street for his most vigorous denunciations.[80]

Without impropriety it may be said, *there* is the place where *Satan's seat is. There* awful impieties prevail; and all conceivable abominations are practiced; *there* the depravity of the human heart is acted out; and from this sink of sin, the seeds of corruption are carried into every part of town. Five and twenty or thirty shops are opened on Lord's days from morning to evening and ardent spirits are retailed without restraint, while hundreds are intoxicated and spend the holy sabbath in frolicking and gambling, in fighting and blaspheming; and in many scenes of iniquity and debauchery too dreadful to be named . . . Here, week after week, whole nights are spent in drinking and carousing; and as the morning light begins to appear, when others arise from their beds, these close their doors . . . Here in one compact section of the town, it is confidently affirmed and fully believed, there are *three hundred* females wholly devoid of shame and modesty. . . . Multitudes of coloured people, by these examples, are influenced into habits of indolence.[81]

It should be noted in passing that a considerable proportion of the colored people, who, as barbers, waiters, musicians, laundresses and seamen, fitted usefully and harmoniously into the Boston scene, were concentrated on the north slope of the hill, chiefly in Belknap (now Joy) and Southack (now Phillips) Streets.[82]

Another contemporary Jeremiah [83] reported: "As respects *The Hill,* it consists principally of drunkards, harlots, spendthrifts, and outcasts from the country; in truth, Beelzebub holds a court there and almost every Town in the Commonwealth has a representative." Mayor Josiah Quincy, although informed that the dozen disorderly houses in this region could not be put down without a military force, organized a House of Correction in 1823, and soon cleaned up the area.[84]

The river front north of the West Boston Bridge was the site chosen for the Massachusetts General Hospital. Although incorporated in 1811, no attempt at construction was made during the War of 1812. In December 1816 the versatile Bulfinch was sent by the hospital board to visit New York, Philadelphia and Baltimore hospitals "to observe," as he recalled, "their construction and to get a knowledge of their expenses and management." [85] Although this mission led to his drawing plans for the McLean Hospital for the Insane in Somerville, and for the superb granite building of the Massachusetts General Hospital, it also led, by accident, to his leaving Boston. While in Baltimore he could not resist visiting Washington. President Monroe received him in an amiable manner, on 7 January 1817, and had him conducted over the ruins of the Capitol. The following July when Monroe visited Boston, Bulfinch, as Chairman of the Selectmen, was much in his company. So it came about that Bulfinch was, in January 1818, appointed Architect of the Capitol at a salary of $2,500 plus traveling and moving expenses. For one in his straitened circumstances, the opportunity could not be disregarded, and during the next twelve years and a half he spent in Washington what he regarded as the happiest period of his life.

His services to Boston cannot be measured in terms of building alone, for, as Mayor Josiah Quincy wrote: "During the many years he presided over the town government, he improved its finances, executed the laws with firmness, and was distinguished for gentleness and urbanity of manners, integrity and purity of character." Quincy expressed the widespread feeling of his contemporaries in the words: "Few men deserve to be held by the citizens of Boston in more grateful remembrance than Charles Bulfinch." [86]

CHAPTER IV

Cutting Down the Hills
to Fill the Coves

WHEN LAFAYETTE returned to the United States in 1824, Boston was in an uproar of excitement. Early in the morning of 24 August the Boston Light Infantry, accompanied by a cavalcade of twelve hundred horsemen, proceeded to the Neck to meet the General, who had spent the night with Governor Eustis in Roxbury. At the city line, the municipality refreshed them with free bread, cheese and punch. Josiah Quincy of the Harvard class of 1821 — son of the mayor of the same name — noted with pleasure "the carters and woodwharfingers of the city, dressed in frocks of snowy whiteness," who were conspicuous among the horsemen. When Lafayette arrived, in an open barouche drawn by four white horses, bells, cannon and human lungs hailed him with deafening enthusiasm.[1] The general excitement with which all classes in the population greeted the beloved figure recalls Washington's visit of 1789, yet the town that welcomed the first president was a very different place from the city that honored his ancient comrade-in-arms thirty-five years later. For one thing, the population had more than tripled. The 18,320 inhabitants recorded by the 1790 United States Census had increased to 33,787 in 1810, to 43,298 in 1820. A City Census of 1825 was to show a population of 58,277.[2] In 1822 town government had been replaced by a city charter, with John Phillips as the first mayor,[3] followed in 1823 by Josiah Quincy and in 1829 by Harrison Gray Otis. Thomas Pemberton's optimistic remark "the town is capable of great increase" no longer rang true, for the large spaces of vacant land that gladdened his sight in 1794 were no longer vacant, and Boston had already embarked upon its perennial occupation of making room for itself. Genesis i.9 would have made a good motto for the seal of the new city:

Let the waters under the heaven be gathered together unto one place, and let the dry land appear: and it was so.

The insular quality of the water-ringed peninsula, which was first challenged by the Charles River and West Boston Bridges, rapidly diminished as new routes of access by land were created. The Mount Vernon Proprietors' private development of Beacon Hill soon suggested that there was profit for the town in the improvement and sale of unlikely land that had remained in public possession. With space growing scarce on the peninsula, rope makers, candle manufacturers and the like began to eye the waste lands where the Neck widened as it approached Roxbury (Fig. 39), which a 1797 town meeting had begun to consider as a "very valuable property of the town." [4] The Selectmen, under Bulfinch's chairmanship, presented to the March 1801 town meeting a plan for developing the Neck into streets laid out in a regular rectangular pattern. The monotony was to be varied by Columbia Square, an oval grass plot bounded by four streets, with Washington Street running through its center, on the site of the present Blackstone and Franklin Squares.[5] Thus on 22 May 1801 a committee of six was appointed to serve with the Selectmen, to "lease and manage said lands in such a manner as shall appear to them for the interest of the Town." [6] Being forcibly struck with the importance and value of these lands," this joint committee urged, during the town meeting at which they were appointed, "that the land be laid out in streets and lots" at their discretion.[7] Although

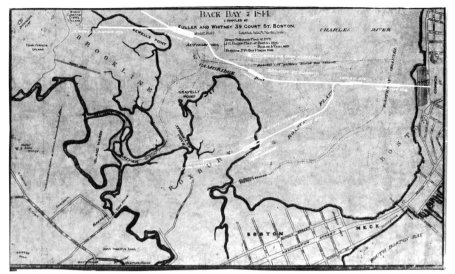

Fig. 39. The Back Bay in 1814

the distinction of Columbia Square was chiefly apparent on paper for many years, thirteen thousand dollars was realized in land sales in the first decade. At this time it appeared that between forty and fifty acres of land upon the Roxbury side of the Neck had been "judiciously laid out into streets and lots," for which, unfortunately, the 16 May 1811 town meeting was told, "there is at present no demand." [8]

The lack of demand for town lands on Boston Neck may not have been unrelated to simultaneous private real estate competition on Dorchester Neck, now South Boston. Being part of Dorchester, this peninsula had not appeared on the Bonner map. Although remote from Boston by land, it was near enough as the crow flies to have served Washington as a gun position that forced the British evacuation of the town. Actually it was separated from Boston only by mud flats and a narrow channel. As Dorchester Neck boasted only about ten families at the end of the eighteenth century, an occasional rowboat crossing at high tide furnished adequate communication until the advent of real estate speculators.

Joseph Woodward of Tewksbury, who was one of the Mount Vernon Proprietors,[9] began buying land on Dorchester Neck, in happy anticipation of the expansion of Boston in that direction. Woodward persuaded Harrison Gray Otis and Jonathan Mason, his associates in the development of Beacon Hill, Copley's son-in-law Gardiner Greene, and William Tudor to follow his lead in snapping up this area. They acted with dispatch both in private purchases and political maneuver, for on 6 March 1804 an act annexing Dorchester Neck to Boston was signed over the loud protests of the town of Dorchester, which received no compensation whatsoever for the loss of its territory.[10] Land values immediately rose.

The General Court, simultaneously with the annexation, authorized the construction of a toll bridge to South Boston, as the area was renamed. Tudor, Otis, Mason and Greene, who were named as proprietors in the South Bridge Act, were allowed seventy years improvement of their investment. Even running east from the Neck at the present Dover Street, where the distance between the peninsulas was the least, a bridge 1,551 feet in length was required. It was completed at a cost of $56,000, and opened with a military display and sham fight on 1 October 1805.

The South Boston Bridge had little success in attracting settlers to South Boston, but for some years it furnished a fashionable promenade for Boston residents because of its agreeable view of the town (Fig. 40). Bulfinch's brother-in-law Joseph Coolidge walked every afternoon from his house in Bowdoin Square to Dover Street.[11] On the bridge, in 1821, Josiah Quincy, Jr., had his first vision of the ravishing Emily Marshall, walking with a gentleman known as Beau Watson. Quincy tells us the walk was "then known in popular parlance (out of compliment to the lovers who were to be met there) as the Bridge of Sighs." [12] One should remember, however, that Miss Marshall, with whom every young man in Boston except William Amory [13] thought himself in love, eventually married William Foster Otis, son of the instigator of the bridge.

For direct communication with the center of Boston the new bridge left much to be desired. Its critics alleged, with reason, that had it been a continuation of Federal Street, the bridge would

Fig. 40. Boston from the South Boston Bridge

have been longer, but the total mileage to South Boston far shorter. Such a location would, however, have jeopardized the waterfront rights of the Front Street Corporation, which had been chartered iɪ 1804 in the legislative package-deal that annexed South Boston, and incorporated the proprietors of the South Boston Bridge. This corporation Edward Stanwood described as "the first systematic and co-operative enterprise having in view the enlargement of the limits of Boston by making new land." It consisted mainly of owners of shore front property east of Washington Street and south of Beach Street, who were collectively engaged in constructing a new thoroughfare, parallel with Washington Street, on the mud flats. The space between this new Front Street (which was renamed Harrison Avenue in April 1841, immediately after President William Henry Harrison's death) and the original shore line was to be filled individually by each owner of adjacent property. The street

was begun in May 1804 and completed in October 1805. Edward
Stanwood observed that "the agreement of owners to build no structure less than ten feet from the line of the street was probably
the first instance of a restriction upon real estate in Boston which
had in view the symmetry and appearance of a street when fully
built upon." Thus nine acres of new land were obtained at a cost
of $65,000 to the persons who had enclosed the mud flats lying
before their original property. By this means, Boston Neck began
to widen.[14]

Verbal brickbats were exchanged in town meeting and in pam-
phlets [15] between the Front Street Corporation and proponents
of a more direct bridge to South Boston which would bar access to
the new shore line of Front Street. Arguments continued for two
decades until a charter for a second and free bridge from the end
of Federal Street was granted in 1826. The opening of this more
direct bridge, in 1828, immediately undermined the property of
the South Boston Bridge Corporation, which never had paid divi-
dends. In 1832 the first bridge was sold to the city for $3,500 —
6 per cent of its cost — and opened for free travel. Tudor, Otis,
Mason and Greene derived a handsome loss for themselves from
this venture, but they had provided Emily Marshall's admirers
with a fine promenade.[16]

In the West End a second toll bridge across the Charles River
was opened in the summer of 1809. This, which was known as
Canal or Craigie's Bridge, ran from Barton's Point in Boston to
Lechmere's Point in Cambridge. 2,796 feet in length and 40 feet
in width, it connected on the Cambridge side with Charlestown
by means of the 1,821-foot Prison Point Bridge. Such improvements gave great satisfaction to Bostonians of the time. Dr. Caleb
H. Snow, in his *History of Boston,* proudly observed: "All these
bridges are well lighted by lamps when the evenings are dark, and
the lights, placed at regular distances, have a splendid and roman-
tic appearance." [17]

The Mill Pond, occupying the triangle between Craigie's Bridge
and the Charles River Bridge, was the next point attacked in the
current enthusiasm for increasing the land area of Boston. It was,

of course, an artificial pond, created by damming the marshy North Cove one hundred and sixty years before. Its mills were useful, but as the town had grown and bridges multiplied, there seemed less need for mills and more for land. When the question of filling it was raised at the 29 February 1804 town meeting, a committee of five, headed by Hon. Thomas Dawes, was appointed to investigate.[18] While this committee was deliberating, the mill proprietors, who were the successors of Henry Symons and his associates who had created the Mill Pond in 1643, obtained an act on 9 March 1804 incorporating them as the Mill Pond Corporation.[19] The purpose of their association appeared to be filling the pond with soil from Beacon Hill, rather than continuing to operate it as their predecessors had done. After a turbulent town meeting on 10 May 1804, extended by recounts and reconsiderations, an adjourned meeting on 14 May finally passed a vote for filling up the pond, and appointed Dawes and five other citizens to be a committee with the selectmen to treat "with the supposed Proprietors."[20] Finally in 1807 seven commissioners, including John Davis and John Quincy Adams,[21] concluded an agreement whereby the whole pond was to be filled at the expense of the mill proprietors within twenty years, the town receiving one eighth of the entire filled area. The Mill Creek was to be continued to the Charles River, streets were to be laid out according to a plan by Bulfinch, and accommodation made for the Baptist churches that had settled along the pond for convenience in baptizing.[22] Bulfinch's plan for the development (Fig. 41) shows a triangular pattern with Causeway Street following the line of the dam, and Canal Street running alongside the canalized Mill Creek.

Having completed the agreement, the next problem was to secure the fill for this area of some fifty acres. The leveling of the western peak of the Trimountain by the Mount Vernon Proprietors caused sheep's eyes to be cast at the remaining peaks. As early as 1758 one Thomas Hodson had made himself unpopular with his fellow townsmen by turning land that he owned on the north side of Beacon Hill into a gravel pit. Although he professed "a readiness to dispose of his right therein,"[23] he kept on digging, to a

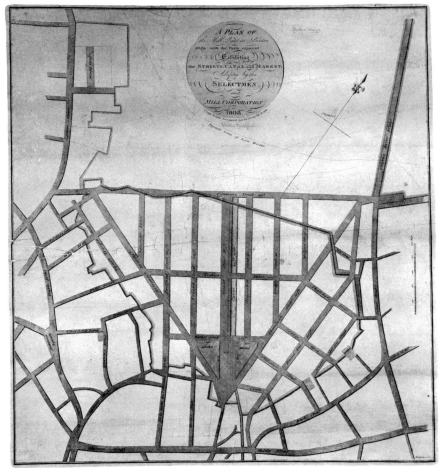

Fig. 41. Charles Bulfinch's plan for the Mill Pond

point where in 1764 the town claimed that the hill was "in very grave danger of being destroy'd" through his activities.[24] No agreement was reached, for town meetings in 1765, 1772, 1774 and 1779 were still concerned with the nuisance that he caused.[25] William W. Wheildon was of the opinion that gravel from this pit had been used to fill marshy ground around the Town Cove during eighteenth-century wharf improvements.[26]

At the close of the Revolution the beacon still stood on the top of Beacon Hill. Part of the land on the slopes of the summit was owned by John Hancock and other private citizens, with the rest believed to be the property of the town. In earlier years this had aroused no great concern, for the hill-top was used as a common pasture.[27] A thirty-foot way led up to the beacon, which stood in an area six rods (99 feet) square.[28] When that undecorative and no longer useful pole blew down, on the night of 26 November 1789, Charles Bulfinch, with the memory of European monumental columns in mind, proposed replacing it by a commemorative Doric column sixty feet high, including base and pedestal, surmounted by an American eagle standing on a globe. The four sides of the pedestal contained inscriptions commemorating "the train of events which led to the American Revolution and finally secured liberty and independence to the United States." With his customary energy, Bulfinch designed the column and superintended its construction. When the new State House was built in 1795 in Governor Hancock's pasture, it was on the southern slope of the hill, with the ancient peak and Bulfinch's monument rising behind it.[29] This classical monument, which so well typified the aspirations of the young Republic, was, however, to survive for hardly a quarter of a century before it was (to the shame of the town) legally pulled down by diggers of gravel bent on filling the Mill Pond.

John Hancock's heirs were ready and willing to turn a penny by providing fill from the top of Beacon Hill. Even in the governor's lifetime there had been question of what he and what the town owned.[30] The Selectmen, being informed on 9 September 1807 that "the Heirs of Governor Hancock had signified their intention to enter into the inclosed part of Beacon Hill tomorrow morning to dig away the earth and take possession, the Chairman [Bulfinch], Mr. Oliver & Mr. Wright were appointed a Committee to repair to the Hill, with Peace Officers & proper Witnesses to maintain the Towns rights and prevent any encroachment thereon."[31] On the sixteenth, Bulfinch reported to the Selectmen a ludicrous scene that had occurred the previous day.

The Committee had repaired to Beacon hill, & there met with Ebenezer Hancock, Esq. & John Hancock & Mr. Samuel Spear who appeared to claim

& enter upon the enclosed part of the Hill in behalf of the Heirs of the late Governour Hancock. Messrs Hancock & Spear each of them took a Shovel full of Earth & threw it into the Cart of Mr. James Bird. The Chairman [Bulfinch] then forbid them to proceed & ordered them to withdraw in the name of the Town & the Committee taking each of them by the Arm led them from the enclosed part of the Hill into the Street, & ordered them not to enter again for any such purpose.[32]

The extended litigation that followed resulted in a victory for the Hancock heirs,[33] who in 1810 were employing "a number of persons in digging and carting away their land on Beacon Hill." [34] A town committee charged with staking out the six-rod square on the summit and the thirty-foot passage leading to it, which indubitably belonged to the town, found in December 1810 that "a large portion of the northeast corner of the land had caved away . . . and that on the southwest corner about fifteen feet at the extreme angle had been taken away by Messrs. Hancock." [35]

Maintaining the summit of a hill when its approaches are being undermined is no easy task. Moreover, as the town was feeling poor in the spring of 1811,[36] it voted to sell various town lands to decrease its debts to banks. Thus at a public auction on 20 June 1811 John Hancock and Samuel Spear, who had been warned off by the Selectmen four years earlier, bought the six-rod square at the summit of Beacon Hill for $9,300 and proceeded to its demolition.[37]

The scene is familiar from a series of five chromolithographs published by J. H. Bufford in 1855, under the title of "Old Boston," that are derived from contemporary sketches made by an English artist, J. R. Smith.[38] Thus we see the area behind the State House as it appeared in the autumn of 1811, with Bulfinch's noble column precariously perched on a half demolished peak, beneath which men are filling two wheeled tipcarts (Fig. 42). William Thurston's fine house above Bowdoin Street, on a site with the finest view in Boston, teeters on the edge of a gravel bank (Fig. 43). Unfortunately, Thurston had built it — in 1804 — within two feet of the monument lot, so that when the Hancock heirs dug sixty feet below the original level immediately to the

Fig. 42. Cutting down Beacon Hill

Fig. 43. Mr. Thurston's house in Bowdoin Street

west, the poor man's house became unsafe and had to be taken down. This was the occasion of a celebrated lawsuit,[39] and a good deal of general disgust.

The monument was demolished by November 1811, although the eagle and tablets were preserved within the State House,[40] but its disappearance began to be regretted, and in 1865 an act was passed authorizing it to be rebuilt. Finally in 1898 the Bunker Hill Monument Association erected, upon the same site, a replica from designs made by the Boston architectural firm of Little and Browne.[41] When accepted by the Commonwealth, the new monument stood in an agreeable little park. Today it resembles a cormorant perched on a spar buoy that rises out of a sea of parked cars, many of whose occupants doubtless think of it chiefly as an obstacle to traffic. Sorry sight that it is today, the monument is at least a reminder of the time when Bulfinch's column rose from a summit that was close to sixty feet higher.

For more than a dozen years Beacon Hill continued to be trundled down to the Mill Pond in tip carts, for it was 1824 before the hill had been reduced to its present height and the streets laid out.[42] The changes around the Mill Pond proceeded slowly. A Pond Street Corporation, incorporated in 1806 to make a direct street from the Charles River Bridge to Hanover Street, had completed what is now Endicott Street, along the northeast shore of the pond, in 1809.[43] The center of the pond continued for a number of years to receive oyster shells, rubbish and street sweepings, as well as Beacon Hill gravel.[44] A sketch of the late twenties (Fig. 44), looking south from the region of Copp's Hill, shows Traverse Street as a dreary waste. Although this filling added close to fifty acres to the city, the real development of the new area began in the thirties, with the coming of the railroads.

Tinkering with the shore line increased on a lordly scale in the first quarter of the nineteenth century. Soon after 1800 some of Copp's Hill was dug away, and new brick buildings were built in 1806 on both sides of Lynn (now Commercial) Street in the North End.[45] The greatest change occurred, however, in Town Cove through the activities of the Broad Street Association, incor-

Fig. 44. Beacon Hill seen across the filled Mill Pond

porated in 1805. The leading spirit of this group was Uriah Cotting, a man of tremendous imagination and energy, to whom N. I. Bowditch, with cause, accorded the title of "Chief Benefactor of Boston." [46] With Bulfinch as planner, Cotting and his associates, who included Harrison Gray Otis, Francis C. Lowell and Rufus G. Amory, changed the face of the waterfront north and south of the Long Wharf, transformed an area of small and dilapidated buildings and wharves into one of broad streets and brick warehouses (Figs. 45–47). One can best picture these changes through

Fig. 45. India Wharf

the eyes of Shubael Bell, Senior Warden of Christ Church, who in 1817 wrote to a friend who had lived in Smyrna for thirty years of the transformation that had occurred during his absence:

India Wharf is spacious and extensive, it supports a long tier of buildings five stories high, and runs from the South Battery, in a southeast direction towards the channel. It has depth of water, sufficient for ships of the greatest burthen. At this wharf the Amorys, the Perkins, the Higginsons and other respectable Merchants transact business.

Broad Street was built a few years since, and extends at right angles, from near the bottom of King street (now State street) South, to the head of India Wharf. This street is made on a place which recently was occupied by a few zigzag wharves and ordinary buildings, and is from eighty to one hundred feet in breadth. The buildings on either side are from four to five stories in height, and constructed in a uniform and elegant style. They are chiefly occupied as stores and ware houses.

India Street, commences at the bottom of King street and extends, fronting the harbour to India wharf. The east side of it is crowded with vessels, which are protected from the violence of storms by the adjacent wharves. The proprietors of India & Central wharves have a design of converting the intermediate space into a wet dock. The buildings on this street front the water, and are constructed in a similar style with those on Broad street.

The space between India and Broad streets, at convenient distances, is intersected by cross streets, the principal of which is called Custom-House Street.

The new Custom-house in this street is a spacious building with compartments, suitable to the business of the different Offices of the customs. It was designed by Mr. Cotting . . . and built by the Broad street corporation. It is the property of the United States.

This, it should be noted in passing, is a predecessor of the present Doric granite temple, built in 1838 from plans of Ammi B. Young,[47] that is now surmounted by the first Boston sky-scraper.

In the course of the last year, Central Wharf, and the extensive range of Stores which it supports was begun and compleated. The completion of this undertaking, unparalleled in commercial History, is a proof of the enterprize, the wealth, and persevering Industry of Bostonians. The number of stores are fifty four, and the length of the tier nearly thirteen hundred feet, of four Stories. The wharf is considerably longer, and about one hundred and fifty feet in breadth, inclosed by a strong stone wall. The

Fig. 46. India and Central Wharves in 1857

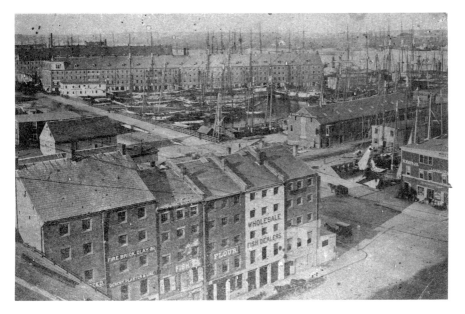

Fig. 47. Commercial and T (Snow's) Wharves about 1865

buildings are supported on piles and have water proof cellars. The wharf is already lined with vessels and crowded with business.

Under an elevated centre is an arch making a convenient passage way from one side of the wharf to the other.

Over this are three rooms nearly sixty feet square, calculated for public sales. From an octagon cupola over the pediments, you have a charming view of the Harbour and neighboring towns, and the liberality of the proprietors has furnished it with a telescope and other apparatus for the accommodation of the public.[48]

Most of this superb waterfront development lost its shape with the filling of Atlantic Avenue in 1868, which banged through the middle of India and Central Wharves as ruthlessly as the elevated highway has recently sliced the State Street block. The east end of India Wharf survived to 1962,[49] providing an echo of the scale of Cotting's conception and the dignity of Bulfinch's design. Cotting was indeed, as Shubael Bell wrote, "a man of great genius and industry" who "with an ardent imagination, ever under the control of a sober judgment, . . . conceives great undertakings, and they seem to be almost simultaneously completed." He had opened Brattle Street and Cornhill, owned lands at Leverett Street and the Neck, and was involved in the development of lower Federal Street that led to the second South Boston bridge.[50] Bell noted his plans for developing Commercial Street as a North End counterpart to India Street, from the Long Wharf to the North Battery; of carrying India Street southerly across the South Cove to the new Front Street, and, finally, of "building a permanent Causeway over the bay on the western side of the town to extend from the end of Beacon Street to the shore of Brookline." [51] Not all of these projects could be carried out by Cotting, but he had, before he died of consumption in 1819, embarked upon the greatest of them — the causeway or Mill Dam across the Back Bay — which was to change the shape of Boston more completely than any other single undertaking in its history.

This enterprise began, not with the idea of creating new land, but of providing water power for mill sites to replace, on a vastly greater scale, what was being lost by the filling of the old Mill Pond. When Isaac P. Davis "and others" — including, naturally,

Cotting — petitioned for "liberty to build a Mill Dam and Turn-pike Road from the bottom of Beacon-Street, and for other Mill improvements," the 11 June 1813 town meeting referred the matter to a committee of the Selectmen plus a representative of each of the twelve wards of the town. The original plan was in-deed grandiose. It called not only for a dam through the Back Bay along the present line of Beacon Street from Charles Street to Kenmore Square, but another from Boston to South Boston that would exclude tides from South Boston Bay. Having thus created great basins on both sides of the Neck, connected by raceways, mills would be built on town lands on the Neck running south from the narrowest point to the present Northampton Street. Water, at high tide, would enter the Back Bay basin through inward-opening gates from the Charles River, run through the raceways across the Neck, thus providing power for the mills, into the empty South Boston basin from which, at low tide, it would drain into the harbor through outward opening gates.

The town committee, under Bulfinch's chairmanship, approved the main points of the petition on 12 October 1813, as did a Joint Committee of both Houses of the Legislature, headed by Thomas Handasyd Perkins, the following year.[52] Perkins forestalled the question as to "whether extensive manufacturing establishments are not injurious to morals, and on that account not to be encour-aged by a wise government" with the answer that this

cannot . . . be considered so much an argument against encouraging the growth of cities and the assembling of workmen in factories, as in favor of an increased vigilance, on the part of a Legislature, to provide, in season, competent regulations and authority for their good government; otherwise, with equal reason, the same objection might be urged against the endow-ment of Colleges and Schools, it being to say, in other words, that the con-gregating together of a great number of persons, is a sufficient objection to an institution of any kind.[53]

Benjamin Weld and other citizens of Roxbury submitted a re-monstrance to the General Court urging that the plan be reversed by making the Back Bay an empty basin, and on the South Boston side a full basin, which could then serve not only as a mill pond but as a wet dock for vessels.[54] The legislative Joint Committee concurred in this modification, and a bill drawn accordingly was prepared.[55]

An even more elaborate network of basins, canals and mill sites was outlined in a plan [56] (Fig. 48) published by Benjamin Dearborn in February 1814, which proposed in addition to the South Boston and Back Bay basins, cross dams across the Charles River (close to the line of the present Harvard Bridge) that would create additional basins connecting by a long canal with Barrell's Creek in Cambridge, which flowed into the Charles near Lechmere's Point. Two more dams would create a basin out of Barrell's Creek and a Charlestown Mill Pond, which would in turn be connected by canals.

Not all Bostonians agreed with Thomas Handasyd Perkins's conviction that "a disposition in the people, to change the channels of their industry, is the best possible evidence of the necessity or utility of such change." One of the opposition vigorously reminded his neighbors, in a letter to the *Daily Advertiser* of 10 June 1814, of the filthy mess these so-called improvements would create.

Citizens of Boston! Have you ever visited the Mall; have you ever inhaled the Western breeze, fragrant with perfume, refreshing every sense and invigorating every nerve? What think you of converting the beautiful sheet of water which skirts the Common into an empty mud-basin, reeking with filth, abhorrent to the smell, and disgusting to the eye? By every god of sea, lake, or fountain, it is incredible.[57]

Although this gentleman proved to be quite right, as his fellow citizens eventually came to agree, the bill for incorporating the Boston and Roxbury Mill Corporation was run through a weary legislature in the closing hours of its session, the House passing it when less than fifty out of more than five hundred members were present and voting.

Although this charter was granted on 14 June 1814,[58] seven years were to pass before the principal Mill Dam was opened. The war, and the complexities of planning slowed down even Uriah Cotting, who issued in January 1818 a persuasive prospectus [59] presenting arguments and forestalling objections.

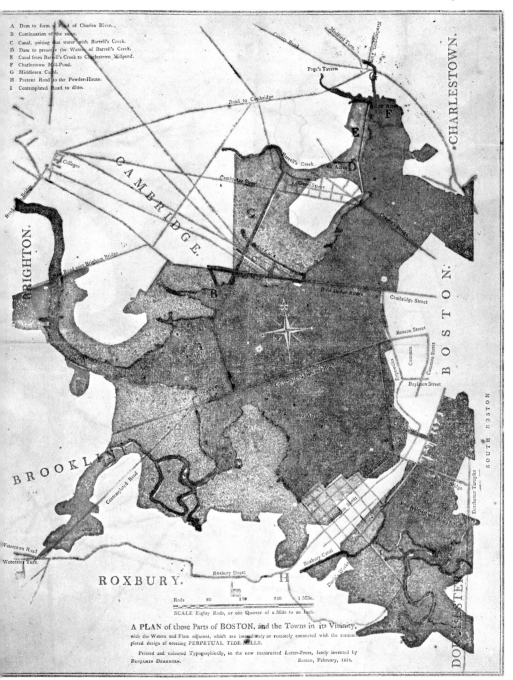

A Dam to form a Pond of Charles River.
B Continuation of the same.
C Canal, uniting that water with Bartell's Creek.
D Dam to preserve the Waters of Bartell's Creek.
E Canal from Bartell's Creek to Charlestown Millpond.
F Charlestown Mill-Pond.
G Middlesex Canal.
H Present Road to the Powder-House.
I Contemplated Road to ditto.

A PLAN of those Parts of BOSTON, and the Towns in its Vicinity,
with the Waters and Flats adjacent, which are immediately or remotely connected with the contemplated design of erecting PERPETUAL TIDE-MILLS.

Printed and coloured Typographically, in the new constructed Letter-Press, lately invented by
BENJAMIN DEARBORN.   Boston, February, 1814.

Fig. 48. Proposal for Mill Dam published by Benjamin Dearborn in 1814

It has been said by some that it will cost double the money. But ask these people, How long the dam is to be? They answer, *They do not know.* How deep is the mud and water? *They do not know*; they only know, *that it will cost double the money.*

Cotting cited his accomplishments with the Broad Street Association, India Wharf and Central Wharf, and his estimate of the eighty-one mills that might be created by his new project, among them six grist mills, eight flour mills, six saw mills, sixteen cotton and eight woolen mills, twelve rolling and slitting mills, as well as many others for turning cannon, making anchors, scythes, grindstones, grinding paints and heaven knows what not else. This remarkable document wound up —

Is there a single person in Boston or the neighboring towns, who can spare eighty dollars, who would not wish to have it said hereafter that he had had a share in this great improvement?

The question has been frequently asked, *How shall the citizens of Boston fill their empty stores?* The answer is easy, — ERECT THESE MILLS, AND LOWER THE PRICE OF BREAD. If the public do not have all these improvements it will not be the fault of

URIAH COTTING

When subscriptions for stock were opened, the scramble was so great that one determined investor climbed into Cotting's office through a window! [60]

The plan actually followed (Fig. 49) was considerably less elaborate than the original proposal, for everything was concentrated in the Back Bay. A main dam, fifty feet wide and a mile and a half long, carrying a toll road, which ran along the line of Beacon Street from Charles Street to Sewell's Point in Brookline, enclosed about six hundred acres of the Back Bay. A cross dam running out from Gravelly Point in Roxbury on a line roughly corresponding to the present Massachusetts Avenue, subdivided this area into a westerly full basin and an easterly receiving basin. The mill sites were located along Gravelly Point. At high tide water was admitted to the full basin by fitting sluices just west of the cross dam; it then passed through the mill sluices into the easterly receiving basin from which it drained back into the

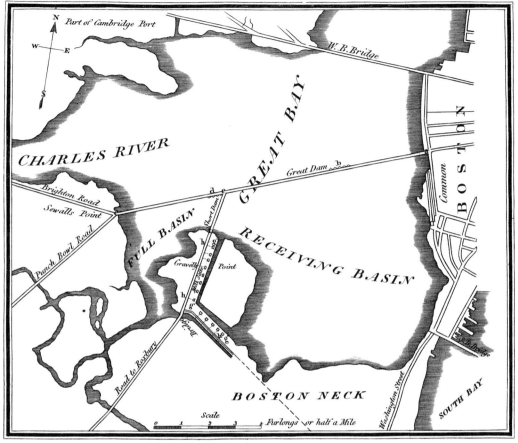

Fig. 49. The Mill Dam as built

Charles by emptying sluices in the main dam at about the present level of Exeter Street.[61]

Upon Cotting's death in 1821, Colonel Loammi Baldwin took over as engineer. The stone for building the dam was brought from Roxbury and Weymouth. A small part of the fill for the toll road, which was known as Western Avenue, came from Beacon Hill. Once the water had been shut off from the Back Bay, the flats of the receiving basin dried up and clouds of fine dust blew in every direction, creating such a nuisance that a sluice-way had to be built to keep them covered with water at all times.[62]

Western Avenue was opened to travel on 2 July 1821 with a

modest parade. Whatever the future of the mills might be, the Boston and Roxbury Mill Corporation had opened another highway from the Boston peninsula to the surrounding country. General William H. Sumner, the Chief Marshal of the day, in his address [63] recalled the state of Boston thirty-four years earlier, when the only passage from the town to the mainland had been by the Neck.

It was then, [he said] our town resembled a hand, but it was a closed one. It is now opened and well spread. Charlestown, Cambridge, South Boston, and Craigie's Bridge have added each a finger, and lately our enterprising citizens have joined the firm and substantial *thumb* over which we now ride.

CHAPTER V

Railroads and Immigrants

HARVARD COLLEGE has recently named its eighth House in honor of Josiah Quincy. The presidency of Harvard, which he occupied from 1829 to 1845, was but one phase of the career of this upright and versatile man. As Member of Congress from 1805 to 1813, President of the Boston Athenæum from 1820 to 1829 and Mayor of Boston from 1823 to 1828, he deserves quite as much grateful remembrance in Boston as in Cambridge. The existence of the Boston Athenæum today is largely due to the vigorous battle that he fought in 1853 — at the age of eighty-two — against its absorption by the newly created Boston Public Library.[1] While the magnitude of his efforts as the city's second mayor to convert Boston into a safer and more healthy city, which are recorded in his *Municipal History of the Town and City of Boston during Two Centuries*, are largely forgotten, the great granite market that he built facing Faneuil Hall remains as a permanent monument to his efforts.

Charles Bulfinch's enlargement of Faneuil Hall in 1805, and his construction of new markets in the South and West Ends, had only temporarily solved the victualing problems of the growing town. The region around Faneuil Hall, having been built largely in the seventeenth century, had changed relatively little. The

Town Dock served chiefly as a receptacle for dead cats and other rubbish, its watercraft consisting of a pair of scows moored for the sale of oysters, wholesale and retail. Those who wished could, as an early nineteenth-century visitor observed, eat them on the spot at a "rough bench furnished with saucers and forks, vinegar cruet and pepper box, and a plate of hard biscuits, called crackers." [2] Temporary wooden sheds cluttered the region, and on high market days farmers' carts completely obstructed all adjacent streets. When a drove of pigs passed through the streets, boys would shout "Here come the Charlestown folks," grabbing the smaller pigs by the tail, tossing them into shop doors or scattering them over the sidewalks, to the peril of pedestrians. [3] Uriah Cotting's activities had introduced order into the waterfront south of Long Wharf; north of it colonial chaos prevailed.

To remedy this, Mayor Quincy undertook a major piece of city planning that involved filling the Town Dock and building over the wharves between it and the Long Wharf, thus creating space for a new two-story granite market house, 555 feet long and 50 wide, that was flanked by harmonious granite warehouses, fronting on the newly created North and South Market Streets (Figs. 50–51). The whole series of buildings, which were designed by Alexander Parris, provided Faneuil Hall with an approach from the harbor of extraordinary dignity and beauty. Moreover, this effort, involving the creation of six new streets and the expenditure of upwards of $1,100,000, was accomplished without any tax or debt upon the city's resources. The cornerstone of the market was laid on 27 April 1825 and on Saturday morning, 26 August 1826, the first customer bought his leg of lamb. [4] Here, as in the older market, the traditional delights of shopping remain. Many a tourist, as well as many a native, has hurried up the stairs to eat at Durgin-Park's dining rooms in North Market Street without pausing to observe the great architectural distinction of these granite buildings. Although one can no longer see them from the harbor, with the bowsprits of square riggers projecting across Commercial Street — which was their finest vantage point — they remain one of the principal ornaments of Boston,

Fig. 50. Quincy Market between South and North Market Streets

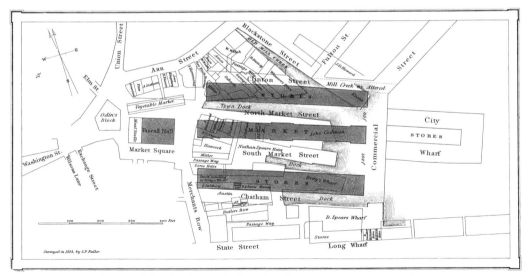

Fig. 51. Plan of the Quincy Market development superimposed
on the old waterfront

and perhaps the finest architectural composition of the period surviving in the United States. Fortunately they have not been mo-
lested by the elevated highway, which has wiped away so much
of this region. Those who care for the historic associations of
Faneuil Hall could not do better than to insure the restoration
and permanent preservation of the noble setting that Mayor
Quincy provided for it.

Boston also owes its Public Garden to Mayor Quincy's foresight. We have seen how in 1794, out of a mixture of sympathy
for the unfortunate and a desire to get an unsightly nuisance into
a remote spot, the town had imprudently granted limited and
qualified rights to the flats at the foot of the Common for the
construction of ropewalks. Thirty years later in February 1824,
when the site so cheerfully granted away was no longer remote,
the city regained this land by paying the occupants the large sum
of $55,000. With a marked difference of opinion among inhabi-
tants about the future of the tract, Mayor Quincy submitted the
problem to a general meeting of the citizens on 26 July 1824,
which overwhelmingly sustained the view that the land now comprising the Public Garden should be annexed to the Common
"and forever after kept open and free of buildings of any kind,
for the use of the citizens." Thus the notions, current at the time,
of dividing the area into streets or making it into a cemetery were
effectively squelched. "The result of the meeting," Mayor Quincy
wrote, "was to deny the expediency and withhold the right from
the City Council of making sale of the land west of Charles
Street."[5]

During the last year of Josiah Quincy's service as mayor a second bridge from Charlestown was completed. The Warren Bridge,
opened as a public highway on Christmas day 1828, ran into
Causeway Street in the center of the Mill Pond development. The
importance of new bridges and toll roads was soon to be overshadowed by the railroads, which during the thirties brought about
major changes in the topography of Boston (Fig. 52). The idea,
oddly enough, first developed in Massachusetts as a practical out-
come of historical piety. The approach of the fiftieth anniversary

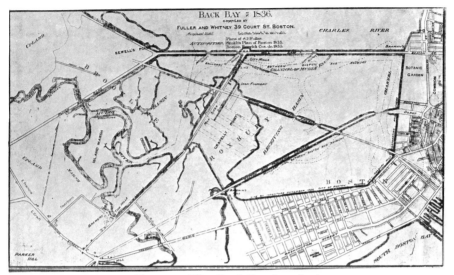

Fig. 52. The Back Bay in 1836

of the Battle of Bunker Hill led to the planning of the monument that today dominates Charlestown. As the granite quarry in Quincy that was to furnish the stone was four miles from the water, Gridley Bryant — a self-educated engineer from Scituate — proposed the idea of a horse-drawn railroad to simplify the movement of the material. With the backing of Thomas Handasyd Perkins, Bryant had his granite railway in operation in the autumn of 1826.[6] Four years later passenger travel by steam-driven cars was being seriously planned, for a Boston and Lowell Railroad was incorporated in June 1830, followed a year later by the Boston and Worcester and Boston and Providence lines.[7] All three opened for travel in the summer of 1835, within a few days of each other.

The Lowell road brought its tracks across the Charles River just east of Craigie's Bridge to a station on Barton's Point, reached from Causeway Street by a new Lowell Street, created by filling into the Charles parallel to Leverett Street. The Eastern Railroad,[8] which was opened as far as Salem in 1839, originally brought its trains to East Boston, from whence ferries conveyed the travelers to Lewis's Wharf on Commercial Street, in the North

End. By 1854, the Eastern, having re-routed its tracks by a
circuitous route through Chelsea, Everett, Somerville, and Charlestown, succeeded in bringing its trains into Boston by a bridge
parallel to that of the Lowell road, and thence to a station on
Causeway Street. The Boston and Maine Railroad [9] and the Fitchburg Railroad first entered Boston from the north in 1845, by
bridges over the Charles paralleling the Boston and Lowell. The
Boston and Maine came way into Haymarket Square, the entire
length of the filled Mill Pond, although, as a city ordinance for-
bade locomotives to cross Causeway Street, the trains were for
a time hauled in and out of the imposing classical station by
horses. The Fitchburg station was a crenelated Gothic affair on
the corner of Causeway and Haverhill Streets. Thus all four of
the northern lines eventually came into the old Mill Pond region
and early gave Causeway Street the railroad terminal character
that it has today. Although their tracks somewhat encroached upon
the Charles River, none of these railroads affected the character
and future development of the city as did the southern and western lines, which, by crossing the Back Bay (Fig. 53) in their approach to Boston, very seriously jeopardized Uriah Cotting's vision
of industrial water power from the new Mill Dam.

Near the junction of the Mill Dam and the Cross Dam, two
City Mills ground flour for a time, before turning to the production of paints and dyes; an iron foundry and other industries
were established on Gravelly Point, but the scores of mills anticipated by Cotting never came into being.[10] It was the distant water
of the Merrimac River rather than that of the Back Bay tides that
supplied the power for the numerous textile mills established by
Bostonians in succeeding years. Within the decade following the
completion of the Mill Dam, the mixed nature of its business led
to the splitting from the Boston and Roxbury Mill Corporation
of a new Boston Water-Power Company.[11] Neither proved financially profitable. The best that one could say of the venture
was that Western Avenue furnished both a convenient route to
Brookline and, with water on both sides and a distant view of
Longwood, which was then open country, an agreeable prome-

Fig. 53. Trains crossing the Back Bay in 1844

nade, or route for drives and sleighrides, particularly in the late afternoon with the setting sun. Fashionable young people came to prefer the Mill Dam to the South Boston Bridge for their strolls. Thomas Handasyd Perkins's granddaughter, Caroline Gardiner Cary (later Mrs. Charles Pelham Curtis), recalled that in the forties the walk to Dover Street "being in an entirely different direction from the Common and its vicinity, . . . was considered as rather an unfrequented stretch and had the credit of being the resort of couples on the eve of an engagement, though as yet unannounced. The mill-dam walk meant there was nothing more to fear from observation." [12]

The Boston and Worcester Railroad, incorporated in 1831 and operating as far as Needham in 1834,[13] entered Boston from the west through the Back Bay on today's familiar Boston and Albany line. From Sewell's Point (close to Kenmore Square) it crossed the Full Basin to Gravelly Point by a 170-foot trestle, known as the "dizzy bridge" from its length, lack of railings and the view, through its widely spaced cross timbers, of the water below.[14] From Gravelly Point it ran diagonally (northwest to southeast) across the Receiving Basin, on an embankment pierced by bridges

Fig. 54. Boston and Providence Railroad Station in Park Square

over channels, to the shore near Castle Street, and thence to its station at Lincoln and Beach Streets.

The Boston and Providence Railroad, incorporated in 1831 and opened in 1835,[15] came through Roxbury and cut diagonally (southwest to northeast) across the Receiving Basin to a station in Park Square (Fig. 54). The Worcester and Providence tracks, which intersected in mid-bay (near the present Back Bay Station) formed a great St. Andrew's cross of railway lines through the Back Bay which not only jeopardized the flowage of water for mill purposes but led eventually to the filling of the entire area. Moreover, the routes followed by these railway lines have materially affected the street plans of the South End and Back Bay districts as we know them today.

The Old Colony Railroad, which was opened between Boston and Plymouth in 1845,[16] entered through South Boston. After crossing the intervening channel, its tracks led first to the Boston and Worcester station and then, after June 1847, to its own terminal in Kneeland Street. Thus, fifteen years after the incorporation of the first railroad in Massachusetts, seven separate

lines had established terminals in Boston. There was no increase
for a decade until the Boston and New York Central (later known
successively as the Boston, Hartford and Erie and the New York
and New England) opened service between Boston and Putnam,
Connecticut, in January 1855. Its tracks crossed South Boston,
parallel to B Street, and then swung into the harbor in a great arc,
to reach a terminal in Broad Street in the vicinity of the South
Station.[17]

The Boston and Worcester Railroad caused greater change in
the topography of Boston than any of the other lines. Not only

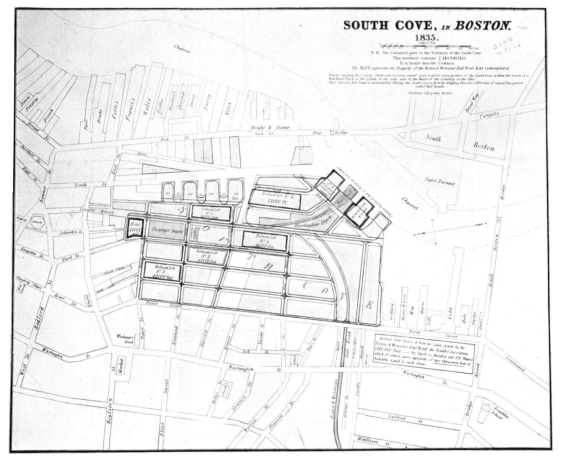

Fig. 55. Plan of South Cove in 1835

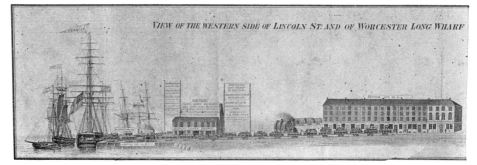

Fig. 56. The projected South Cove development

did it charge across the Back Bay, to the detriment of water flowage, but it also led to a considerable widening of the Neck. The Front Street Corporation had begun this process in 1804 by filling what is now Harrison Avenue as a new street (parallel to Washington), encroaching upon the waters of the South Cove. In 1833 the South Cove Associates, organized with a capital of $414,500 to provide the railroad with a terminus and yard space, undertook practically to obliterate the South Cove (Fig. 55).

After purchasing seventy-five acres of mud flats lying south of Windmill Point and east of Front Street, they brought fill from gravel pits in Roxbury and Dorchester by boat, and from Brighton by rail, to such purpose that by November 1839 they had created Lincoln and Albany Streets and the present Chinatown. In six years fifty-five acres of land, containing three miles of new streets, had been reclaimed from dock tidewaters, a railway station provided, and a wharf constructed that was to carry railroad service around the world, or packet service inland to Worcester, depending on the way one looked at the matter.

An ungainly lithograph (Fig. 56) owned by the Boston Athenæum, issued as "promotion literature" for the South Cove Associates' activities, shows Liverpool packets loading cargo from a "Merchandize Depot," liberally plastered with signs of New York, New Orleans, Baltimore, Charleston, Savannah, and Nova Scotia packets, not to mention the "St. Louis, Missouri, Rail-road Transportation Line." The staggering total of one hundred railroad

AND OTHER CHANNEL-WHARVES ON THE SOUTH COVE.

A promoter's dream of the 1830's

passengers a day to and from Worcester in 1838 made it obviously desirable to build the United States Hotel — then the largest in the country — at Lincoln and Beach Streets. The South Cove Associates were full of expansive ideas involving warehouses, markets and other major structures, optimistically set forth in this lithograph, many of which, thanks to the panic of 1837, never got built. The wharf proved an unsatisfactory inspiration, for vessels reached it only after passing through a dubious channel and various draws. By the fifties it was considered a nuisance, but the monumental United States Hotel offered hospitality of sorts well into the present century.[18]

From the Boston and Worcester Railroad grew the Western Railroad which, by the winter of 1841–1842, had reached Albany.[19] The spectacular nature of this link with the west inspired the local imagination to give the names of New York towns and cities to the new streets in the South Cove area. Thus Erie, Oneida, Oswego, Genesee, Rochester and Troy were commemorated in Boston, in catharsis of the emotion aroused by the marvels of rail transportation.

The disappearance of the last peak of the Trimountain was at least partially due to the coming of the railroads. Although the peak of Mount Vernon had been moved down to make Charles Street early in the century, and the peak of Beacon Hill had been trundled to the Mill Pond in the next decade, Cotton or Pemberton Hill, the eastern peak, remained untouched until the thirties.

Cotton Hill, and the ridge linking it with Beacon Hill, had long been an area of large houses, set in spacious gardens. On the site of the east wing of the State House William Molineaux, a merchant of Huguenot origin, had built in 1760 one of the most pretentious houses of its time, which, after the Revolution, was occupied for forty years by Daniel Dennison Rogers.[20] Opposite, on the eastern corner of Bowdoin and Beacon Streets, stood Governor James Bowdoin's house, with gardens extending behind it up the ridge and down its northern slope as far as what is now Ashburton Place. Adjoining this was the great house of Edward Bromfield, Jr. (Fig. 22), which passed to his son-in-law, William Phillips, in 1763. The present site of the Boston Athenæum once served as Lieutenant-Governor Phillips's pasture.

On the eastern corner of Beacon and Somerset Streets, where the stone house of the Reverend James Allen (1632–1710) of the First Church had stood, David Hinckley built in 1810 a double granite house (Fig. 57), which was subsequently occupied by Benjamin W. Crowninshield, Madison's Secretary of the Navy, and by John Lowell Gardner, East India merchant and son of Samuel Pickering Gardner, who lived in the great wooden Vassall house in Summer Street. Although this was thought to be the finest Boston house of its time, it should be noted that (unlike its earlier neighbors) it was built close to the street, as an element in a block, rather than sitting back in gardens. Upon Crowninshield's death in 1851 the newly founded Somerset Club bought his house and occupied it until 1872, when the Club moved to David Sears's house at 42 Beacon Street.[21]

The land on the east slope of Cotton Hill, upon which the Reverend John Cotton, Governor John Endicott, Sir Henry Vane, and the mint-master John Hull, among others, had lived in the colonial period, was purchased by Gardiner Greene in 1803. Joining it with other properties that he had bought, he developed behind his house on Tremont Street a hillside garden that was one of the wonders of the first third of the nineteenth century, where terraces with ornamental trees, flowering shrubs, Black Hamburg grape vines, peacocks and greenhouses led up to a vantage point

Fig. 57. Houses at Somerset and Beacon Streets

where one had a splendid view in all directions.[22] Charlestown, Boston, the wharves crowded with shipping, and the harbor, were all spread out before the eye, with Nahant in the extreme distance. At the very top of the hill, seventy feet above its present highest point, stood a summer house which was in the neighboring garden of Ebenezer Francis [23] (Fig. 58).

After Gardiner Greene's death in 1832 the property was bought by Patrick Tracy Jackson, who had been one of the founders of the textile mills at Lowell, and Treasurer of the Boston and Lowell Railroad from its incorporation in 1830. Jackson's motives were speculative rather than horticultural, for he proposed to shave off the top of the hill to fill new land north of Causeway Street, where the railroads from the north were coming in, and, on the decapitated hill, to develop Pemberton Square as a desirable residential area. For this purpose Jackson summoned a Wilmington

Fig. 58. View from the summit of Pemberton Hill

farmer, Asa G. Sheldon, who had previously bossed forty oxen and fifty men for him in grading the Lowell railroad.

Sheldon, in 1862, published an autobiography [24] which is a diverting record of what a determined Yankee could do with only manpower and oxen to aid him. Apropos of nothing in particular, he turned, in his "tenth link in the chain of life" to the subject of demolishing the hill, in the following manner:

In the spring of 1835, I received a letter from Jackson, desiring me to come to Boston, stating that he had a week's work for me to do. When there, he informed me that he wished me to ascertain what it would cost to move Pemberton Hill into salt water, north side of Causeway Street.

After probing the hill in several places and walking over the ground as fast as an ox team would walk, to ascertain how many times they could go in a day, the result of my investigations was that it could be done for 25 cents a yard. [25]

He got the job, although at 28 cents rather than 25. It involved nothing short of demolishing Gardiner Greene's house, the old Faneuil house in Tremont Street (Fig. 21), Dr. Lloyd's house and two others in Somerset Street, and carting the top sixty-five feet of the hill to the Charles River north of Causeway Street. Sheldon, in his laconic way, observed: "The whole area, including Streets adjoining, was upwards of four acres, and it made in the water, eight acres, fourteen feet deep." [26] Wearing his teamster's blue and white striped frock, he bought one hundred and twenty-six oxen, hired sixty Yankees and one hundred and ninety-nine Irishmen, and turned Dr. Lloyd's house, which he bid in at auction, into a boarding house for his men. The first shovelful of dirt was thrown on 5 May, and the last on 5 October 1835. This five-month operation, which cost around thirty thousand dollars, netted a profit of two thousand and seven hundred dollars, of which Jackson took a thousand dollars, leaving the rest for Sheldon. The following spring Sheldon worked for Jackson for five dollars a day, making Lowell, Nashua, Haverhill, Andover and Billerica Streets on the new land that had been created by the moving of the hill.[27]

At ten o'clock on Tuesday morning, 6 October 1835 — just twenty-six hours after Asa G. Sheldon had loaded his last ox cart — building lots on the site that he cleared were sold at auction "under a pavilion on the premises." [28] The main feature of the development was an enclosed place half way up the hill, first called Phillips Place but in 1838 renamed Pemberton Square. The auction catalogue stated:

Twenty-five lots front on Phillips Place, which with its Avenues is on a more extensive scale than any other in the City. The Place is in Crescent form, and measures at the greatest breadth of the area one hundred and nine feet, narrowed at each end to seventy five feet and is four hundred feet in length; ten feet of the width on each side is included in the given contents of lots, and is to be fenced in by the purchasers for grass plots or shrubberies.

The place was approached by an "avenue" leading up from Scollay Square into the center of the eastern side, while another street

Fig. 59. Pemberton Square

continued from the southwest corner up the hill to Somerset
Street. The lots for sale, which included not only the place and
its approaches, but twenty-five below, fronting on Tremont Street,
and ten above, facing Somerset Street, were carefully covered by
restrictions designed to assure uniform and harmonious architectural treatment. Thus Pemberton Square (Fig. 59) became
bordered with high-ceilinged red brick houses not unlike those of
its contemporary, Louisburg Square. In the half century that
elapsed before the present Suffolk Court House was plumped down
in the region, obliterating all sense of proportion, Pemberton
Square more than lived up to its promoter's aspiration of furnishing "sites for dwelling houses not surpassed if equalled by any
in the City for elevation, retirement, and proximity to business."
Ebenezer Francis, a retired East India merchant — reputed at
mid-century to be one of the two richest men in Boston[29] —
whose garden house on the summit of the hill had been imperiled

by Sheldon's excavation,[30] came down from his dangerous heights on Somerset Street and settled at 8 Pemberton Square. Robert Bennet Forbes, shipmaster and China Trade merchant, lived here for a time in the forties, before settling in Milton. The merchant Nathaniel Goddard, who had long lived at the corner of Kingston and Summer Streets, moved in 1843, at the age of 76, to 22 Pemberton Square.[31] Robert C. Winthrop, sometime Member of Congress, N. I. Bowditch the conveyancer, Amos A. Lawrence and his partner Robert M. Mason, John Amory Lowell, and Joseph Coolidge — grandson of the Joseph for whom Bulfinch had built the great house in Bowdoin Street in 1792 — were all living in Pemberton Square by 1850. On the last vacant lot, No. 11, Francis B. Crowninshield built a house in the early fifties.[32]

The pattern of brick blocks set by Pemberton Square soon spread around the other slopes of the hill. Charles Bulfinch, who had returned from Washington to pass the last years of his life in Boston, wrote on 12 June 1843 to his son:

The alterations here surpass all you can conceive. I have this morning viewed those going on in Bowdoin Street. Mr. Coolidge's noble mansion, trees and all, are swept away, and 5 new brick houses are now building on the spot. The same changes are taking place in Summer street, — Mr. Bussey's, Mr. Goddard's and Mr. Ellis' houses are giving room to a great number of modern houses, — so that you can see, although crowds assemble nightly to hear predictions of the speedy end of the World, still there are enough of unbelievers to go on making earthly habitations.[33]

The ridge connecting the former peaks of Cotton and Beacon Hills, on whose eastern slope the Bromfield and Bowdoin houses stood, was leveled in 1845, and Ashburton Place cut through from Bowdoin to Somerset Streets. As we admire the red brick houses around Beacon Hill today, it is well to remember that to Bulfinch, and those of his contemporaries who survived into the 1840's and '50's, these same houses connoted horrid crowding upon sites that had once been shaded by great trees where birds had sung, and made fragrant by the perfume of roses and honeysuckle.

This was, alas, the penalty of a growing population that was being steadily swelled by immigration. The 58,277 inhabitants of 1825 had become, by 1840, 93,383 and in 1850, 136,881. Oscar Handlin's *Boston's Immigrants 1790–1880*, which has recently been issued in a revised edition by Harvard University Press, describes graphically the changes brought about by the ever increasing numbers of newcomers. Early immigrants who had arrived in Boston mostly moved on to regions of greater opportunity. The great exodus from Ireland, however, brought here thousands of strangers who, having only the funds for the passage, and no skilled craft or trade to make them in demand in the newer parts of the country, remained in Boston to eke out a miserable existence by unskilled labor. By 1837 the *Boston Morning Post* was publishing a supposedly humorous reprint of selections from its court reports of the previous three years, in which the unhappy Irishman was all too often the protagonist by reason of drunkenness, fighting or pilfering, like the poor innocent fellow who went into a lumberyard " 'to pick up a few chips to boil his taykittle in the morning,' but, by mistake or absence of mind, carried off a mahogany plank ten feet long." [34] Professor Handlin finds that "by 1850, about 35,000 Irish were domiciled in the city; five years later there were more than 50,000 — almost all natives of the southern and western counties." [35] As fifty thousand is twice the entire population of Boston in 1800, it is easy to see that, even with the land that had been added and the houses that had been built during the intervening half century, the crowded housing of these newcomers was bound to change the character of certain regions at devastating speed. It was in the North End and the region of Fort Hill that the Irish early settled, with some expansion into the West End.[36]

The North End had never entirely recovered from the Revolution, for many of the Loyalists who accompanied the British to Halifax in March 1776 had occupied some of the best houses in that region. The post-Revolutionary shipping families that succeeded to the leadership of Boston — many of whom had moved in from Essex County — settled in other parts of town, as the tides of fashion turned southward and westward. Thus Hanover and

Salem Streets became a region of small merchants, tradesmen and artisans, interspersed with a few conservative families of larger resources who were blessed if they would budge.

The Second Church in North Square, when its wooden meeting house was pulled down for fuel by the British during the winter of 1775–1776, united with the New Brick. From 1829 to 1832 Ralph Waldo Emerson occupied its pulpit in Hanover Street, but under his successor, Chandler Robbins, the congregation migrated out of the North End to a new Gothic building in Bedford Street, dedicated in 1852. The New North (which like the Second Church had become Unitarian) had had Bulfinch build them a fine new meeting house in Hanover Street in 1804. Nevertheless by 1822 the church was complaining that "the young gentlemen who have married wives in other parts of the town have found it difficult to persuade them to become so ungenteel as to attend worship in the North End." [37] The Reverend Francis Parkman, father of the historian, who was minister of the New North from 1813 to 1849, preferred to live in the region of Bowdoin Square. In 1862 the building was sold to Bishop Fitzpatrick and became St. Stephen's Roman Catholic Church. Christ Church, Salem Street, still hobbled along, although with increasing lameness, until rescued in 1911 by Bishop Lawrence.[38]

Ann Street early in the century degenerated into a rough waterfront region of disorderly houses and brawls. Eyewitnesses have cherished the memory of a riotous descent upon an establishment called the Beehive, on the night of 22 July 1825, which led to "old marm Cooper scudding through School alley under full sail at a rate that would have done credit to a privateersman." [39] Indeed "the nymphs of Ann Street" remained a subject of complaint and police interest well into the fifties, and the name a byword for sordidness until it was, in 1854, changed to North Street.

Abner Forbes's and J. W. Greene's gossipy pamphlet *The Rich Men of Massachusetts*, issued in 1851, listed five hundred residents of Suffolk County reputed to be worth $100,000 or more. Seven were still living in the North End. Jonathan Parker, described as "Started poor. Hard-ware dealer, probably the oldest in the city," [40] who was alleged to have a capital of a quarter of a million, not only lived in Salem Street but stayed there through the sixties. Isaac Harris, mast-maker, who had lived in North Bennet Street soon after the War of 1812, resolutely remained there for more than half a century. In spite of such obstinate exceptions, the natural tendency was to move out of the North End, particularly as retail business and tenements began to encroach.

The process was more gradual in the South End, for Summer Street (Fig. 60) long retained its agreeable character. As late as 1838, E. C. Wines, coming from Philadelphia, noted:

Another pleasant feature of Boston is the many green and shady front yards which relieve and refresh the eye, as you wander through its winding streets. More or less of these are met with in every part of the city; but Summer street, on both sides, is lined with them from one end to the other. This, to my taste, is decidedly the handsomest street in Boston. Town and Country seem here married to each other, and there is no jar between the husband and the wife. It is a harmonious union, and the source of many pleasures. [41]

In addition to these houses surrounded by gardens, the region of Summer Street also had, in Chauncy Place, Winthrop Place and Otis Place, blocks of early nineteenth-century brick houses, similar to those on Beacon Hill, that survived longer because they occupied less space (Fig. 61).

The slopes of Fort Hill changed more rapidly during the thirties and forties. The Pearl Street houses, built after the burning of the ropewalks in 1794, stood in generous grounds, with the unencumbered slopes of the hill above them. Caroline Gardiner Curtis describes Fort Hill as "a remnant of Revolutionary days, still showing the remains of fortifications, though overgrown with grass, making a pretty little park with a beautiful view over the harbor." [42] Here her grandfather, Thomas Handasyd Perkins, would stroll after dinner. Once on a spring afternoon, when accompanied by Harrison Gray Otis, he had the pleasure, after watching a ship in its progress up the harbor, of recognizing it as one of his own, arriving from China "in advance of her time and just a year from the time she sailed away." [43] In 1808 a circle

Fig. 60. Houses at Summer and Kingston Streets

Fig. 61. Church Green opposite Summer Street in 1858

Fig. 62. Fort Hill in 1860

of houses, first known as Washington Place, had been begun on the hilltop. Later, with a lordly disregard for geometry, the name was changed to Washington Square. Shortly before his death in 1822, James Perkins had given his house at 13 Pearl Street to the Boston Athenæum, which had since its incorporation in 1807 been first in Scollay's Buildings for two years and then for thirteen in the Amory house in Tremont Street, adjoining King's Chapel Burying Ground.[44] Eleven years later, in 1833, James Perkins's brother, Thomas Handasyd Perkins, gave his house at 17 Pearl Street to the school for blind children that subsequently adopted his name, and moved to Temple Place[45] where he built himself the house now occupied by the Provident Institution for Savings. One by one the private residents of Pearl Street moved away.[46] By 1839 the New England Institution for the Education of the Blind had moved to larger quarters in South Boston,[47] and the Athenæum was, "because of the increase of business and the erection of warehouses in the vicinity," thinking of going elsewhere.[48]

Ten years passed before the Athenæum finally moved to its present building at 10½ Beacon Street, overlooking the Granary Burying Ground. Its Pearl Street property, which had been carried at $22,890 in Treasurer's reports in the twenties, was sold in 1850 for $45,000.[49]

With land values rising in this way, absentee owners of private houses would have little desire to improve or even maintain their property. Their natural instinct would be to sell for business purposes, or get what they could out of renting the houses as they stood, while waiting to sell. Thus Fort Hill (Fig. 62), like the North End, was ripe for receiving the incoming immigrant horde. As Professor Handlin has observed:

In this transition originated the Boston slums — precisely the housing the Irish needed. Near the wharves and cheap in rent, these localities became the first home of such immigrants in Boston. Newcoming Irishmen, nostalgic for the Emerald Isle, gravitated towards these vicinities, augmenting the number of Irish already there, and making their countrymen reluctant to leave the home-like community even when they could. As a result, there were few natives in the North End and Fort Hill and even fewer non-Irish aliens, for these groups fled, sacrificing other interests in order to avoid the decline in social status that resulted from remaining.[50]

CHAPTER VI

The Flight from the South End

THE LATE GEORGE APLEY, that well-documented creation of John P. Marquand's accurate recollection, settled down one evening in his Beacon Street library, "walled in by the leather backs of good books, with the prints of sailing ships above the shelves and his collection of shaving mugs just below them," to write for his children an account of their ancestors. When he reached the stage of describing his own father's houses, he wrote:

Your grandfather, also, bought this house on Beacon Street when the Back Bay was filled in, and this leads me up to a single amusing instance of his unfailing business foresight.

Shortly before he purchased in Beacon Street he had been drawn, like so many others, to build one of those fine bow-front houses around one of the shady squares in the South End. When he did so nearly everyone was under the impression that this district would be one of the most solid residential sections of Boston instead of becoming, as it is to-day, a region of rooming houses and worse. You may have seen those houses in the South End, fine mansions with dark walnut doors and beautiful woodwork. One morning, as Tim, the coachman, came up with the carriage, to carry your aunt Amelia and me to Miss Hendrick's Primary School, my father, who had not gone down to his office at the usual early hour because he had a bad head cold, came out with us to the front steps. I could not have been more than seven at the time, but I remember the exclamation that he gave when he observed the brownstone steps of the house across the street.

"Thunderation," Father said, "there is a man in his shirt sleeves on those steps." The next day he sold his house for what he had paid for it and we moved to Beacon Street. Your grandfather had sensed the approach of change; a man in his shirt sleeves had told him that the days of the South End were numbered.[1]

This, in Marquand's novel, occurred in 1873, but, as early as 1863, William Dean Howells's hero, Silas Lapham, had "bought very cheap of a terrified gentleman of good extraction who had discovered too late that the South End was not the thing, and who in the eagerness of his flight to the Back Bay threw in his carpets and shades for almost nothing." [2]

At this point it becomes necessary to indicate the bounds of the area from which George Apley's father fled so precipitately, thus creating a good buy in real estate for the Silas Laphams who were appearing on the scene. In seventeenth- and eighteenth-century Boston, before anyone had tinkered with the outline of the Shawmut peninsula, filled land or built bridges, the term South End was applied to the region between the present State Street and the Neck, from the Common eastward to the harbor. As the narrow outline of the Neck was obliterated (Fig. 63), first by the filling of Front Street and the South Cove, and then by the making of land south of the narrowest point, the traditional balance between the North, South and West Ends was upset, just as in Washington the northwest region, by spilling over to engulf Georgetown and points beyond, has rather completely demolished the symmetry of the l'Enfant plan of the District of Columbia. The creation of all this new land in the direction of Roxbury led to some ambiguity in geographical terms during the nineteenth century. As the private houses of Franklin, Pearl and Summer Streets gradually gave way to business — a process that was made final by the great fire of 9 November 1872 — there was an increasing tendency to think of this area as an extension of the downtown center of Boston, and to apply the term South End more specifically to the newer lands further south. One might squander considerable time in an effort to define the popular conception of the shifting boundaries of the South End, decade by decade. For the purposes of this study, I propose, after 1850, to apply it solely to the new lands south of Dover Street, developed in the area where the Neck widened as it approached Roxbury.[3]

These Neck lands, which in the eighteenth century were often overflowed by high tides, to the considerable inconvenience of travelers approaching Boston by land from Roxbury, only began to become useful after the Revolution when a sea wall was built

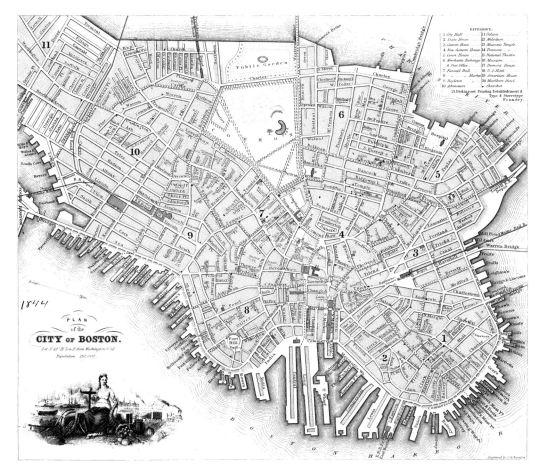

Fig. 63. The Boynton map of 1844

to cut off the tides.[4] During the first half of the nineteenth century, the area, although laid out into streets (Fig. 64), developed slowly, but, beginning with the fifties it rapidly grew into a region of symmetrical blocks of high-shouldered, comfortable red brick or brownstone houses, bow-fronted and high-stooped, with mansard roofs, ranged along spacious avenues, intersected by cross streets that occasionally widened into tree-shaded squares and parks, whose central gardens were enclosed by neat cast iron fences. Yet this seemingly attractive new South End never fulfilled its promise, for it began to slip into grubbiness while still comparatively new — a future that may be confidently predicted for some of the rows of ranch houses with which speculative developers have defaced the suburbs of Boston in the years since World War II. Before the end of the century, settlement houses were attempting to alleviate the squalor of slum conditions in the South End. Robert A. Woods, head of the South End House, was only being coolly descriptive when in 1898 he entitled his settlement study of the region *The City Wilderness*. Professor Albert B. Wolfe's *The Lodging House Problem in Boston*, published in 1906 in the *Harvard Economic Studies*, drew its sordid material from the only recently new South End, while today, after the passage of a century, the caption of "Arabia deserta" that Rudolph Ruzicka applied to his engraving of Worcester Square, seems only too appropriate.

To return to the beginning of the nineteenth century, the Neck lands had naturally been laid out in relation to Washington Street (once Orange Street), which was, originally, the only thoroughfare in the region. Columbia Square appeared on a plan of 1801, on the site of the present Franklin and Blackstone Squares, not far south of the point where the Neck began to widen. From Columbia Square, Suffolk Street (now a part of Shawmut Avenue) was laid out west of, and parallel to, Washington Street as a new road leading toward the Roxbury meeting house.[5] A survey by Osgood Carleton,[6] who died in 1816, shows a certain amount of scattered building in the Washington-Suffolk Street region between Northampton and Lenox Streets (Fig. 65).

Fig. 64. The Neck from the J. G. Hales map of 1814

Fig. 65. The Neck in the early nineteenth century

The damming of the Back Bay induced some random filling along the western shore of the Neck which permitted the continuation of Suffolk Street (Shawmut Avenue) through to Castle Street, and the extension of Tremont Street through the Neck lands to Roxbury. Thus in the thirties, in place of but one road across the Neck, there were, with the widening and filling, four parallel highways — Tremont Street and Shawmut Avenue west of Washington Street and Front Street (later Harrison Avenue) east of it. Newly laid out city lands were sold at auction, sometimes producing better bargains for the purchaser than the city; witness the occasion on a rainy day in November 1830 when Lucius Manlius Sargent, driving to his country house, almost inadvertently picked up nearly four acres between Shawmut Avenue and Tremont Street at a poorly attended auction for the trifling sum of $269.80.[7]

The region built up slowly, but in the late forties it showed momentary promise of attracting purchasers who wished to have rather more land around their houses than was easily possible in the older parts of the city. Beacon Hill was fast being covered with solid blocks, while the Summer Street gardens were, one by one, disappearing as land values increased. Thus in 1848 when Peter Parker, a merchant living at 46 Beacon Street, next door to Harrison Gray Otis, undertook to build a handsome house for his daughter and son-in-law Mr. and Mrs. Edward Preble Deacon, he chose a site on Washington Street in the new South End. There, from designs of M. Lemoulnier of Paris, he built a brick house standing in grounds enclosed by a high brick wall that was entered, through double gates guarded by a porter's lodge, from Concord Street. The Deacon house, for its scale and for its handsome French furnishings, was one of the wonders of the mid-century. Passing sleigh riders admired it (Fig. 66); friends who frequented the house found it even more intriguing because of its quite un-New England suggestion of handsome extravagance. Caroline Gardiner Cary (later Mrs. Charles Pelham Curtis), who was

SLEIGH RACING ON THE NECK, BOSTON, MASSACHUSETTS.

Fig. 66. The Deacon house in Washington Street

twenty-one when the house was built, recalled years later that it was "much beyond, in pretension and reality, any house that Boston has known since." In her *Memories of Fifty Years* [8] she wrote of it and its builder:

Mr. Deacon, the son-in-law, was a handsome, attractive man, but without visible property, as I remember was said, when he appeared in Boston, coming from one of the Middle States. As stories went abroad of the extravagant ordering of furniture from Paul, the upholsterer of the day, there was a saying that this was really "robbing Peter to pay Paul," for it was very certain to be the father-in-law who paid the bills. Whoever paid, the planning and carrying out of the plans showed a great deal of taste, and it was said that it was all done by Mr. Deacon. Certainly, to reproduce a swell Paris house out on Washington Stret, and not only that, but to maintain the establishment after the French model, showed a certain amount of force both of brain and will.

One entered through a gateway into a courtyard of fair size and drove under a porte cochere (I think the first one ever seen in Boston), and within the illusion was well carried out: the great hall with a gallery running around the top, drawing room, ballroom, dining room, boudoir, all furnished appropriately. What I especially remember were the boudoir — walls covered with quilted satin, ceiling dotted over with butterflies — and some beautiful panels painted by Fragonard. . . . Beside a beautiful ball given there, I especially remember some charming small dances, ending in a supper, announced to us by tall French footmen in livery.

This elegance was short-lived, for the family after a brief period went to Europe, and Mr. Deacon soon died. "With him," Mrs. Curtis recalled, "went the chief attraction of the house," for although Mrs. Deacon lived on there for a time "she was too queer to be popular." Eventually she returned to Europe to live permanently. After Peter Parker's death the house and its contents were sold at auction in February 1871. Ten years later the Massachusetts Normal Art-School moved there.[9] Although part of the building is reputed to be standing — at the point where one sees from the Forest Hills elevated train the sign "Deacon Halls" — the best suggestion of the elegance of the house survives in the Museum of Fine Arts in the splendid eighteenth-century carved and gilded panels from the Hotel de Montmorency that once decorated the walls of the Deacon house.

Nothing else on this scale was ever again built in the South End, which instead developed into more modest blocks. In 1850 the city took steps to improve the public lands in the region, and through the work of the engineers E. S. Chesbrough and William P. Parrott a varied street plan was developed which stimulated the sale of building lots. Chester Square and East Chester and West Chester Parks (now parts of Massachusetts Avenue) were established in that year, while in 1851 Worcester Square and Union Park were laid out and sold at auction.[10] One by one the streets and squares built up, nearly always with due regard to the architectural unity of the blocks (Figs. 67–68). *Ballou's Pictorial*, presenting a view of Blackstone Square in 1855, proudly observed that this "serves as the type of construction which is rendering the south end of our city what upper New York is to the older portions of that great metropolis" and referred with pardonable pride to the

Plan of a Series of Dwelling Houses Designed & Erected in 1857 & 58 by Nathaniel J. Bradlee, Archt.

Boston, December 4, 1858.

Fig. 67. South End blocks designed by N. J. Bradlee

Fig. 68. South End blocks designed by N. J. Bradlee

screening, by such buildings, of "that mournful and inodorous Lake Asphaltics — Back Bay, with its mud, it creeks, the mud-larking boys, and its occasionally good shooting during an easterly turn in September and October." [11]

The sad fact that, after thirty years, it was abundantly clear that while Uriah Cotting's mill dam had not developed a great series of factories driven by water power, it had, by confining the tides, turned the Back Bay into an unsightly and stinking nuisance. The railway lines that crossed it only increased the nuisance to a point that eventually required, on grounds of public health, the filling of the entire area. A legislative commission, reviewing in 1852 the history of the Back Bay and the various rights involved in it, proposed that the Boston and Roxbury Mill Corporation and the Boston Water-Power Company should abandon their business as mill and water power owners, but should be allowed to hold and use their property for land purposes, under the authority and direction of the state, filling their basins with clean gravel, making provision for perfect drainage. Commissioners who were appointed to determine the rights of the various parties claiming an interest in the flats, and to devise a plan for the filling and laying out of the new lands, made agreements which placed the majority of the unfilled lands in the hands of the Commonwealth. A good deal of hassling between city and Commonwealth ensued. Finally in 1857 authority was granted the commissioners to let contracts for filling, to sell the new land as soon as it was made and to use the sums obtained for the next stages of the filling.[12] As this in the end proved to be purely a state matter, in which the city had no share, plans for the new Back Bay developed with singularly little coordination with what the city was doing in the South End. The regions were, in the first place, separated from one another by the Providence and the Worcester railway lines. Moreover, as the main avenues of the South End ran parallel to Washington Street, and those of the future Back Bay development would reasonably run parallel to the Mill Dam, the different axes of the two areas, which converged on the older city at a 45 degree angle, made it relatively difficult to connect the two sets of streets. Thus the two areas developed separately — the South End from the fifties and the Back Bay from the sixties — with little connection between them (Fig. 69).

To dispose of the unsightly flats between Tremont Street and the Boston and Providence Railroad tracks, Columbus Avenue was, in 1860, projected from Park Square to the Roxbury line, over land of the Boston Water-Power Company. This thoroughfare, which ran parallel to the railway tracks, was begun in 1868 and completed in the following decade, after the land in question had been transferred to the city by the company.

The third quarter of the nineteenth century saw almost continual building in the South End. The 1850 city population of 136,881 had risen to 341,919 by 1875. Business was engulfing Bulfinch's handsome rows of houses. The Tontine Crescent and Franklin Place were demolished in 1857–1858 to make way for

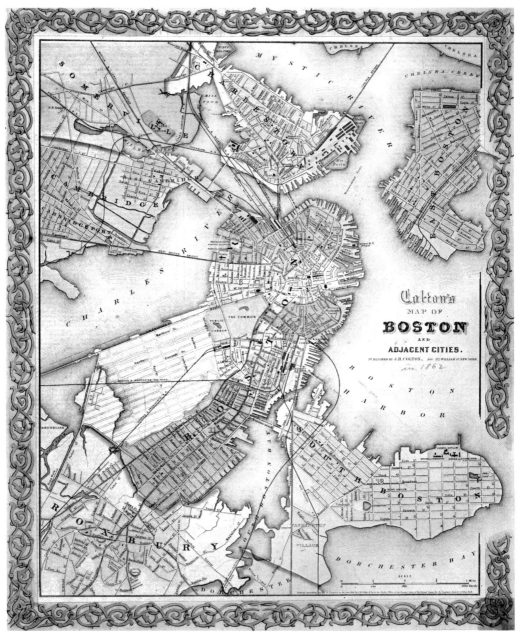

Fig. 69. The Colton map of 1855

blocks of stone stores and warehouses in Franklin Street.[13] The days of Colonnade Row as a pleasant residential area were numbered. Moreover, the horse cars of the Metropolitan Railroad, which began to operate from Scollay Square to Roxbury late in 1856, brought the South End into convenient communication with the center of the city.

Furthermore, the great growth in strength of the Roman Catholic Church, brought about considerably by immigration, led to important institutional developments in the South End. The imposing granite Jesuit Church of the Immaculate Conception (Fig. 70) in Harrison Avenue, designed by P. C. Keeley of Brooklyn, New York, was completed in 1861. Boston College, administered by the same order, was established in 1863 in an adjacent red brick building.[14] With the changes that were occurring in Franklin Street, the wholly charming Cathedral of the Holy Cross that Charles Bulfinch had built for Bishop Cheverus early in the century became surrounded by business blocks. As it was, moreover, entirely too small for the needs of the fast-growing diocese, a new Catholic cathedral, of the same dedication, was begun in Washington Street at the corner of Waltham Street, in 1867.

Fig. 70. Church of the Immaculate Conception and Boston College

This very large Gothic building, dedicated in 1875, was, like the Immaculate Conception, designed by P. C. Keeley.[15]

A considerable number of Protestant churches were either founded in the new South End in the third quarter of the nineteenth century, or moved there during this period from the region between Boylston and Dover Streets. A new Unitarian Church of the Unity, founded in 1857, was soon built in West Newton Street.[16] James Freeman Clarke's Church of the Disciples, founded in 1841, moved from Freeman Place on Beacon Hill to Indiana Place, near the Boston and Worcester tracks, and finally in 1869 built on the corner of Warren Avenue and West Brookline Street.[17] The South Congregational Church, which, with the engaging logic of Boston nomenclature, was Unitarian and quite without relation to the Old South Church which *was* Congregational, moved from the region of Boylston Market, during the pastorate of Edward Everett Hale, to Union Park Street, where it built a large church that was completed in 1862.[18] Theodore Parker's Twenty-eighth Congregational Society, also Unitarian, founded in 1845, moved in 1873 to Parker Memorial Hall, on the corner of Berkeley and Appleton Streets.[19]

Congregationalism was represented by the Shawmut Congregational Church, organized in 1849, which built a large brick meeting house on the corner of Tremont and Brookline Streets in 1864;[20] by the Berkeley Street Church, founded in Pine Street in 1827, which moved in 1862 to what was then believed to be the largest Protestant church in New England, at the junction of Warren Avenue with Tremont, Dover and Berkeley Streets;[21] and by the Union Church, formed in Boylston Hall in 1822, which built at Columbus Avenue and Newton Street in 1870.[22]

The Methodist Church on Tremont Street between Concord and Worcester, a piece of Hammatt Billings's Gothic, was completed in 1862,[23] while the Gothic building in Columbus Avenue of the Second Universalist Church was occupied ten years later.[24] The First Presbyterian Church settled at the corner of Columbus Avenue and Berkeley Street, and the Evangelical Lutheran Zion Church at the corner of Shawmut Avenue and Waltham Street.[25]

It will be noted that all of the preceding Protestant religious societies in the South End had been of nineteenth-century foundation. Only in the case of the Baptists, who had moved to the region in large numbers,[26] did churches founded in the colonial period migrate there. A Shawmut Avenue Baptist Church at the corner of Rutland Street, founded in 1856, was absorbed in 1877 by the First Baptist Church of 1665, which had left the North End for Somerset Street in 1853. Within five years, however, the combined society moved on to the Back Bay.[27] The Federal Street Baptist Church of 1827 moved to the South End, where it settled on the corner of Clarendon and Montgomery Streets, become known as the Clarendon Street Baptist Church,[28] while in the seventies two colored Baptist societies, the Ebenezer and the Day Star, were founded in West Concord and Appleton Streets.[29]

The handsomest development of the South End was furthered between 1861 and 1864 by the building, near Boston College, of the Boston City Hospital (Fig. 71) on a seven-acre tract bounded by Concord, Albany and Springfield Streets and Harrison Avenue.

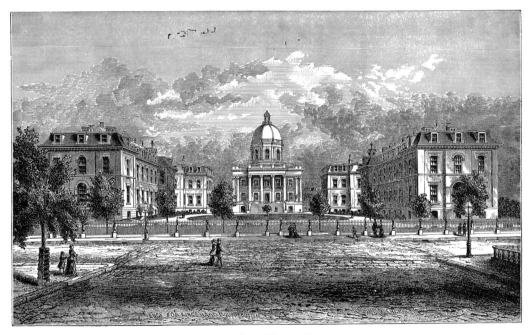

Fig. 71. Boston City Hospital

Its domed central administration building, connected with pavilions by curving arcades, was designed in a strongly French vein by Gridley J. F. Bryant, son of the engineer who had devised the Granite Railway at Quincy a generation earlier. In the years following Bulfinch's migration to Washington the architecture of Boston had splintered off into a variety of styles, Greek revival, Gothic revival and what Walter F. Kilham, in his succinct and informative little book *Boston After Bulfinch*, calls "Plain American." To these, in the sixties, was added a strong dose of French Renaissance as seen through the eyes of the Second Empire. The present City Hall on School Street, built in 1862 by Bryant in association with Arthur Gilman, shows the very marked inspiration of the Tuilleries and the new Louvre in Paris. Although now abandoned by municipal administration, the old City Hall is a handsome building in itself as well as a landmark in the development of local taste. Bryant's original brick buildings of the City Hospital, before they were overwhelmed by later construction, were similarly a handsome addition to the South End, approached as they were through the tree-shaded Worcester Square.[30]

The splendor of the French Second Empire was reflected in the marble-faced Commonwealth Hotel (Fig. 72), on Washington

Fig. 72. Commonwealth Hotel

Street between Worcester and Springfield Streets, and in the great brick St. James Hotel upon Newton Street facing Franklin Square. The St. James, built by M. M. Ballou and opened in the spring of 1868, boasted over four hundred rooms, reached by a steam-operated passenger elevator. Although General Grant honored it with his patronage while president, the St. James had a short life as a hotel, for in 1882 it was taken over by the New England Conservatory of Music.[31]

The Girls' High School settled in 1870 into a mansard-roofed structure on West Newton Street that was at the time claimed to be "the largest, most substantial, and costly school edifice in the United States." [32] The marvels of this were soon to be eclipsed by the even larger structure, begun in 1877 to house the Boston Latin and English High Schools, which undertook to be "the largest in the world used as a free public school." This double building, fronting on Warren Avenue, Dartmouth and Montgomery Streets, was designed by George A. Clough, the city architect.[33] It was indeed so large that soon after its dedication in 1881 the City Council, seeing pupils rattling about in its fifty-six rooms, considered adapting it for the use of the Boston Public Library, which was seriously overcrowded in its 1858 building on Boylston Street, facing the Common. Although William H. Whitmore, who was one of the Library trustees, strenuously favored the plan, his colleagues disagreed and the school remained there for more than half a century.[34]

The casual visitor, wandering through the streets of the South End today and finding so many remnants of a handsome past, may well wonder why the region so soon fell into decay. The solid and dignified aspect of its blocks have, I suspect, somewhat beclouded the issue, for as nearly as I can discover from rummaging in directories, the South End never was, with the solitary and premature exception of the Deacon house, a really fashionable area. Some young couples set up housekeeping, and Silas Laphams aplenty were to be found in the South End, while some elderly people, pushed out of their former haunts by the spread of the business district, ended their days there. With the destruction of

Franklin Place, John G. Torrey, President of the Columbian Bank, moved to the corner of Washington and Canton Streets, while his lawyer-neighbor Henry B. Smith went to new quarters at 190 Shawmut Avenue. Some scholars enjoyed the quiet streets of the South End; in the sixties Justin Winsor, the great Superintendent of the Boston Public Library, was living in West Brookline Street and the Reverend Robert C. Waterston in Chester Square; but I fail to find any trace of China Trade families or the reputed holders of great fortunes having migrated in this direction.

When Abner Forbes and J. W. Greene published *The Rich Men of Massachusetts* in 1851, seven out of the five hundred residents of Suffolk County reputed to hold property of one hundred thousand dollars or more were sticking it out in the North End, while only three appeared to be living in the new South End beyond Dover Street.[35] Daniel Weld, wholesale grocer, and George May, son of the merchant Perrin May, who had been living in Washington Street not far from Dover Street in the thirties, when the Neck still retained some of its original character, were still there in 1851. Edward D. Peters, a retired commission merchant, said to have had a capital of three hundred thousand dollars, who had formerly lived in Rowe Place, off Bedford Street, was in 1851 living at the corner of Washington and Canton Streets. Seventeen of the men listed by Forbes and Greene who were recorded as living in other parts of Boston in 1851 (including John G. Torrey and Henry B. Smith) moved to the South End in the course of the fifties and sixties. The fortunes of two of these were estimated in 1851 at two hundred thousand dollars; [36] five were reputed to have property of one hundred and fifty thousand,[37] and ten of one hundred thousand dollars each.[38] Yet in the same year Forbes and Greene estimated that there were forty-one men in Boston worth between half a million and three million each. These were without exception firmly distributed around Beacon Hill, Park Street, Pemberton Square, Colonnade Row, Temple Place and the region of Summer Street. Mrs. Charles Pelham Curtis recalled the way in which, down to the fifties, Boston had been "very limited in its residential region" with "different streets . . . given over, as it were, to different clans."

Summer Street was the home of the Sam Gardner family; Lees, Jacksons and Putnams, all related to each other, congregated about Chauncy Place and Bedford Street; Perkinses in Temple Place; Lawrences and Masons in the part of Tremont Street between West and Boylston, then called Colonnade Row; Eliots in Park and Beacon; Amorys in Franklin Street (then such a pretty place with a little grass park down the middle); the head of the Sears family lived in the house of the Somerset Club . . . , and their married children lived on each side; Curtises and Lorings were in Somerset Street.[39]

In the next quarter of a century when any of these clans budged, it was toward the Back Bay or the country rather than the South End.

Even so, it is not easy to see how a region so substantially and amply built slipped into lodging houses so fast. The most convincing explanation I have yet seen is that offered by Professor Albert B. Wolfe,[40] who blamed it chiefly on the panic of 1873.

The immediate occasion for the change seems to have been the real-estate situation on Columbus Avenue. This street was put through as far as Northampton Street about 1870, and was immediately built up with a somewhat cheaper style of houses than those on the older streets. Most of these new houses were built on mortgages, and after the panic of '73 had broken over the city most of them were in possession of banks. The banks sold them for what they would bring, and the result was an acute drop in the value of Columbus Avenue real estate, and in the character of the immediate locality. The shock thus felt on Columbus Avenue with such force gradually had the effect of disturbing the equilibrium in the rest of the South End.

Thus, one by one, houses began to change hands, perhaps not with the instantaneous decisiveness attributed by George Apley to his father, but inexorably.

Professor Wolfe, who estimated that "by 1885 the South End had become dominantly a lodging house section," demonstrated in detail the transformation of Union Park between 1868 and 1902 by a study of the real estate transfers. His chart of that pleasant square shows solid private occupancy through 1872, two lodging houses creeping in during 1874, and the change steadily continuing until in 1902 only seven out of fifty-three houses remained as private residences. The same transformation occurred

in other parts of the South End, although at a different pace.
The streets toward Chester Square (now Massachusetts Avenue)
lost their character more slowly. Walbridge A. Field, lawyer, of
the Dartmouth class of 1855, settled at 43 Rutland Square in the
seventies and was, as Chief Justice of Massachusetts, still there
at the end of the century.[41]

The region between Dover Street and Boylston was considerably
altered in the last three decades of the century. In 1869, Broadway, which was the main thoroughfare through South Boston, was
carried over the Fort Point Channel to Albany Street. In the same
year a regrading operation, known as the Church Street improvement, was completed by the city in the region where the Boston
and Albany tracks crossed Columbus Avenue and Tremont Street.
As a result of changes brought about by the filling of the Back
Bay, this area had become hardly above tide level in general, and
in some instances below it. To improve sanitary conditions, more
than two hundred brick buildings were raised to new foundations,
then to fourteen feet above their former levels (Figs. 73–75). At

Fig. 73. Church Street alterations in 1868

Fig. 74. Church Street before   Fig. 75. Church Street after

the same time seven streets were widened, and Columbus Avenue extended through to Park Square. Between 1870 and 1872 a comparable enterprise was carried out in the Suffolk Street district, involving the regrading of thirty-two acres between Dover, Tremont, Pleasant and Washington Streets. About one hundred and fifty buildings in this area were demolished, another six hundred were equipped with new and higher foundations, and many streets were altered. A part of the quarter of a million cubic yards of fill required came from the leveling of Fort Hill. Suffolk Street, which had formerly ended at Castle Street, was cut through to Tremont Street to become a northern extension of Shawmut Avenue.[42]

The area comprised in this regrading had never had a very marked character. Its proximity to the railroad did it no good, and it soon lapsed into a slum region of tenements and lodging houses. Mary Antin, whose parents migrated from Polotzk, within the Pale, to "the promised land," described the air in Dover Street as "heavy with evil odors of degradation."

Outwardly, Dover Street is a noisy thoroughfare cut through a South End slum . . . Dover Street is intersected, near its eastern end, where we lived, by Harrison Avenue. That street is to the South End what Salem Street is to the North End. It is the heart of the South End ghetto, for the greater part of its length; although its northern end belongs to the realm of Chinatown. Its multifarious business bursts through the narrow shop doors, and overruns the basements, the sidewalk, the street itself, in push-carts and open-air stands. Its multitudinous population bursts through the greasy tenement doors, and floods the corridors, the doorsteps, the gutters, the side streets, pushing in and out among the pushcarts, all day long and half the night beside. Rarely as Harrison Avenue is caught asleep, even more rarely is it found clean. Nothing less than a fire or flood would cleanse this street.[43]

From this ghetto she would, after dark, go to the South Boston bridge, when the confusion at home drove her out or when she needed fresh air. This was, one must remember, the spot where Josiah Quincy, Jr., had seen Emily Marshall three quarters of a century earlier. But instead of a view across water to a serene and compact Boston, the bridge now provided a vista of railroad yards.

I liked to stand leaning on the bridge railing, and look down on the dim tangle of railroad tracks below. I could barely see them branching out, elbowing, winding, and sliding out into the night in pairs. I was fasci-nated by the dotted lights, the significant red and green of signal lamps. These simple things stood for a complexity that it made me dizzy to think of. Then the blackness below me was split by the fiery eye of a monster engine, his breath enveloped me in blinding clouds, his long body shot by, rattling a hundred claws of steel; and he was gone, with an imperative shriek that shook me where I stood.

So would I be, swift on my rightful business, picking out my proper track from the million that cross it, pausing for no obstacles, sure of my goal.[44]

CHAPTER VII

The Filling of the Back Bay

WILLIAM LAWRENCE, seventh Bishop of Massachusetts, remembered his childhood drives across the Back Bay between the house in Pemberton Square where he was born in 1850 and his father's country place in Longwood. To a very small boy it seemed a long journey, but there was a good deal to be seen in the drive along the Mill Dam, which is now Beacon Street.

On the south side was the Back Bay, and on the north the Charles River. A plank walk ran along the south side of the road and a line of poplar trees. Driving out from Boston on a winter day was a cold trip. The northwest wind swept down the Charles River unobstructed, and the great mass of snowy ice caused by the tides on the flats gave the scene an Arctic look, for Cambridgeport was well back of the river across water and marsh. To the south one's vision swept across the Back Bay to the Neck two miles away, and the Roxbury Meeting House stood out against the sky. Through holes cut in the ice men were spearing eels, and boys were skating. Halfway across the Dam was the tollgate, where every team and carriage stopped to pay toll; and just beyond, where at flood tide the Charles rushed in under a cut in the road to fill the Back Bay, and at ebb tide rushed out again, were the mill and mill-wheel which ground corn hauled in from Brookline and Newton by the farmers. At the fork the 'Brighton Road' ran out where Commonwealth Avenue now is, and the 'Punch Bowl Road' to the left, leading to the Punch Bowl Tavern in Brookline.[1]

Fig. 76. The Back Bay from the State House in the late fifties

The appearance of the Back Bay, as the young William Lawrence saw it, is preserved in one of a series of photographs (Figs. 76–79) taken in the late fifties from the dome of the State House,[2] which shows the region on the eve of its final filling. Land has already considerably encroached upon water, for the Public Garden has been created and the shore line is now at Arlington rather than Charles Street.

The City had no sooner recovered the sites granted for rope-walks in 1794, at the foot of the Common, than various eager persons began to daydream about building upon these lots. Even though the citizens of Boston had in 1824 upheld Mayor Quincy's view, denying the City Council the right to sell the land west of Charles Street,[3] Dr. Caleb H. Snow's A History of Boston, published the following year, contained in some copies an illustration

Fig. 77. Looking east from the State House in the late fifties

Fig. 78. Looking south from the State House in the late fifties

Fig. 79. Looking southwest from the State House in the late fifties

by Abel Bowen of proposed development in the region (Fig. 80) that is startlingly prophetic of what happened thirty-five years later.[4] The notion of using the land as a garden came from Horace Gray and other amateur horticulturists, who in 1837 petitioned the City for a lease of the land. Gray, who had a collection of camellias in the conservatory of his town house in Kingston Street, and various varieties of hothouse grapes at his country place in Brighton, envisioned on the site a botanic garden similar to those in European cities. By an act of the Legislature passed on 1 February 1839, he and George Darracott, Charles P. Curtis, and others, were incorporated as the Proprietors of the Botanic Gardens in Boston, and the group built a greenhouse and set out various ornamental trees and plants. A large circus building, just north of Beacon Street and west of Charles Street, was converted into an immense conservatory for plants and birds — containing over a thousand camellias, some of tree size — and was a great attraction until its destruction by fire. But the idea of profiting from the land died hard. In 1842, 1843, 1849 and 1850 the City Council made attempts to sell the garden. A *Report of the Joint Committee on Public Lands in relation to the Public Garden, July 1850,* published as City Document No. 18 for that year,[5] went so far as to present a plan showing the garden divided into house lots, with new streets between Beacon and Boylston that bear a considerable resemblance to Marlborough Street, Commonwealth Avenue and Newbury Street. In spite of the alluring estimate of a possible million and a half to be realized from the sale of lots, these miserable proposals went down to defeat.

In the decade following the construction of the Mill Dam, houses began to be built on the north side of Beacon Street, west of Charles. The six fine granite houses beyond River Street — numbers 70 to 75 — were built in 1828 by the Mount Vernon Proprietors, although the other Beacon Street lots facing the Public Garden remained vacant until the forties.[6] The nine great brick houses designed by George M. Dexter — numbers 92 to 99 — built in 1849–1850, were conceived on a noble scale, yet their surroundings left something to be desired. Diagonally across from them, Bishop Lawrence recalled, "was the city dump, where ashes and other refuse were thrown by tipcarts into the Back Bay." [7] Wharf rats scampered in and out of the sea wall on the westerly side of the Public Garden, while a common sewer, which entered the bay at the present corner of Beacon and Arlington Streets, did little to improve the atmosphere.[8]

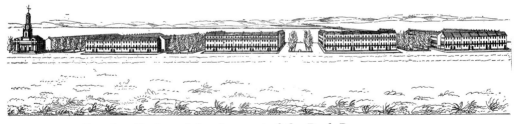

Fig. 80. Projected development of the Back Bay

There was no doubt that something needed to be done about the Back Bay. Of all those who ventilated suggestions, the most imaginative and far-seeing was a visiting Scot, Robert Fleming Gourlay, who in 1844 proposed a grandiose plan (Fig. 81) that would not only improve the Back Bay but provide for the future

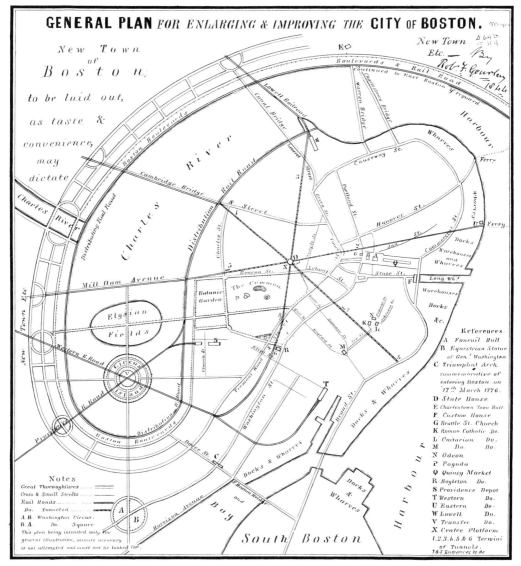

Fig. 81. Robert F. Gourlay's plan for Back Bay development

expansion of Boston through a network of suburban railway lines that would be carried into the city through subways. Devoted to what he termed "the science of city building," Gourlay had evolved plans for the improvement of his native Edinburgh, and of New York, before tackling the problems of Boston. His chronic insomnia, which was the subject of a report in the *Boston Medical and Surgical Journal,* gave him double the average man's time for thought. Indeed in 1843 he claimed to have slept but two hours during the preceding five years and eight months. During 1843 and 1844, while staying at the Marlborough Hotel — a strict temperance hostelry in Washington Street — Gourlay bombarded the Mayor and citizens of Boston and the Governor and legislators of Massachusetts with a series of proposals that were at once visionary and prophetic. Some, like his pagoda and flower garden for the Common, or his triumphal arch proposed for the intersection of Washington and Dover Streets to commemorate Washington's entering Boston on 17 March 1776, were more ornamental than necessary. Others of an intensely practical nature sought to solve the overcrowding of the city brought about by natural growth and heavy immigration, and to provide commodious suburbs, by means of the recently arrived railroads.

During the last twenty years, [he wrote in 1844] Boston has doubled its population; but now, the ratio of increase must be greater far. Fifty years hence it will contain 500,000 souls; and within a century, a million at least. The Peninsula is already crowded; and here, want of forethought has caused confusion past remedy; but there is a field beyond, which may be planned out, and built on, with every advantage. Seventy years ago, the capital of Scotland was noted for discomfort. The necessities of a warlike age had driven the people within narrow bounds, to have protection from rocks and ravines. Bye-and-bye, buildings shot up to giddy heights, for want of room; but, at last, a stupendous bridge gave access to a plain, whereon a new town grew up, on a regular plan, unrivalled for beauty and convenience. So it may be here, more easily, and on a grander scale.[9]

In the middle of the Back Bay, at the intersection of the railroad lines, Gourlay proposed a "Circus Island" with a concealed sunken railroad "transfer depot" in the center, around which would be built two rings of houses. From this island "Distribution" and "sub-urban" railroads were to sweep around both banks of the Charles River as well as into the city, where they would dive into subways that connected with the various railway terminals. A subterranean "Centre Platform" at the State House is a curious prophecy of the role of the Park Street subway station, then half a century in the future. By this means, through travelers from Lowell and Portland could proceed directly to Providence and New York without fighting their way through the narrow streets of Boston. "Already," Gourlay wrote, "Washington Street is crowded to excess; and, every day, we witness inconvenience from the noise and collision of carriages. What would it be were there a million of residents, and tens of thousands of visitors?"

From the Public Garden south along the shore of the Back Bay and along the Cambridge and Charlestown shores of the Charles River, "continued to East Boston if required," were to be a band of "Boston Boulevards," with a railway line skirting the water, a tree-shaded park two hundred feet wide, and a forty-foot street, along which houses were to be built, with other streets be-

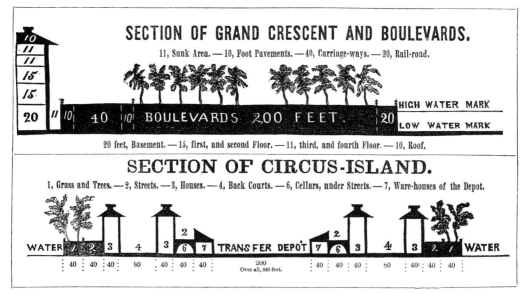

Fig. 82. Details of Robert F. Gourlay's plan

hind (Fig. 82). By this planning for suburban development, served by the "steam horse," a greater Boston would come into being.

The high grounds near Roxbury, Chelsea, &c — Mount Auburn, Fresh Pond, Spy Pond, &c — the streams, the islands, and the promontories; — all may be made to harmonise, in one grand panorama, — to display striking and enchanting scenes, such as imagination, once awakened, may conceive better than it is possible to describe.

How easily could PATHS, and RIDES, and DRIVES be conducted round about, and among all these fascinating objects! How agreable would it be to have public carriages, hourly, to carry us to each place, in turn, — allowing sufficient time for strangers to be satisfied: — to have a steamboat, in connection, running from Squantum Point: touching at certain promontories, islands, &c; and landing at Winthrop head! [10]

The Back Bay was to be dredged, and kept filled "for health, cleanliness and beauty" with three or four feet of clear water, while the mud dredged up would be used for the construction of an oval island to be known as the Elysian Fields, centered upon today's Copley Square. Boylston Street would run across the Bay, parallel to the Mill Dam, while Dartmouth Street would similarly cross the Bay from the Mill Dam to Circus Island.

Sadly enough, nothing came of all this imaginative planning. Even Gourlay's name is completely forgotten. All that remains is his pamphlet and the lithographed *General Plan for Enlarging and Improving the City of Boston* that he inscribed for the Reading Room of the Athenæum in 1844.[11] But if his shade still suffers from insomnia in another Elysian Field than the one he projected for the Back Bay, today's traffic congestion and debates over MBTA extensions must give Robert Fleming Gourlay a certain wry satisfaction.

David Sears, who incidentally had bought up a number of the mud flats in the Back Bay, came forward in 1849 with a plan for filling the area but leaving a 75-acre oval "Silver Lake" in the center, to secure the supposed sanitary benefits of fresh air passing over salt water. Boylston Street, in this plan, would lead to the center of the eastern shore of the lake, while a new Sears Avenue would run south of it in the region of St. James Avenue. David

Sears's plan (Fig. 83), lithographed by Toppan and Bradford, and dated 4 June 1849,[12] suffers from a certain amateurishness in design. It is not, for example, clear what he proposed to do with the Boston and Providence Railroad tracks, which simply vanish into space rather than leading to a station.

By mid-century the unsanitary aspects of the Back Bay forced public action. The Boston Board of Health had, in 1849, described its condition as "one of nuisance, offensive and injurious to the large and increasing population residing upon it." [13] Resolution of the conflict of public and private rights in the area was not easy. The Commissioners on Boston Harbor and the Back Bay, appointed under the Resolves of 1852, chapter 79, whose title was changed in 1855 to the Commissioners on the Back Bay, had their hands full. Finally, as ex-officio members of a Committee ap-

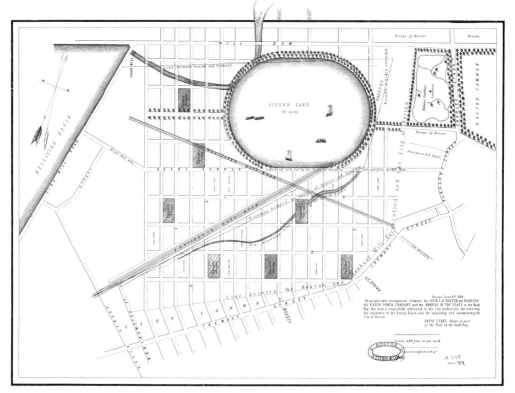

Fig. 83. David Sears's plan for Back Bay development

pointed under the authority of the Resolves of 1856, chapter 76, they succeeded in achieving a tripartite indenture of 11 December 1856 between the Commonwealth, the City, and various private proprietors, that opened the way for the filling of the area.[14] This division gave to the Boston and Roxbury Mill Corporation the flats north of their Mill Dam, which were soon to be known as the "water side of Beacon Street"; to the Commonwealth the area roughly between Beacon and Boylston Streets from Arlington Street on the east to an irregular line between Exeter and Fairfield Streets to the west; and to the Boston Water-Power Company the rest of the Back Bay. The city, which had been uncooperative throughout, and rapacious in its demands, was excluded from the distribution of land for filling, although it and the Commonwealth agreed to build jointly the new Arlington Street, from Beacon to Boylston Streets, west of the Public Garden.

The Legislature in May 1857 confirmed the tripartite indenture of the preceding December, and authorized the Commissioners on the Back Bay to fill and to sell the Commonwealth's lands there.[15] Their plan, which was adopted in 1856, provided for four new streets parallel to the Mill Dam, which were to be intersected at intervals varying from 548 to 600 feet, by cross streets. Commonwealth Avenue, which ran west from Arlington Street, at the center of the Public Garden, was not only two hundred feet wide, with a park between the roadways, but its lots were restricted so that all houses had to be set back twenty feet from the property line. Beacon and Boylston Streets were continued west on paper, while the names Marlborough and Newbury, which had in the colonial period been applied to portions of Washington Street, were revived for the streets north and south of Commonwealth Avenue. Public alleys running behind the houses provided inconspicuous access to kitchen doors for deliveries. This imposing plan, with its long vistas and suggestion of French boulevards, is generally credited to the architect Arthur Gilman, although the architect George Snell and Messrs. Copeland and Cleveland, landscape gardeners, appear to have made suggestions regarding Commonwealth Avenue.[16]

Here was an extremely handsome area on paper, but as no money had been appropriated for the filling, the Commissioners were reduced, as their seafaring ancestors had been, to the technique of parleying nothing into something by way of exchange. They treated with a Vermonter, Norman Carmine Munson, born in Hinesburg in 1820, who with his partner George Goss was established as a contractor at 22 Congress Square. Although Goss and Munson had carried out various railroad filling contracts, they had never undertaken anything of the magnitude of this job. Finding private financial backing for the necessary equipment and materials, they contracted with the Commissioners, in July 1858, to fill the whole area of Commonwealth land between the Public Garden and Clarendon Street, in return for four blocks of land amounting to 260,000 square feet. This left the Commonwealth 793,000 square feet for sale, exclusive of space allocated to streets, parks and passageways. During the summer of 1858 the Commissioners also sold, for $75,000, the block on the land side of Beacon Street between Arlington and Berkeley, to William W. Goddard and T. Bigelow Lawrence, who also made a contract for filling with Goss and Munson. By these transactions the Commissioners found funds for further work without expense to the Commonwealth.[17]

Twenty-three years earlier, Asa G. Sheldon had removed Pemberton Hill with the help of New England farmers, Irishmen, and oxen. The Boston hills were by 1858 too completely built over to permit further digging; and Goss and Munson were obliged to go some distance for their fill. In doing so they used two new techniques — the railroad and the steam shovel. Railway lines already obligingly crossed the Back Bay, while John Souther (1816–1911), who built engines at the Globe Locomotive Works in South Boston, was just putting a steam shovel (Fig. 84), invented by William Smith Otis of Philadelphia, into active production.[18] The process followed was well described in *Ballou's Pictorial* for 21 May 1859.

The gravel is brought from Needham, near the line of Newton, a quarter of a mile from the Upper Falls Depot, and nine miles distant from Boston.

Fig. 84. John Souther's steam shovel loading gravel for the Back Bay

One hundred and forty-five dirt cars, with eighty men, including engineers, brakemen and all, are employed, night and day in loading and transporting the gravel over the road. The trains consist of thirty-five cars each, and make, in the day time, sixteen trips, and in the night nine or ten, or twenty-five in twenty-four hours. Three trains are continually on the road during the day, and one arrives at the Back Bay every forty-five minutes. The excavators for loading the cars work by steam, and perform the work with rapidity and ease. There are two of them, both of which are propelled by engines of twenty-five horse power. The gearing of the engines is so arranged, however, as to greatly augment their power. When an empty train arrives at the pit, it is divided, and one half is fed by one excavator and the other half by the other. A locomotive is attached to each half, and the cars are drawn past the excavators, to be filled. Two shovels-full fill a car, the operation being very much like that of a dredging machine. As the shovel is elevated from the pit, it is turned towards the car, and

when directly over it the bottom is opened, and thus the gravel is de-
posited. The time occupied in loading an entire train of thirty-five cars is
about ten minutes. The excavators do the work of two hundred men.
The process of loading the cars, though very simple, is curious and interesting. During the year the contractors have been at work, there have been
taken out of the hills of Needham about three hundred thousand yards of
gravel. Some of the sand-hills which have been levelled were fifty feet
high, and the plain which has been made by the machines in excavating,
is about twelve acres in extent. The farm from which the sand and gravel
are taken belongs to the Charles River Railroad Company. When the contractors commenced operations there was a mortgage upon the land. They,
the contractors, agreed, on their part, to lift the mortgage, and the Railroad
Company agreed without further compensation to give the sand. It is believed that the excavation and filling in are going on at a more rapid rate
than has ever been known in the history of any similar contract in the
country. The contractors make, in the Back Bay, on an average, about
twenty-five hundred cubic yards, or forty-five hundred superficial feet per
day. This is equal to nearly two house lots. About fourteen acres of land
have been made already. At the rate the work is progressing, the hundred
acres belonging to the State will be completed in about four years more
time. The land made is measured on the first day of every month by an
engineer, under the direction of the Commissioners, and the contractors
draw their pay once a month, averaging from ten to twenty thousand dollars. They have drawn, in cash, only fourteen thousand dollars from the
State treasury, and this was received during the first two months of the
year. They have, however, purchased land of the Commissioners to the
amount of three hundred thousand dollars, one hundred and twenty thousand dollars worth of which they themselves have sold for cash. As they
settle now each month with the State, they receive, of course, deeds of
land instead of cash. The Commissioners have sold in all about five hundred
thousand dollars worth of land. They have received the cash for two hundred thousand dollars' worth over and above the amount sold to Goss &
Munson. It is estimated that the hundred acres will realize to the State,
when all completed, the handsome sum of three millions.

The following year, 1859, Goss and Munson signed a contract
with the Boston Water-Power Company for filling on their lands.
Albert Matthews (1860–1946), son of Nathan Matthews, sometime President of the Boston Water-Power Company and Mayor
of Boston, recalled that each car of the gravel train had "N. C.
MUNSON" painted on its side, and that the locomotives were

Fig. 85. Back Bay scavengers of the 1850's

dignified, like ships of the Royal Navy, with such high-sounding names as AJAX.

To get some idea of the appearance of the Back Bay in the course of filling, one has only to drive south from Boston over the Morrissey Boulevard today and watch the filling of marshy ground. The process by which the Boston College High School and the new plant of the Boston Globe have emerged rapidly from dumps closely parallels the sequence of events in the Back Bay a century ago. The main difference between the present and past operations is that one misses today the eager scavengers depicted by Winslow Homer in 1859 on the Back Bay lands (Fig. 85). In this sketch, engraved after his drawing for *Ballou's* issue of 21 May 1859, Homer has caught the "operations of the *chiffoniers,* these 'pickers up of unconsidered trifles' " in the areas where rubbish supplemented Needham gravel. Rubbish must have been fairly widespread, for Albert Matthews recalls that when "he was young enough to play baseball and football on vacant lots, hoopskirts were occasionally seen sticking up and oyster shells were plentiful." [19]

As profits began to be realized from the sale of Back Bay lands, the Legislature generously turned them to good purpose. The Acts of 1859, chapter 154, provided for payments of profits to the Massachusetts School Fund, the Museum of Comparative Zoology, Tufts, Williams and Amherst Colleges, and the Wesleyan Academy in Wilbraham. Moreover chapter 210 assured the future of the Public Garden, by providing that no building save a City Hall might be thereafter erected between Charles and Arlington Streets.[20] This blocked the way for such contraptions as the cruciform glass house designed by William Waud that was injudiciously proposed in the same year as a Massachusetts Conservatory of Art, Science and Historical Relics (Fig. 86). Fortunately a new City Hall was built in School Street in 1862, so that the Public Garden has continued as such; equally fortunately the municipal gardeners have been both careful in their work and conservative in their tastes, so that the Public Garden's gaudily brilliant flower beds, like its swan boats, irresistibly recall a French park of the Second Empire[21] (Fig. 87).

While filling was under way in the early blocks of the Back Bay, George H. Snelling presented an emotional Memorial to the Legislature,[22] dated 5 April 1859, pleading that the center of the Back Bay not be filled and that a basin of water seven hundred feet wide be substituted for Commonwealth Avenue. Snelling based his argument on the ground that the southwest wind "blows directly over the Common; and, taking its bracing qualities from the wide area of water over which it now passes — water renewed from the ocean twice in twenty-four hours — it bears health and refreshment to every part of this crowded and closely built city." [23] Although supported by various friends, Snelling's proposal failed, perhaps for the reason suggested by Albert Matthews years later.[24]

Not the least curious feature about it is the remark about the tide. The latter might "bring in clear water twice daily," but how about the mud left, also "twice daily," by the tide when it went out? In the old days before the dam was built, "twice daily" the mud flats on either side of the Charles were an offense to the eye and a dire affront to the nose.

Thus filling and building proceeded according to the 1856 plan. Their progress can best be comprehended by reference to a series of maps prepared in the eighties by the engineering firm of

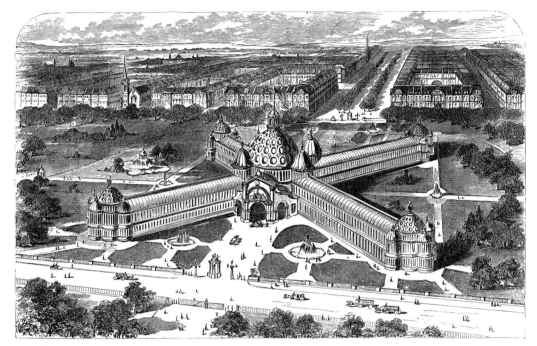

Fig. 86. Proposed Massachusetts Conservatory of Art, Science, and
Historical Relics in Public Garden

Fig. 87. Public Garden in the 1860's

Fuller and Whitney, showing the Back Bay at ten-year intervals.[25] In 1851 there is nothing filled west of the Public Garden. In 1861 (Fig. 88) the shore line of the Receiving Basin is just west of Clarendon Street. In 1871 (Fig. 89) Boylston and Newbury Streets and the south side of Commonwealth Avenue are filled only to Exeter Street, while the north side of Commonwealth Avenue reached Gloucester Street and Marlborough and Beacon Streets are filled as far as Hereford Street. This is the situation shown in an 1869 photograph (Fig. 90) where the eastern blocks of the Back Bay seem substantially completed, although water is plainly visible in the background. The 1882 map shows the entire area filled, although not necessarily built upon.

South of Boylston Street the railway lines not only prevented any symmetrical continuation of the Back Bay streets, but created a dreary kind of no man's land that was unconducive to handsome treatment. Similarly, west of the Cross Dam the marshes of the Muddy River, richly fragrant with sewage, presented a considerable obstacle to any consistent expansion in that direction. West Chester Park (now Massachusetts Avenue), the last well-designed thoroughfare of the South End, was in 1873 continued

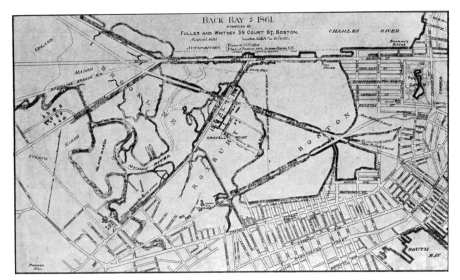

Fig. 88. The Back Bay in 1861

northeast across Gravelly Point to Beacon Street, creating a new
ninth cross street in the Back Bay grid, parallel to and west of
Hereford Street. Thus confined by the Public Garden on the east,
the Charles River on the north, the Muddy River on the west, and
railway lines on the south, the Back Bay developed in splendid
isolation. While the magnificent breadth of Commonwealth Avenue swept one naturally into the Public Garden and the Common, only Berkeley and Dartmouth Streets and Massachusetts
Avenue clumsily bridged the railway barrier to the South End.
In consequence, the region bounded by Arlington and Beacon
Streets, Massachusetts Avenue and Boylston Street, developed as
a well-defined unit which retained for many decades a reputation
for social homogeneity that lived up to the handsome appearance
of its buildings.

The lots on Arlington Street, facing the Public Garden (Fig.
91) were filled during the early sixties by large and dignified
five-story houses of brown standstone, whose French inspiration
is apparent in more respects than the mansard roofs. In the early
blocks of Commonwealth Avenue, and of the water side of Beacon
Street, brownstone houses of similar dignity were built during

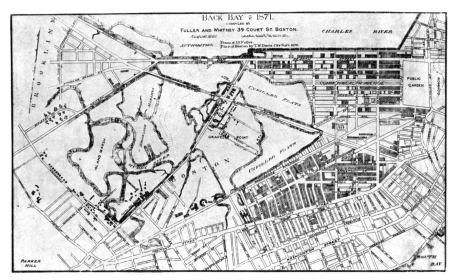

Fig. 89. The Back Bay in 1871

Fig. 90. The Back Bay in the early 1870's

Fig. 91. Arlington Street in the 1870's

Fig. 92. The John L. Gardner house at 152 Beacon Street

the first decade after the filling. While not by any means identical in design, or even in height, the houses in the new streets had a certain grandiose unity of feeling that set a tone for the Back Bay. For an example of a type new to Boston, one may take 152 Beacon Street (Fig. 92), built by David Stewart of New York for his daughter Isabella, who married John Lowell Gardner, Jr., on 10 April 1860. Although Mr. Stewart bought the land in November 1859, Mr. and Mrs. Gardner did not move into the new house until 1862. The façade, with its shuttered windows, is thoroughly French; it is reported that its little yellow drawing room seemed more like Paris than Boston. In 1880, to provide a music room, Mr. Gardner bought the adjacent house, number 150, and added it to his own, although as the floors were on different levels little flights of stairs were necessary to connect the rooms. While living in these houses, Mrs. Gardner assembled the works of art now exhibited in Fenway Court.[26] It is perhaps worth

Fig. 93. An attempt to be Gothic at 165 Beacon Street in 1869

observing that two thirds of Mrs. Gardner's life in Boston — including her most active years — were spent in 152 Beacon Street.

Individualism, within the limits of building restrictions, soon began to show itself in the Back Bay. Consider, for instance, the gandery attempt to be Gothic in brownstone that was achieved in 1869 at 165 Beacon Street (Fig. 93), with a lordly disregard for what might be placed in the vacant lots on either side. Fortunately this effort attracted few followers. The seventies saw the construction of a considerable number of brick houses, in local modification of the French academic tradition. Of these perhaps the handsomest is 163 Marlborough Street (Fig. 94), built in 1871 for Thomas F. Cushing by Snell and Gregerson. This corner house, which formed an original and harmonious composition with neighboring ones at 326 and 328 Dartmouth Street, was bought in 1897 by Hon. William Crowninshield Endicott, whose daughter-in-law continued to occupy it until her death in March

1958, in her ninety-fourth year. Through continuous occupancy by two families over eighty-seven years, the unusually fine original interiors long survived unchanged.[27]

Photographs of the Back Bay in the sixties and seventies show a rich profusion of vacant lots. As land was filled, and as the likelihood of sales appeared to warrant, the Commissioners would offer various lots at public auction. The photograph of Commonwealth Avenue at Dartmouth Street in the mid-seventies (Fig. 95) shows a vacant center of the block between Dartmouth and Exeter Streets. Ten of these lots — numbers 161 to 179 — were offered

Fig. 94. The William C. Endicott house at 163 Marlborough Street

at auction on 27 December 1870, together with five lots on the south side of Beacon Street west of Exeter, and two lots on the north side of Newbury west of Clarendon, that had remained unsold from an earlier auction of 5 February 1870.[28] Between 1872 and 1883 the entire Dartmouth-Exeter Street block shown in this picture was built up. In spite both of this piecemeal method of selling land and of the variety of individual tastes, Commonwealth Avenue (Fig. 96) and the water side of Beacon Street built up into reasonably harmonious blocks, as did some parts of Marlborough Street. Most houses in these streets were built by those who were to occupy them, although one sees the less inspired results of mass building by developers on the land side of Beacon Street in the late sixties, in Marlborough Street above Fairfield in the seventies, and, to an excessive and dreary extent, in Newbury Street west of Dartmouth in the eighties.

As Summer Street, Pemberton Square and the West End ceased to be pleasant residential districts, and as it became clear that the South End was never likely to live up to its rather pleasing appearance, the attraction of the Back Bay increased. Conservative persons comfortably settled upon Beacon Hill tended to remain there. There is, indeed, a tale of a gentleman who, within the present century, firmly told a prospective son-in-law, who proposed to build a house in the Back Bay, that he could not consider having his daughter live on "made land." In consequence of this the newly married couple settled on the lower slopes of Beacon Hill. Such compunctions were not, however, general, and as apartments were slow to take hold in Boston, the normal means by which comfortably situated Bostonians sheltered themselves down to World War I was by buying or building houses in the Back Bay.

The tone of the Back Bay was early set by the number and the character of the churches and institutions that flocked there. Almost on the wheels of the gravel cars came the Unitarians of the Federal Street Church, over which William Ellery Channing had presided from 1803 to 1842. This congregation began to build in 1859, at the corner of Arlington and Boylston Streets, the present Arlington Street Church (Fig. 97), in which the architect, Arthur

Fig. 95. Commonwealth Avenue in process

Fig. 96. Commonwealth Avenue completed

Gilman, pleasingly combined Georgian and Italian elements in the local brownstone.[29] Around the corner, in the first block of Newbury Street, Emmanuel Church, a Gothic building of Roxbury conglomerate stone designed by A. R. Estey, was consecrated on 24 April 1862. The first rector of this new Episcopal parish was the Reverend Frederic Dan Huntington, who had previously been Minister of the Unitarian South Congregational Church and Preacher to Harvard University. Indeed the new Back Bay church had been organized in 1860 with the expectation that Dr. Huntington, who was leaving the Unitarian ministry and seeking Episcopalian ordination, would become the rector.[30] A contemporary observer who disliked what he considered "the poor, homely appearance" of Emmanuel, which was squeezed lengthwise, although not unpleasantly, into the middle of a block of houses, remarked that the church "might better have paid Richard Upjohn $5000 and got a good church."[31] Neighbors did just that, for a few years later Richard Michell Upjohn designed a Gothic building with a very striking 236-foot spire for the Central Congregational Church at the corner of Newbury and Berkeley Streets. This congregation, organized in 1835, which had formerly worshiped in Winter Street, moved to its new church in the Back Bay in 1867.[32]

There was indeed a kind of mass migration of religious groups, for during the sixties and seventies the First, Second and Third Churches, as well as two others of colonial origin, moved to the new lands. The First Church of 1630, originally near the Town House and since 1808 in Chauncy Place, bought land on the corner of Berkeley and Marlborough Streets in 1865 and built thereon a Gothic church, designed by Ware and Van Brunt, that was dedicated on 10 December 1868.[33] The Second Church of 1660 — the oldest "Old North," the church of the Mathers — which had in mid-century abandoned the North End for Bedford Street, also joined the trek and built in Boylston Street between Clarendon and Dartmouth, during 1872–1874, a spireless Gothic church designed by N. J. Bradlee.[34]

The Third Church — unlike the First and Second, which had become Unitarian — had remained Congregational. It had, more-

Fig. 97. The Arlington Street church in the early 1860's

over, continued to occupy the Old South Meeting House at the corner of Washington and Milk Streets long after its older sisters had abandoned their eighteenth-century buildings. In the end, however, the historic Revolutionary associations of the old meeting house failed to outweigh the inconveniences of the site, when to these were added the seductive prospect of getting an inflated price, with which to build in the Back Bay, for the land. In 1869 the society bought lots at the northwest corner of Dartmouth and Boylston Streets and built upon them the New Old South Church, which was dedicated on 15 December 1875. The North Italian Gothic design by Cummings and Sears included a striking campanile which overshadowed the Second Church in much the way that Upjohn's Central Church spire carried the eye away from Emmanuel. The move of the Old South Church from Washington Street to the Back Bay was not accomplished without acrimonious dissension, both private and public, which in the end led to the preservation of the Old South Meeting House as a historic monument, through the offices of the Old South Association in Boston, a corporation formed for the purpose, which raised four hundred thousand dollars to save the building from the hands of the wreckers to whom it had been consigned by the church. This is worth remembering as the first instance in Boston where respect for the historical and architectural heritage of the city triumphed over considerations of profit, expediency, laziness and vulgar convenience.[35]

The Brattle Square Church (Unitarian) sold its colonial meeting house of 1772, in 1871, in favor of a new Romanesque church, designed by H. H. Richardson, at the corner of Commonwealth Avenue and Clarendon Street. The construction of this great building, whose tower was adorned with a frieze by Bartholdi, with trumpeting angels which inspired the irreverent nickname of "Church of the Holy Bean Blowers," proved too great a financial burden for the congregation, which in 1876 ignominiously dissolved. The building remained an imposing white elephant until the winter of 1881–1882, when the First Baptist Church, having realized the unwisdom of its previous move to the South End, bought it.[36]

Trinity Church, the Episcopal parish of the colonial South End, began to consider moving from Summer Street to the Back Bay soon after Phillips Brooks became its rector in 1869. In 1871 the church bought a triangular lot on the east side of what is now Copley Square — then, as Bishop Lawrence recalled, "a desert of dirt, dust, mud and wind" — for which Richardson designed the masterpiece of his short career. This great building, in which the Romanesque masses of Auvergne are blended with the *Torre del Gallo* of Salamanca and the portal of St. Gilles to provide the exterior for an auditorium capable of accommodating Phillips Brooks's devoted followers, was consecrated on 9 February 1877.[37]

In 1884 the Hollis Street Church migrated to the southeast corner of Newbury and Exeter Streets, opposite which in 1885 was completed the equally unattractive temple of the Working Union of Progressive Spiritualists. In 1887 the Reverend Edward Everett Hale's South Congregational Church, like the First Bap-

Fig. 98. The Museum of Natural History in 1864

tist Church and George Apley's father, decamped from the South End and united with the Hollis Street congregation.[38] Their building, destroyed in 1966, for a time housed the Copley Methodist Episcopal Church (now merged in the West Church), while the Spiritual Temple across the way is now the Exeter Street Theatre.

Secular institutions gravitated to the Back Bay as eagerly as did churches. The Boston Society of Natural History, organized in 1830 and housed in Mason Street since 1848, received from the Legislature in the winter of 1860–1861 a grant of land on Berkeley Street extending from Boylston to Newbury. Upon this site the Society soon built a three-story brick museum (Fig. 98), designed by William G. Preston, which now houses Bonwit Teller's shop. The remainder of the block was devoted to the Massachusetts Institute of Technology, which had been incorporated by an act of 10 April 1861, and whose first building was authorized in 1863. This building, designed by Preston, in singularly felicitous relation to its neighbor, was named in honor of William Barton Rogers, the founder of the Institute. In 1872 the Rogers Building was still the last structure west on Boylston Street, but three years later the Institute built a slate-roofed drill hall and gymnasium, of wood covered with corrugated iron, which was moved in 1883 to the site of the Hotel Lenox to make way for the Walker Building.[39]

While Back Bay south of Boylston Street was still an untidy waste, a persuasive musical promoter, P. S. Gilmore, talked his fellow citizens into constructing in what is now Copley Square a vast temporary Coliseum (Figs. 99–100), in which a National Peace Jubilee was held in June 1869, with the favoring presence of President U. S. Grant. The American passion for bigger and better elephants has scarcely ever been more startlingly seen than in this venture, for Gilmore had the genius for the super-colossal that was in the next century to flower in Hollywood. Witness, for a single example, the performance on 17 June 1869 of the Anvil Chorus from *Il Trovatore* by an orchestra of one thousand musicians, a chorus of ten thousand singers, supplemented by organ, drum corps, the ringing of church bells and the firing of cannon (electrically controlled from the platform), and one hundred Boston firemen beating rhythmically upon anvils with sledge hammers.[40] This gargantuan extravaganza, which drove John S. Dwight, "the chief apostle of music in Boston," to refuge in Nahant, surprisingly broke even — but a similar International Peace Jubilee in June 1872, by which Gilmore sought to celebrate the conclusion of the Franco-Prussian War, rolled up a whopping deficit, even with Johann Strauss present to lead his own compositions.[41] So the Coliseum, which looms up in the background of Fig. 90, disappeared to give place to the first building of the Museum of Fine Arts. This institution, which was incorporated in 1870, was first housed at 10½ Beacon Street in the top floor galleries of the Boston Athenæum, of which it was an outgrowth. Sturgis and Brigham designed for the Museum one of those striped red brick and terra cotta Victorian Gothic structures that make one wish John Ruskin had never visited Italy. With this building, which was opened to the public in the summer of 1876, on the south, Trinity Church on the east (Fig. 101), and the Second

Fig. 99. The Peace Jubilee Coliseum

Fig. 100. Interior of the Peace Jubilee Coliseum in 1872

and New Old South Churches on the north, Copley Square which — unlike the rest of Back Bay — had never been properly or reasonably laid out, was beginning to stumble into shape. The makings of a handsome square had been, largely by accident,

Fig. 101. Copley Square in the 1880's

achieved. An important open space at this point had not been contemplated in the original planning of the Back Bay. It was simply one of those awkward spots — like the intersection of Columbus and Warren Avenues in the South End — where a projected street, in this case Huntington Avenue, started off at an angle different from its neighbors. Indeed it was 1883 before the triangular lot bounded by Huntington Avenue, Dartmouth and Boylston Streets, which was originally planned to be built upon, was purchased by the city and named Copley Square. Although two years later the opposite triangle, bounded by Huntington Avenue, Trinity Place and St. James Avenue was added, thus completing the square, it was never given any adequate monumental treatment.

The Harvard Medical School, which had formerly been close to the Massachusetts General Hospital, moved in 1883 to a new building at Boylston and Exeter Streets, with the fond expectation of getting ample room for expansion in a site approximately half way between the Massachusetts General and the City Hospital in the South End.[42] With the Medical School a block west and M.I.T. and the Boston Society of Natural History one block to the east, Copley Square had, by the mid-eighties, become the major intellectual as well as religious center of Boston. This role was to be confirmed by the location on its west side of the new building of the Boston Public Library, which had first opened to readers in Mason Street in 1854 and had, since 1858, been located in Boylston Street on the site of the Colonial Theatre. The Commonwealth granted land in Copley Square to the library in 1880. After a series of bumbling political and architectural misadventures, which wasted seven years and considerable money, the library trustees succeeded in engaging McKim, Mead and White to plan the great building in Copley Square that was first opened to readers in 1895.[43] With these institutions a new heart of the city had been created in what a few short decades before had been a stinking eyesore.

CHAPTER VIII

The Westward Movement

AFTER SEVERAL DECADES of wandering about the South End and the Back Bay, we must return briefly to the old center of the city to note simultaneous developments there. At the conclusion of Chapter V, I called attention to the manner in which the once fashionable region around Pearl Street and Fort Hill (Fig. 102) was, in the forties, giving way to business. A corollary to this was the temporary subletting of houses, no longer occupied by their owners and being held for future sale at higher price, to the very numerous immigrants who were obliged to shelter themselves wherever and however they could. Professor Handlin has pointed out[1] the way in which "enterprising land-owners utilized unremunerative yards, gardens, and courts to yield the maximum number of hovels that might pass as homes," and how "the abundant grounds surrounding well-built early Boston residences, and the hitherto unusable sites created by the city's irregular streets, once guarantees of commodious living, now fostered the most vicious Boston slums." Thus the area around Fort Hill became crowded with "tottering rookeries" with their backs flush to the slopes of the hill, that were jammed with unfortunate Irish families. Conditions were so unsavory that in the fall of 1866 the city began clearing the entire area. John Souther, whose steam shovels had loaded

Fig. 102. Fort Hill in 1858

the gravel cars for the filling of the Back Bay, dug away at Fort Hill, until in the summer of 1872 the entire elevation had been leveled (Figs. 103–104). Part of the earth thus obtained was carried by an elevated railroad down to the adjacent shore front to fill in Atlantic Avenue, which was laid out in 1868 across the cove that had, in the original state of the Shawmut peninsula, separated the South and North Ends. The remainder was carted away to be used in raising the ground level in the Church and Suffolk Street improvements.[2] Thus Fort Hill disappeared and the last trace of the colonial waterfront in the region of the Long Wharf was buried under new streets.

The great fire of 9 November 1872 completed the obliteration of early landmarks in the area between Summer and Pearl Streets from Washington Street to the harbor. Although the fire stopped just short of the Old South Meeting House, it destroyed Trinity Church, burned out the *Transcript* and *Pilot* newspaper offices and devastated many stores, business blocks and warehouses.[3] Even before the fire Trinity Church and the Old South were planning to move to the Back Bay.[4] Within a few years after it, the

Fig. 103. Taking down Fort Hill in 1869

Fig. 104. Oliver Street during demolition of Fort Hill in 1869

greater part of the private residents and noncommercial institutions between the Common and the harbor, even in those streets that had been spared by the fire, moved to the westward, leaving the colonial South End to offices and retail and wholesale trade.

The tides of immigration during the second half of the nineteenth century inundated the North End, as they had the region of Fort Hill. Of the 23,000 persons living there in 1850 half were Irish, but as decades passed they were succeeded by Russian and Polish Jews, and, toward the end of the century, by Italians who, displacing the earlier comers, have made the region their own.[5] Something of the same pattern followed in the West End, with new-coming immigrant groups pushing out earlier arrivals, although the process began later there than it had in the North End. While the great gardens around Bowdoin Square were being filled with blocks of brick houses in the forties, the region held its own for another quarter of a century. Kirk Boott's house in Bowdoin Square was, for example, enlarged into the Revere House in 1846, which in 1860 enjoyed sufficient reputation as a hotel to be chosen for the lodging of the future Edward VII during his visit to Boston on his tour of the United States as Prince of Wales.[6] The Church of the Advent, with Richard Henry Dana, Senior, as its first Senior Warden, was founded in 1844 for the purpose of bringing some of the principles of the Oxford Movement to the Episcopal church in Boston. For close on forty years it was situated in the West End, only being moved to its present site at the corner of Mount Vernon and Brimmer Streets in 1883.[7] But by 1892 the West Church, at Cambridge and Lynde Streets, whose pulpit had been ornamented by Jonathan Mayhew and Charles Lowell, closed its doors for want of congregation in the neighborhood. Its handsome meeting house, built in 1806 by Asher Benjamin, was bought, to prevent its destruction, by Andrew C. Wheelwright, who, with outstanding public spirit, held it until the Boston Public Library took it over in 1894 for conversion to a West End Branch, whose distinguishing specialty was for years a fine collection of Judaica.[8] By the end of the century the North and West Ends had become predominantly areas of tenements and lodging houses, with the newer South End lagging only slightly behind. Thus the supremacy of the Back Bay as a residential district was established, for most persons who wished to live with a certain decorum but whose resources did not permit them to settle in the Back Bay had, with increasing railway and ferry service, migrated out of Boston proper to suburbs and outlying towns.

The Back Bay as originally conceived amounted to an island of elegance limited by water on the north, ill-smelling marshes on the west and railroad lines on the south. Hopeful cartographers under the compelling necessity of doing something with the triangular no-man's land that divided the Back Bay from the South End, outlined on maps (such as Fig. 69) additional streets, to the south and west continuing the Back Bay grid, with a lordly disregard of the inescapable problems of grade crossings and the bridging of the Muddy River. The Boston and Providence Railroad tracks, cutting diagonally across the unfilled Back Bay from Roxbury to Park Square since the mid-thirties, were obviously there to stay and could not be ignored. So, just as Columbus Avenue in the South End had been laid out parallel to them, Huntington Avenue, to the north of them, was projected from Copley Square to the Brookline line. In Fuller and Whitney's survey of 1871 (Fig. 89), Huntington Avenue extended but a single block to Exeter Street. As the unused flats that flanked the Boston and Worcester tracks (which by then had become, as today, the Boston and Albany), were filled, the railroad acquired them for train yards. Thus, when Huntington Avenue bridged the tracks and was laid out beyond Exeter Street, it was separated from Boylston Street — the southernmost frontier of the Back Bay — by an impenetrable barrier of railroad yards that has had to this day strong psychological and social as well as physical connotations.

The Massachusetts Charitable Mechanic Association, which, upon its foundation in 1795, had elected Paul Revere as its first president, was the first institution to venture upon Huntington Avenue. The Association had, between 1857 and 1860, completed a handsome building, from Hammatt Billings's design, at the corner of Bedford and Chauncy Streets, adjoining the Second

Church. Its triennial exhibitions, which required great elbow room, were held in Faneuil Hall and the hall above Quincy Market. Although its building was untouched by the great fire of 1872, the general westward movement, combined with the need of more exhibition space than was available above the markets, led the Association to contemplate a move to the Back Bay. In 1880 it bought a triangular two and one half acre plot of land on Huntington Avenue, at the corner of West Newton Street, which had been extended through from the South End by bridging the Boston and Providence tracks in 1878. On this site was built in 1881 a vast brick hall, designed by William G. Preston, which contained sufficient floor space not only for the Association's exhibitions, but for most of the elephantine assemblies that took place in Boston during the next seventy-five years.[9] At the laying of the cornerstone on 15 March 1881, Charles W. Slack, President of the Association, observed with pride that

The stranger who visits our "burnt district" or "Back Bay" area — having had some experience abroad — looks upon our substantial warehouses and our comfortable residences with admiration. He sees, in the tasteful ornamentation of the one, a reminder of Parisian elegance; while, as he gazes upon the strength of the other, he recalls the solidity of London or St. Petersburg.[10]

When opened, the Mechanics' Building was the only structure on Huntington Avenue south of the bridge over the Boston and Albany tracks, but within ten years the avenue had been built up nearly solid as far as West Chester Park, now Massachusetts Avenue. St. Botolph Street was laid out as a parallel thoroughfare between Huntington Avenue and the Boston and Providence Railroad, and lots in this region were sold at public auction during the eighties — in the manner of earlier sales in the Back Bay — by the Trustees of Huntington Avenue Lands.[11] Both architecturally and socially this Huntington Avenue development left a great deal to be desired, for, as Walter F. Kilham has written: [12]

Huntington Avenue came into popularity at a moment when "French flats" were the last word, particularly for medium-priced habitations, and it was rapidly built up with apartment houses of the four- or sometimes

five-story "walk-up" type of building, often regrettably the products of
real-estate offices rather than those of architects. This moment also happened to coincide with the confusion caused by the impact of the "Queen
Anne" movement upon the still only slightly understood Romanesque, with
the result that the avenue's architecture, while interesting as a document
of the time, possessed neither the restful, if slightly soporific, regularity
of Columbus Avenue on the one hand, nor the ambitious variety of Commonwealth Avenue on the other.

For the various streets running off West Chester Park between
Huntington Avenue and Boylston Street that were laid out in the
eighties — Westland Avenue, Falmouth and Caledonia Streets
and the like — even less could be said.

As vacant lots in the Back Bay decreased through the seventies,
the problem of extending the area west of its original limits became more pressing. The Full Basin of Cotting's Mill Dam scheme,
which became useless for mill purposes once the greater part of
the Receiving Basin was filled in, survived as an unsavory sedi-
mentation basin for all the sewers of Roxbury and some of those
of Brookline and Brighton, and as the receptacle of any pollution
that might be carried in the waters of Muddy River. It was feel-
ingly described as

The foulest marsh and muddy flats to be found anywhere in Massachusetts
without a single attractive feature; a body of water so foul that even clams
and eels cannot live there, and a place that no one will go within a half
mile of in the summer time unless absolutely necessary, so great a stench
was there.[13]

Moreover, if Commonwealth Avenue were continued west into
this Stygian morass, the extension would collide at an awkward
angle with the Boston and Albany tracks in a few hundred yards.[14]
Parisian boulevards and grade crossings are highly incompatible,
but the difficulty was solved in a most ingenious manner in the
early eighties by the landscape architect Frederick Law Olmsted,
in the course of an imaginative and large-scale design for city
parks. As part of a coordinated system that would link Franklin
Park and the Arnold Arboretum with the Back Bay, the Public
Garden and the Common, Olmsted — by means of skilful drain-

age and unobtrusive improvement of the natural contours —
converted the noxious flats of the Muddy River into a healthy and
decorative park known as the Back Bay Fens, skirted on the east
by an avenue designated as the Fenway, which followed the wind-
ings of the now more cleanly Muddy River off to Brookline and
Jamaica Plain. By shifting the axis of Commonwealth Avenue
from west to northwest at West Chester Park, Olmsted found the
means of continuing that boulevard without collision with the
Boston and Albany tracks, which, on its new course, the avenue
paralleled (Fig. 105). After bridging the Muddy River at Charlesgate, which was that stream's new and respectable approach to the
Charles, Commonwealth Avenue continued on to Sewell's Point
in Brookline (now Kenmore Square), where it crossed Beacon
Street and continued out toward Longwood as a broad avenue
along the line of the old Brighton road.[15]

Once Olmsted had solved the problem of the westward expansion of the Back Bay any number of things began to happen. The
Charles River Embankment Company, incorporated in 1881 by
a group of owners of property on the Cambridge bank of the
Charles River, persuaded the Legislature in 1887 to authorize

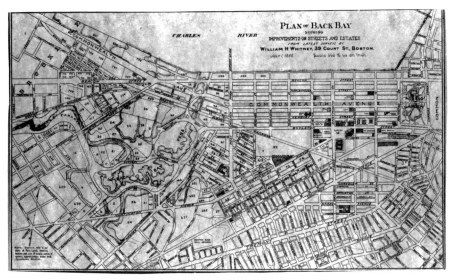

Fig. 105. The Back Bay in 1888

the cities of Cambridge and Boston to build a new bridge across
the Charles that would connect West Chester Park in Boston with
Massachusetts Avenue in Cambridge. This bridge, named in honor
of John Harvard, was opened to public travel in the autumn of
1891. Three years later the city changed the names of West
Chester Park and its connecting streets in Boston to Massachusetts
Avenue, so as to form a continuous route, bearing the same name,
from Edward Everett Square in Dorchester to Arlington.[16]

The Charles River Embankment Company undertook the building of a sea wall on the Cambridge shore, west of the Harvard
Bridge, in the course of which, with a view to economy in filling,
a suction dredge of a type used in San Francisco was used. As the
river bottom on the Cambridge shore proved too hard for this piece
of equipment, the Riverbank Improvement Co., of which John
Quincy Adams (of the Harvard class of 1853) was president,
who owned certain flats on the Boston shore, persuaded the dredge
owners to move their equipment across the river and try their luck
there. On the Boston shore, which had a softer bottom, the dredge
worked admirably, although in pumping up some of the sewage
near the mouth of the Muddy River it produced such a stench that
attempts were made to stop the work. However, the fill was completed just as the dredge was destroyed by fire. Thus was created
Bay State Road, running from Beacon Street just beyond Charlesgate along the Charles, parallel to the extension of Commonwealth
Avenue.[17] As this new street, which was laid out in its first blocks
in 1889, had the same view as the water side of Beacon Street,
several extremely large and handsome houses were built there
during the nineties and the early years of this century. The architect Arthur Little built himself a house at the corner of Bay State
Road and Raleigh Street in 1890. In 1900 Dr. Charles G. Weld
built at the corner of Sherborn Street the great Georgian house
that is now the Faculty Club of Boston University, and in 1905
Mr. and Mrs. William Lindsey — the parents of Leslie Lindsey,
drowned in the sinking of the *Lusitania,* in whose memory the
Lindsey Chapel of Emmanuel Church was given — built a Gothic
manor house on the corner of Granby Street. As in Beacon Street,

the water side of Bay State Road built up more handsomely and completely than the lots across the way, some of which remained vacant for many years. Although the Bay State Road houses were often handsome, they were rather a long way off; somewhat too far for convenient calling in the days of horse-drawn vehicles. Thus the street never fulfilled the complete hopes of its earliest settlers.

Some very large town houses were built on the north side of Commonwealth Avenue between Massachusetts Avenue and Charlesgate during the nineties. A similar development which was envisioned for the Fenway proved even more abortive than the move to Bay State Road. The Massachusetts Historical Society, which had left the arch over the Tontine Crescent in 1833 for 30 Tremont Street, adjoining King's Chapel Burying Ground, moved in 1899 to a new building at 1154 Boylston Street at the corner of the Fenway.[18] The Boston Medical Library, housed at 19 Boylston Place since 1878, had bought a lot at the corner of St. Botolph and Garrison Streets in 1888. In 1896 they considered exchanging that property for land on Caledonia Street, which would have amounted to jumping from the frying pan into the fire, but in 1899 they were seized with the thought of building on the lots next to the Massachusetts Historical Society in the Fenway. At a special meeting, held on 25 May 1899, to consider the move, various arguments, pro and con, were brought forth.

It is objected that this place is not central — never will have around it the population, as it gives on a park and a river . . . that it is bleak and unhandy for seven months in the year, and that it will remain so. . . In rebuttal it is said that this site is the only one worthy of the dignity of the profession, and that a handsome building there will bring us notice, money and reputation.

Hopeful dignity prevailed, and in 1901 the Boston Medical Library dedicated its new building in the Fenway.[19] The architect Robert S. Peabody built himself a substantial town house next door, and a few others followed.

Mrs. John Lowell Gardner, whose art collections had outgrown 152 Beacon Street, bought land at the corner of the Fenway and

Fig. 106. The Back Bay from the State House in 1900

Worthington Street in January 1899 and within the year began the construction of Fenway Court. This great house, planned from its inception as "The Isabella Stewart Gardner Museum in the Fenway," which was formally opened on New Year's night 1903,[20] oddly prophesied the future of the Fenway, which was to become a region of institutions, interspersed (where someone wished to make a quick dollar) by not very distinguished apartment houses. The Back Bay pattern of substantial town houses never took root there, for by the end of World War I the days of building such houses were over. The motor car had brought the country within reach; domestic service had become more expensive and less attainable, and so Bostonians who still could and who still wished to live in this manner bought existing houses rather than building new ones.

From the nineties onward an increasing number of institutions moved out of central Boston to the westward. Since the construction of the Music Hall in 1852, "from which time forward," in M. A. De Wolfe Howe's fine phrase, "it was unnecessary to ask a visiting Jenny Lind to sing in the Fitchburg Railroad Station," [21] the musical life of Boston had centered around that building at Winter Street and Bumstead Place, a stone's throw from the Common. There the Boston Symphony Orchestra had played from its foundation in 1881. In 1893 when the future of the Music Hall was imperiled by proposed street changes, a corporation was formed to provide a new home for the orchestra. Thus Symphony Hall, opened on 15 October 1900, was built at the corner of Huntington and Massachusetts Avenues.[22] Although McKim, Mead and White designed a building that, after nearly seventy years, still admirably serves its purpose, it is unfortunate that it should have been plumped down upon a totally undistinguished site without an inch of ground around it. At the opening concert Major Henry L. Higginson, founder of the orchestra, related how the directors "chose this site as the best in Boston, and in 1893 they bought it at about half the price per foot paid for the opposite lot, where the Horticultural Hall is to stand." [23] One can only wish, in retrospect, that they had taken a little fuller advantage of this excellent bargain.

The Massachusetts Horticultural Society, founded in 1829, had built in 1844 a narrow Corinthian temple for itself in School Street. In 1865 it moved to a more spacious granite Horticultural Hall, built in the prevailing French Renaissance manner, on Tremont Street at Montgomery Place, only a short distance from the old Music Hall. In January 1900 the Society bought land opposite Symphony Hall and built thereon, from designs of Wheelwright and Haven, the present Horticultural Hall. This was an advantageous exchange, for the new building cost (including land) $515,997, while the Tremont Street property sold for $600,000.[24]

Other musical institutions soon followed the Boston Symphony Orchestra to Huntington Avenue. Chickering and Sons, the piano manufacturers, built a new Chickering Hall at 239 Huntington Avenue, adjoining Horticultural Hall, which they opened on 8 February 1901.[25] In 1912 this became the St. James Theatre, and later was renamed the Uptown Theatre. It was demolished in 1968 to make way for the Christian Science Church Center that is described in Chapter IX. The New England Conservatory of Music, which had taken over the St. James Hotel in the South End in 1882,[26] moved in 1902 to a new building in Huntington Avenue at the corner of Gainsborough Street. To this building in 1904 Eben D. Jordan, son of the founder of Jordan Marsh Company, added an auditorium named after himself, Jordan Hall. Jordan was also responsible for the building in 1908–1909 of the Boston Opera House, diagonally across Huntington Avenue from the Conservatory.[27] This great theatre, designed by Parkman B. Haven, on traditional nineteenth-century lines, with eighty-four boxes and 2,750 seats, was leased to the Boston Opera Company, which for a few years under the direction of Henry Russell offered a local opera season. After the demise of the company the house limped along for four decades, and in 1958 was demolished. Like Symphony Hall, the Boston Opera House suffered from tightness of ground and ignoble surroundings. It can only be considered a preposterous piece of New England parsimoniousness to have placed such a building where one was forced to enter a splendid and highly gilded baroque interior by crawling in obliquely from the grimy sidewalk of a crowded street. Once Northeastern University had established its simple but dignified functional campus across the way in 1938, the surroundings were improved, but even so it was a stingy and tasteless absurdity to jam a sizable Opera House between a storage warehouse and blocks of undistinguished apartments.

Indeed the only institution that moved to Huntington Avenue without being unduly parsimonious about space was the Museum of Fine Arts, which as early as 1899 was bursting the seams of its building in Copley Square. In that year the trustees bought twelve acres, running from Huntington Avenue through to the Fenway, on which construction of the present building, from designs by Guy Lowell, was begun in 1907.

The Harvard Medical School in 1906 built new buildings for itself on Longwood Avenue, west of the Fenway. It was followed to the region by the Peter Bent Brigham Hospital, completed in 1912, and by the Children's Hospital, the Collis P. Huntington Memorial Hospital, the Boston Lying-In Hospital and the Beth Israel Hospital. Simmons College and Emmanuel College and the Boston Latin School have all settled in these western reaches of the Fenway.

In the westward movement of the twentieth century some institutions have moved entirely out of the city. The Second Church in 1914 abandoned Copley Square for Audubon Circle in Brookline. The Perkins Institution for the Blind, once in Pearl Street and then in South Boston, moved in 1912 to a hillside above the Charles River in Watertown, where a harmonious set of red brick buildings with a singularly graceful tower, designed by R. Clipston Sturgis, generously delights the eyes of passers-by to compensate for what its inhabitants cannot themselves see.[28] Boston College, after forty-five years in the South End, began in 1909 to build, from plans of Maginnis and Walsh, a new campus on heights in Chestnut Hill, overlooking the Reservoir. The site in the sixties had been on Amos A. Lawrence's farm. His son, Bishop Lawrence, in sending the president of the college a photograph of the farm in 1870, put into words what many others who have enjoyed the silhouette of Charles D. Maginnis's buildings have felt: "Boston College with its beautiful group of buildings has given a grace and benediction to my boyhood haunts." [29]

Boston University began life in a series of separate buildings around the top of Beacon Hill,[30] and later, with its great expansion, fanned out all over the city. Impelled by the energetic determination of President Daniel L. Marsh it undertook in the nineteen thirties to create a central campus for itself on Commonwealth Avenue, east of Cottage Farm Bridge. Previous to this move Commonwealth Avenue west of Kenmore Square had proved a vain hope. The Temple Israel had built there on the corner of Blandford Street in 1907, in marble save on the west where cement was substituted in the confident expectation that the block would soon build up.[31] It never did, for the street remained one of trolley cars, automobile salesrooms and vacant lots until President Marsh began its transformation. From its new buildings, Boston University had spread west to absorb the defunct Braves Field, and east to take in many of the larger houses of Bay State Road. The Lindsey house now accommodates the President of Boston University, the Weld house its Faculty Club. Altogether a street that never fulfilled its original promise is today coming into its own.

The Massachusetts Institute of Technology by 1902 was contemplating a move from Boylston Street. Ten years later it purchased land on the Cambridge shore of the Charles River, east of the Harvard Bridge, and there built a pleasing group of limestone buildings, designed by Welles Bosworth, that were first occupied in 1916. Such a move was made reasonable by the improvement in the Charles River that resulted from the completion in 1910 of a dam that excluded the harbor tides and converted the Charles River Basin into an agreeable body of fresh water (Fig. 107). The

Fig. 107. Charles River Basin in the 1950's

Alster Basin in Hamburg served as the inspiration for this improvement, which eliminated the mud flats that twice daily had made the view from the rear windows of Beacon Street unsightly. With the improvement of the basin came the construction of the Esplanade, originally a narrow concrete walk behind the Beacon Street houses, and, after 1931, through the generosity of Mrs. James J. Storrow, a more spacious park, delightfully planted, with space for outdoor music and refuges for the little boats whose sails give movement to the scene on a breezy spring afternoon.[32] For a few years this improvement lent singular charm to the Basin, which has been lost since the necessities of traffic have brought motor cars into an area that was designed for the sauntering pedestrian.

For two decades after M.I.T. established itself in Cambridge, the Rogers Building continued in use by the Architectural Department, while the Walker Building was leased to Boston University. In 1939 both were demolished to make way for the granite building of the New England Mutual Life Insurance Company that inspired David McCord to compose the clerihew:

> Ralph Adams Cram
> One morning said damn,
> And designed the Urn Burial
> For a concern actuarial.[33]

This move, from the company's old French Renaissance building in Post Office Square, built after the Boston Fire by N. J. Bradlee, formed part of a general change of focus that had been taking place on the edges of the Back Bay (Fig. 108). The houses of Boylston Street and many of those on Newbury were gradually being taken over by shops, particularly of a sort that might appeal to the residents of the Back Bay. Between Boylston Street and Columbus Avenue, from Park Square west, the station and train-yards of the Boston and Providence Railroad occupied a substantial acreage. When the South Station was completed in 1900 as a union terminal for all railway lines from the south of Boston, the original Boston and Providence tracks — that is, the northeast arm of the great St. Andrew's cross of lines that had divided the Back

Fig. 108. Aerial view of the insurance district in the 1950's

Bay — were discontinued, and trains from Providence ran instead up the southwest arm to Back Bay Station, which was at the intersection, and then turned down the southeast — the original Boston and Worcester right of way — to reach the South Station. Nothing was done for a considerable number of years with the Boston and Providence holdings east of Clarendon Street. This sixteen-acre area long sat idle; indeed around 1906 an automobile demonstration track occupied some six acres behind St. James Avenue between Berkeley and Clarendon Streets.[34] When these abandoned lands were finally reclaimed by the construction of the Park Square Building, the Statler Hotel and the John Hancock Insurance Company, this region, which had never had any integral connection with the life of the Back Bay, suddenly emerged as a new business district. The tower of the John Hancock Building, which looks extraordinarily well from a great many angles in dif-

ferent parts of the city (Fig. 109), now overshadows the spires
of the churches that were for three quarters of a century the most
conspicuous elements in the Back Bay skyline.

The acquisition by the Prudential Insurance Company of the
Boston and Albany train yards (Fig. 110) will not only change the
skyline but completely alter the insular character of the Back Bay,
for these yards had for decades protected the Back Bay from the
grubby infringements of Huntington Avenue and the even less
desirable influence of the South End as completely as the Charles
River separated the Back Bay from Cambridge. With the entire
triangle between Boylston Street and Huntington Avenue given
over to this new development (Fig. 111), one may hopefully an-
ticipate that the contagion of improvement may redeem many of
the lost opportunities of Huntington and Massachusetts Avenues,
and some of the drearier stretches between them and the Fenway.

Fig. 109. Public Garden in the 1950's

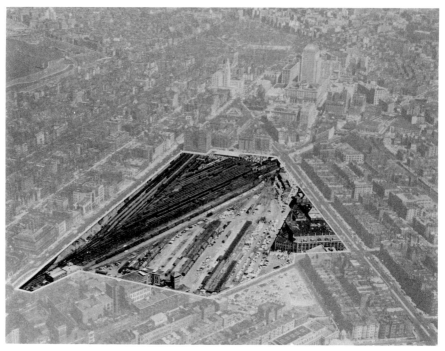

Fig. 110. Site of the Prudential development

Fig. 111. Proposed Prudential development

As we have seen, this region began as a no-man's land, blighted in advance by proximity to the railroads, an area that developed unevenly, due in part to haphazard placing of important institutions on meager sites that had no planned relation to one another. Indeed the only constructive improvements preceding the 1950's were the result of the expansion of Christian Science. Mary Baker Eddy had, in the early eighties, conducted her Massachusetts Metaphysical College at 569 and 571 Columbus Avenue, near West Chester Park, although in 1887 she moved from the South End to 385 Commonwealth Avenue, which was one of a developer's row of houses built soon after Olmsted had projected the avenue beyond its original limits. As early as 1886 she had endeavored to purchase land in Falmouth Street, which led off West Chester Park north of Huntington Avenue, and was about half way between her two places of residence. There the original Mother Church, dedicated on 5 January 1895, was built. Due to Mrs. Eddy's express desire that this building be preserved, even when much greater space was required, a vast domed Extension was added to it between 1904 and 1906.[35] The conversion of the area between the church and Huntington Avenue into a well-planted park, and the construction of adjacent buildings for the Christian Science Publishing Company, have done much to improve the character of the region. With the complete alteration of so much adjacent land by the Prudential development, one hopes that the improvements begun around the Mother Church may spread by contagion to the surroundings of other institutions to the westward.

In the past quarter century greater changes have taken place in the use of buildings on Commonwealth Avenue, Marlborough and Beacon Streets than in their external appearance. Only a fraction of the largest private houses are now occupied in the fashion for which they were built. Some have become apartments, others doctors' and dentists' offices; here and there one even sees the ill-lettered pest signal ROOMS in a ground floor window. Many have been satisfactorily adapted for the use of various schools and colleges. So the principal streets of the Back Bay, although fallen from their original estate, retain a semblance of their former dignity that, on a sunny spring morning when the magnolias are in flower, is almost convincing.

Unfortunately here and there incongruous apartment houses break the symmetry of a block. Equally unfortunately some of the recent buildings, even when designed with care by skillful architects, take too little account of their surroundings. The brick Lutheran church at the corner of Berkeley and Marlborough Streets, which would be an admirable building elsewhere, relates itself with singular infelicity to its neighbors (Fig. 112). Moreover, a tendency to pull down buildings to create parking lots, that has shown itself in two disastrous connections in 1958, will, if continued, quite thoroughly wreck any quality that the Back Bay has preserved. The S. S. Pierce building at the corner of Dartmouth Street and Huntington Avenue, built in 1887 from the de-

Fig. 112. Lutheran church in Berkeley Street

signs of S. Edwin Tobey, was of no remarkable quality in itself, yet it anchored the façade of the Boston Public Library in a useful way (Figs. 113–114). Indeed Charles F. McKim in planning the library must have taken into account the disparate masses offered by the Pierce building and by the campanile of the New Old South. Godding's pharmacy, on the corner of Newbury and Dartmouth Streets, had even less interest in itself, yet without it the neighboring buildings are strangely adrift.

The legislation of 1955 protecting Beacon Hill is based on the assumption that the relation of buildings to each other is of vital importance to the area. Some similar recognition, whether by public opinion, private agreement or legislation, will be necessary if one is to retain any of the character of Commonwealth Avenue, Marlborough Street and Beacon Street. The fate of Tremont Street should be remembered. Bulfinch's Colonnade Row disappeared to make way for haphazard, nondescript, unrelated business buildings, which are now all but derelict, even though they face the finest site in the city.

In the course of these eight chapters we have traveled so far in time as to see certain of the improvements of the nineteenth century becoming obsolete and being demolished. In the area of the New York streets, which excited so much enthusiasm in the early days of railroading, whole blocks have been leveled for redevelopment. A similarly drastic fate soon overtook the West End. This is the less to be regretted in that the area, having been open country in the eighteenth century, had fewer points of historic interest than the other parts of the town; save for the first Harrison Gray Otis house, the West Church and the Massachusetts General Hospital — which will be preserved — the best things were already gone many decades ago.

The North End seems to me quite another affair. On the arrival of the Massachusetts Bay Company in 1630 it was almost an island, for during high tides waves would carry across the low marshy ground between Copp's Hill and the Trimountain. Now, with the development of overhead highways which cut across Hanover and North Streets, it is once again almost an island, where several of the finest surviving monuments of colonial Boston fit harmoniously and sympathetically into the modern life of an Italian-American community. I can only hope that there will be no wholesale redevelopment of the North End by external and arbitrary authority, and that future improvements there will be made by local property owners and occupants in their own way and on their own terms.

In downtown Boston, thanks to the fire of 1872 and the pressure of business, Faneuil Hall, Quincy Market and the granite warehouses of North and South Market Streets constitute the chief group of coherently related buildings that survive. They deserve careful and respectful preservation that will continue the market tradition. Whatever changes take place in the immediate future between Faneuil Hall and the State House should be made in relation to the few important survivals. In Union and Marshall

Fig. 113. S. S. Pierce building in Copley Square

Streets one has the Union Oyster House, the Ebenezer Hancock house and their adjacent streets and alleys to consider, and in Washington Street the Old State House, the Old South Meeting House and the Old Corner Book Store. As one moves toward the hill King's Chapel and Park Street Church and their adjoining burying grounds are monuments that should always command their surroundings. The Boston Athenæum and the Ticknor house are essential elements in the Beacon Hill scene.

The topographical history of Boston over three centuries has been a record of constant change; so has the history of its architecture. I have no desire to see a slavish antiquarianism in new construction, and no inclination to see any part of Boston as another Williamsburg. The tourist-trade architectural style that could best be described as "Madison Avenue Colonial" has no place in a city that has a vital life of its own. Yet I can hope that

Fig. 114. Parking lot on site of S. S. Pierce building in 1958

new buildings in the center of Boston will, in their placing, color and contours, respect and enhance their older neighbors rather than swearing at or overpowering them. I can hope also that the transformation of the Boston and Albany train yards into the Prudential development may lead to a gradual regeneration of the Fenway, where established institutions might well expand into blocks that are now poorly used; that new roads may bring parts of the South End into a new relation to the rest of the city, and provide decorous approaches to the Catholic Cathedral and the City Hospital, with perhaps the revival of a square or two. My greatest hope is that all these changes will be made thoughtfully, with deliberate respect for what is good in the present life of Boston, rather than in a theoretical, arbitrary or speculative manner. American cities today are getting to look all alike. Their individual characters are fast disappearing. Boston still retains a considerable degree of its own flavor and color. It would be a pity to let this be submerged in an "organization man's" impermanent and glittering mediocrity, when there is still time to build soundly upon existing strengths.

Fig. 115. The Back Bay from the State House in 1958

Fig. 116. Aerial view of Boston in 1957

CHAPTER IX

A Decade of Renewal

In March 1958, just as I was beginning the series of Lowell Lectures that form the preceding chapters of this book, the irrepressible H. Daland Chandler published in the *Bulletin* of the Boston Society of Architects this verse concerning the project for a Government Center, still very much in the "talking stage."

> In Scollay Square did Johnny Hynes
> A stately civic group decree,
> Where Sailors and their Valentines
> Now skip it, trip it, fancy free.
>   I wonder, as Time turns the crank,
> Will we be round in nineteen blank
> To greet, — and with undoubted spice,
> This miracle of rare device?
>   Scanning
>   And panning. . .
> (Or will our sailor still be there
> Skipping and tripping in the Square?)

The note of skepticism in the last two lines was not unjustified, for ever since the early years of the twentieth century members of the Boston Society of Architects had been planning "stately civic groups" which never got off the drawing board.[1] But this time, through a combination of circumstances, something happened.

Scollay Square, until 1835 graced by the Gardiner Greene mansion and later in the nineteenth century the neighbor of the dignified Pemberton Square, had in the twentieth century become the Boston center of tattooing parlors, shooting galleries and burlesque houses. Although dear to the hearts of enlisted men and merchant seamen of many nationalities, it had become a shabby, tumbledown area. As early as 1930 William Stanley Parker,[2] then president of the Boston Society of Architects and a member of the City Planning Board, had proposed it as the site for a new Government Center. But the depression, followed by World War II, had prevented action until 1958 when Mayor John B. Hynes[3] again put the plan forward. It was carried almost to completion during the administration of his successor, John Frederick Collins, whose able service as mayor extended from 1959 to 1967.[4]

The Boston Redevelopment Authority (BRA), established in 1957 as an offshoot of the Boston Housing Authority, undertook as its first project the transformation of the New York streets in the South Cove into a modern light industrial and commercial center.[5] Its second effort, with a 48-acre tract that occupied much of the ground between Cambridge and Lowell Streets from Staniford Street to the Charles River, led to the wholesale demolition of the West End, and gained few friends for the new Authority. This project, initiated early in 1958, brutally displaced people, disrupted neighborhoods and destroyed pleasing buildings,[6] only to create a vast approximation of a battlefield in the center of the city. Save for the West Church,[7] the first Harrison Gray Otis House, St. Joseph's Church,[8] the Massachusetts General Hospital and the Charles Street Jail,[9] almost nothing remains of the old West End. Gradually the apartment towers of Charles River Park, with swimming pools, garages and like amenities, have risen on parts of this battlefield,[10] although along Staniford Street there is still (in the summer of 1968) a vast improvised parking lot awaiting "improvement." These towers are, needless to say, beyond the purses of the former residents of the West End. They are, moreover, as complete a break with the traditional architecture and habits of Boston as the adjacent shopping center-motel-movie house in Cambridge Street, which has the air of having wandered in from the suburbs of another city.

The experience of the West End created a widespread conviction that if urban renewal were necessary in Boston some less drastic form must be devised. Total demolition of large areas, without regard for the feelings of people, and their eventual reconstruction — after long periods as a desolate dump — in unfamiliar form for new uses was neither good sense nor good politics. Mayor Collins early in his administration determined that federal funds available for urban renewal must be used in a more imaginative way that would enhance rather than obliterate the unique character of the city. Thus in 1960 he brought to Boston from New Haven a man of outstanding competence, experience and energy — Edward J. Logue — first as consultant and then as Development Administrator, and appointed as Chairman of the Boston Redevelopment Authority the Right Reverend Monsignor Francis J. Lally, the able and respected editor of the archdiocesan newspaper, *The Pilot*.

Armed with extraordinary centralized planning and renewal powers, Logue attacked the multifarious problems of the city with imagination and honesty. On the reasonable theory that plans were more likely to prove practical if the people who made them had the responsibility for their execution, the Redevelopment Authority was merged with the older City Planning Board so that projects could be planned and carried out by the same agency. Logue assembled an able staff, and soon had won the willingness of the financial and business community actively to cooperate in the proposals of the Boston Redevelopment Authority. Avoiding the mistakes of his predecessors in the West End, Logue, throughout his seven years as Development Administrator,[11] continued to emphasize renewal rather than wholesale demolition and rebuilding.

The Boston Redevelopment Authority under Mayor Collins, Monsignor Lally, and Edward J. Logue (Fig. 117) embarked on a wide variety of simultaneous projects throughout the city. "A 90 Million Dollar Development Program for Boston" that Mayor

Fig. 117. Edward J. Logue, Mayor Collins, and Monsignor Lally
at Government Center

Collins announced on 22 September 1960 chose for study ten
comprehensive areas, covering 25 per cent of the land area of the
city. While some of these, like those in Charlestown and Roxbury,
being outside the original bounds of the Shawmut peninsula, are
beyond the scope of this book,[12] others — especially the Government Center project, the first to be undertaken — have been almost as dramatic in their effect upon the topography of Boston as
the filling of the Back Bay.

The City Planning Board had in 1959 released a plan for a new
Government Center in Scollay Square,[13] which did not involve
federal renewal funds. Logue, however, wished not only to bring
this area into his new far-reaching federally assisted renewal program for the city as a whole, but to be certain that the highest
possible architectural standards were maintained in his first, and
most visible, project. Early in his stay in Boston he had said:

Renewal and rehabilitation do not guarantee beauty. It is entirely possible to rebuild Boston in an unattractive, unimaginative way which will make people wonder whether the new is in fact better than the old. This can be avoided with sufficient forethought and courage. It is the function of distinguished architecture and imaginative civic design to see that beauty is the hallmark of the renewed city. Beauty once flourished in Boston. It must again.[14]

His first step in the Government Center was to hire I. M. Pei and Associates of New York City to design the project — "that is, to

Fig. 118. BRA rendering of Government Center

delineate each disposition parcel and establish controls which would limit height, bulk, and setback, and establish a pattern of relationships between each building." [15] Born in China, I. M. Pei had come to Boston in 1935 to study at the M.I.T. School of Architecture during the days of Dean William Emerson.[16] From his student days, he had acquired a singular appreciation of the essential qualities of the earlier life and architecture of the city. He wished not only to preserve the significant historic buildings in the area, but to create spaces in which immense new buildings might be placed in harmonious relation to their older neighbors. As radical revision of the street pattern was necessary, some twenty-two existing streets were reduced to six. Brattle Street, Brattle Square and Elm Street disappeared entirely, as did part of Washington Street and that portion of Hanover Street between Court and Friend Streets [17] (Figs. 118–121).

Fig. 119. BRA model of Government Center

The new City Hall, set in a broad open space, was the keystone of Pei's plan. As this would look upon Faneuil Hall, it was projected as a relatively low building covering considerable ground. Long, low, curving private office buildings were suggested for the west and east sides of this new square, and a new federal office building on the north, while the existing Sears Crescent of Corn-

Fig. 120. BRA model of Government Center

Fig. 121. Government Center in June 1968

Fig. 122. Architects' drawing of City Hall

hill on the south was retained. Pei set height limits upon each part of the Government Center, establishing a subtle balance between low buildings and towers that would relate the new area agreeably to adjacent older parts of the city (Fig. 120). His specifications were included in the national competition for the new City Hall, sponsored by the Boston Society of Architects,[18] which was approved in February 1960 and announced the following November. It attracted 500 applications, 250 preliminary submissions, and 8 final ones. The competition was won on the first ballot by a group of relatively young and unknown architects — Gerhard M. Kallman, Noel M. McKinnell, and Edward F. Knowles, of New York City — who submitted a design for a building that is neither a greenhouse nor a cracker box (Fig. 122). Often in the past the winning design in competition has been laid aside unused. This one was promptly executed. The building is logically planned, with departments receiving many visitors in the great base, which the architects call "the mound"; ceremonial space — mayor's office and council chamber — above; and pure bureaucracy, not requiring much public access, tucked away on the three top floors. The City Hall is low and huge, with Mycenaean or Aztec overtones in its massiveness. In my view, it is as fine a building for its time and place as Boston has ever produced. Traditionalists who long for a revival of Bulfinch simply do not realize how big this building is, and that one does not achieve a handsome monster either by enlarging, or endlessly multiplying, the attractive elements of smaller structures. Although before leaving office, Mayor Collins occupied his new quarters here for a few days in December 1967, almost another year was required to complete the interior finish and the approaches to the building.

To the north of the City Hall is the John Fitzgerald Kennedy Federal Building (Figs. 123–125), consisting of two 26-story towers fronting on Cambridge Street, bridged to two long, low rectangular extensions, running along a new Sudbury Street to Haymarket Square. This striking building, designed by The Architects Collaborative of Cambridge and Samuel Glaser Associates, was occupied in the spring of 1966. Two segments of a handsome crescent-shaped private office building [19] that separates Government Center on the west from the Suffolk County Court House

Fig. 123. Government Center in April 1968

Fig. 124. John Fitzgerald Kennedy Federal Building

higher up Beacon Hill, have been completed (Fig. 123), and the third and final portion will be ready for occupancy in 1969. Pei's plan calls for the eventual construction of a smaller but somewhat similar low office building on the east (Fig. 118) that will serve as a screen between the great scale of Government Center and the diminutive network of colonial alleys — Marshall Street, Salt Lane, Marsh Lane and Creek Square — that form the block be-

Fig. 125. John Fitzgerald Kennedy Federal Building

tween Union and Blackstone Streets. Connected with this on the north there will be a low tower hotel bounded by New Congress, Hanover, Blackstone, and New Sudbury Streets; to the north of this site, and of the low wing of the John Fitzgerald Kennedy Federal Building a huge municipal parking garage and bus terminal at the moment of writing is under construction.[20] Incidentally, these buildings on the east will screen the unsightly John F. Fitzgerald Expressway from Government Center.

Haymarket Square, created as a part of Charles Bulfinch's 1808 plan for filling the old Mill Pond, disappears completely under the parking garage and hotel. It is no loss, for it has had no architectural or topographical merit for many decades. Bowdoin Square — once a handsome residential area but for the past century a pretty complete mess — similarly disappears without regret, although its name still survives below ground in a subway station.[21] The office building of the New England Telephone and Telegraph Company remains, but it is to have as a neighbor on the corner of Cambridge and the relocated Chardon Street a St. Botolph's Chapel that will be one of Dean Sert's experiments in solid geometry. Behind the telephone building, between the new Sudbury and Chardon Streets are an assortment of public and private buildings, some old and some new.[22]

A 22-story State Office Building,[23] completed in 1966, fronting on Cambridge Street between Somerset and Bowdoin Streets, ap-

Fig. 126. BRA model of State Service Center

propriately adjoins Government Center (Figs. 118, 120–121).
The clearing for and construction of this building was an earlier
state venture, unrelated to the Boston Redevelopment Authority.
It swept away everything between Ashburton Place and Cambridge Street, including Allston Street, Allston Place, Bulfinch
Place and part of Howard Street, destroying a number of once
handsome buildings, several of which preserved remnants of the
work of Charles Bulfinch.[24] Across Cambridge Street, within the
area bounded by Cambridge, Staniford, Merrimac and New
Chardon Streets, a State Service Center (Fig. 126) is under construction that is to house three separate agencies, Employment
Security, Health Education and Welfare, and Mental Health. This
was originally conceived as three separate buildings, each with its
own architect. As the area fell within the limits of the Government
Center Urban Renewal Area, the Boston Redevelopment Authority was eventually able to inspire a collaboration that produced
plans for "three buildings merged into one monolithic, monumental whole."[25]

In this connection it is worth noting the points that Edward J.
Logue, looking back over his seven years as Redevelopment Administrator, considered to be the "substantial achievements"[26] of
the Government Center Project.

The Government Center Plan accomplished many "firsts" for the Boston
program, most importantly — early land acquisition and early property
disposition, techniques which made it possible to save over two years in
the execution of this (and other) projects.

Government Center also established Design Review as an ongoing and
successful process and made possible its application to other projects.

But in my view, the most significant achievement of Government Center was our success in obtaining the cooperation of no less than nine gov-
ernmental agencies which participated in the development of the project,
agencies as diverse as the GSA and the MBTA, State Government Center
Commission and City Real Property Department. Each of these agencies
with its own power of eminent domain, agreed to work together and with
the BRA in the furtherance of a plan in which none could play a dominant
role. In a world in which sovereign jealousies are strong, I think this is a
unique achievement.

Also deserving of mention as a significant achievement is I. M. Pei's magnificent design for the Project — a master plan which is proving itself as brilliant in execution as in concept.[27]

Although as of the summer of 1968 there is still so much construction, grading and tidying up to be done that the effect of the Government Center must still be judged from drawings and models rather than photographs, Daland Chandler is around, only a decade after the publication of his verse, to greet "this miracle of rare device," and there is little to attract sailors and their Valentines in what was once Scollay Square. They throng today to a new "combat zone" in that section of Washington Street between Essex and Stuart Streets, for, though one may demolish buildings, honky-tonk goes on forever.[28]

In the Boston Redevelopment Authority's initial plan for Government Center as evolved by I. M. Pei, provision was made for a privately financed office tower at the head of State Street, between the Old State House and the new City Hall (Fig. 120). Although the site, designated as "Parcel 8," had two serviceable buildings on it, Pei had four reasons for marking them for demolition:

The proposed new tower would more than double the tax yield of the site. It and its plaza would also provide a spacious and attractive setting for the Old State House, and symbolize the regeneration of downtown. Moreover, it would block off Washington Street, thereby simplifying and improving the traffic circulation in the area.[29]

What the proposal further accomplished was to safeguard the traditional position of State Street as the financial center of Boston. Bankers and businessman tend to follow each other like sheep. If one shies off in an oblique direction, the others heedlessly follow in hot pursuit. The construction of the Prudential Center raised the specter that banks and law offices would rush pell-mell to the Back Bay, in search of glittering new quarters. At the worst State Street would have become a shambles; at best there would have been the divided confusion that exists today in New York between Wall Street and midtown Manhattan, where the transaction of business may involve needless miles of travel. In a city where men

like to walk, this would have been a calamity. Thus the "Parcel 8"
tower was included in the BRA plans as insurance against such
divisive confusion.

This part of the Government Center renewal plan inspired a
deal of squabbling within and outside the City Council. Before it
was resolved, British investors (Boston British Properties, Inc.),
conjured up by the architect Frederick A. Stahl, undertook to con-
struct a 34-story office building at 225 Franklin Street, across the
way from the Federal Reserve Bank, and only a few blocks from
the middle reaches of State Street. The State Street Bank and
Trust Company leased the lower floors for their headquarters and
gave their name to the building. When such tenants as the law
firm of Ropes & Gray and the engineering firm of Stone and Web-

Fig. 127. View west from Custom House tower in April 1968

ster took space there, a firm anchor was cast.[30] The State Street
Bank Building opened in the spring of 1966, and a chain reaction
has followed. Cabot, Cabot and Forbes have nearly finished the
40-story New England Merchants National Bank Building[31]
(Figs. 121, 127) at 20 State Street (on the "Parcel 8" site) and
are excavating (on the 1640–1808 site of the First Church) for
a second 40-story tower on Washington Street at the head of State
which will contain the main office of the Boston Safe Deposit and
Trust Company, to be known as the Boston Company Building.[32]
The First National Bank is building itself a 37-story tower[33] at
Franklin and Federal Streets, while the National Shawmut Bank
has purchased for construction in the early 1970's the block
bounded by Milk, Federal, Franklin and Devonshire Streets, which
includes the present building of the First National Bank and the
former site of the Stone and Webster building.[34] This lively game
of musical chairs assures the continued integrity of the State Street
region as the financial center of Boston. Without the foresight of
Logue and Pei, however, State Street might have splattered itself
all over the city.

In too many cities of the United States the traditional core has
disintegrated, as retail shops have migrated to suburban highways,
leaving the center of the city to lapse into a few islands of buildings in a sea of parking lots. Bostonians have no desire to see that
happen. Although the larger department stores have established
branches in various suburban shopping centers, the business community has taken active steps to preserve the traditional "four corners" of retail trade — the intersection of Washington, Winter
and Summer Streets and the adjacent blocks. In 1962 a Committee for the Central Business District (CCBD) was formed, under
the chairmanship of Charles A. Coolidge[35] which raised private
funds for a study of the immediate renewal and long-range future
problems of the Central Business District. Working in close cooperation with the Boston Redevelopment Authority, the CCBD
engaged the firm of Victor Gruen Associates, which submitted in
the autumn of 1967 a final report[36] designed to keep the traditional shopping center of Boston where it has always been, with

adequate regard for the improvements of public transportation and the horrendous use of the private automobile.

The basic concept of Gruen's plan is a cluster of "urban sub-areas" each of which by its size, shape and density of activity would permit the walker to remain in possession of his soul.[37] This would be accomplished by closing certain interior streets to vehicles, and circumscribing each area by traffic streets that would take care of the legitimate needs of delivery trucks and the like. The retail, theater and garment districts remain essentially on familiar ground but with expansions and improvements. A large parking garage is proposed at the South Station [38] on air rights over the railroad tracks. To link this with the traditional "four corners," there has been planned a development of new shops, offices and a department store, fronting on an upper-level walk for those on foot. Tremont Street, facing the Common, and Park Square would somewhat resume their nineteenth-century residential character, although with retail shops on the ground floors of apartment houses.

Unfortunately, just as the formal renewal plan for the Central Business District was in process of being approved by the Boston City Council in the autumn of 1967, it was found that the $77,000,000 of federal funds which the plan called for were not available because of the strain on federal resources caused by the Vietnam war, and urban racial problems. Thus the broad plan has been split into a number of "mini projects" which can be executed separately with far smaller federal participation. By this means, and through various private enterprises, some accomplishment in the Central Business District is already visible. A 28-story apartment house on Tremont Street, replacing some of the nondescript business buildings that had supplanted Bulfinch's Colonnade Row, was completed in 1966.[39] Construction began on Washington Street in 1967 for a new Raymond's on the old site "where U bot that hat." [40] The Boston Five Cents Savings Bank is about to embark upon a new addition, designed by the architects of the new City Hall, at the corner of School and Washington Streets on a site resulting from demolition that will link School and Milk

Streets in accordance with the future traffic pattern of the Central Business District. Some years will doubtless pass before walkers have undisputed title to Washington Street from the Government Center to South Cove, and of Winter and Summer Streets from Park Street to the South Station, but the plan exists, an early land acquisition program began in 1965, and it is to be hoped that eventually the federal assistance necessary to carry out the entire project may be forthcoming.

In the introduction to his final report, Edward J. Logue remarked that during his seven years in Boston — "the richest of my life" — he had come to love the city in a very special way and had become "a hopelessly confirmed Bostonian." He continued: "To know Boston is to know her traditions and to honor them. And while it is the new things we do which get talked about, we have been very careful to respect and preserve the good things of the old Boston — even at some expense to the new." [41] The recent history of the Old Corner Book Store is a case in point. In Chapter II, I originally observed: "It still survives as a unique example of

Fig. 128. The Old Corner Book Store in 1960 and 1964

early eighteenth-century domestic architecture in this area, although almost hidden from view by billboards and signs. It deserves a better fate." [42] In the autumn of 1960, when the building was in serious danger of demolition, John Codman, Chairman of the Beacon Hill Architectural Commission, organized an Old Corner Committee, which evolved a plan for buying the building, and restoring it for practical use. Mayor Collins, who expressed the belief that "a City's future is but a logical extension of its past," encouraged the effort, as did the Boston Redevelopment Authority.[43] Over $50,000 for an equity payment was raised in a few weeks, and on 30 December 1960 Historic Boston Incorporated, a non-profit organization which had received its charter from the Commonwealth of Massachusetts the previous day, took title to the building. The exterior restoration of the main body of the building was soon undertaken, and since 1964 the *Boston Globe* has rented the ground floor for its downtown office [44] (Fig. 128). Thus the only example of early eighteenth-century domestic architecture in the Central Business District has been preserved in a manner that is economically useful and self-sufficient and which pays its share of taxes to the city. The Boston Redevelopment Authority plans for the Central Business District have been designed to enhance the appearance of the Old Corner Book Store and its 1729 neighbor, the Old South Meeting House, by creating a small park as a setting for these two significant eighteenth-century survivals [45] (Fig. 129). Similarly, in the Waterfront Project, Logue fully appreciated the necessity of rehabilitating the North and South Market Street buildings and the Quincy Market,[46] which I have described in Chapter V as "one of the principal ornaments of Boston, and perhaps the finest architectural composition of the period surviving in the United States." [47]

In the past century Boston has had two classic examples of overoptimistic planning: the creation of Atlantic Avenue in 1868 and of Bay State Road some twenty years later. The latter provided for extending the Back Bay just as the demand for large city houses was waning: the former enlarged the waterfront almost at the moment when Boston's maritime history was closing.[48]

Fig. 129. BRA proposed park beside Old South Meeting House

The Atlantic Avenue wharves chiefly accommodated coastal shipping and fishermen, for such transoceanic vessels as there were berthed in East Boston. When the major fish dealers moved to the Fish Pier in South Boston,[49] opened in 1914, and the schooners and coasting steamers disappeared, the majority of the Atlantic Avenue wharves lost their reason for being. But fine views of the harbor, combined with low rents, led various venturesome Bostonians to create a *vie de bohème* in the ramshackle buildings of T Wharf and in the nobler warehouses of Long, Commercial and Lewis Wharves.[50]

The BRA Waterfront Project [51] has been concerned with strengthening this area as a residential community, reinforcing the neighboring districts, and opening the city once again to the sea. This called for the relocation of the wholesale food industry [52] which was jammed into traffic-snarling quarters between Faneuil Hall and the waterfront, as well as the realignment of Atlantic Avenue and adjustment of the ramp system of the Central Artery to reduce surface traffic in the region. For living by the sea, the rehabilitation of warehouses was further to be continued, and provision was made for a group of luxurious apartment towers in the area south of Long Wharf. This region would be conveniently adjacent both to the State Street financial district and the new Government Center. To strengthen the existing North End community, a zone of moderate priced new and rehabilitated housing was proposed between the waterfront and the North End. The most significant addition visible at the moment of writing is the impending completion of the New England Aquarium at the end of Central Wharf.[53] The most unhappy loss is the disappearance of the remnant of India Wharf, which was the only example of Charles Bulfinch's work remaining on the waterfront.[54]

Bulfinch has been more respectfully treated in the North End than on the waterfront, for St. Stephen's Church in Hanover Street — the only survivor of the Boston churches he designed — was in 1964–1965 magnificently restored by Richard Cardinal Cushing, Archbishop of Boston (Fig. 130). This was no inconsiderable task, for, as George E. Ryan has written:

By summer's end, 1965, St. Stephen's Church in the North End of Boston had been moved a total of 25 feet — up, down, and backwards — in a history that began more than 160 years ago. The first move, 12 feet back, was effected about 1870 when the City widened Hanover Street. The second, shortly afterwards, when a growing population of Irish Catholics in the North End ran out of space in the main church auditorium and literally "scooped out" a lower church by raising the building 6½ feet and "inserting" another level. The third move — a modern project that restored the venerable edifice to its 1804 condition — dropped St. Stephen's down again, back to the ground-level dictated by the famed Hub architect, Charles Bulfinch.[55]

It is remarkable even for Boston that the same firm — Isaac Blair & Co. — which raised St. Stephen's for Archbishop Williams,

Fig. 130. St. Stephen's Church

lowered it back to its proper foundations for Cardinal Cushing nearly a century later. Across the way the Corporation of Christ Church, Salem Street, is continuing the restoration of the early eighteenth-century Ebenezer Clough house [56] at 21 Unity Street. Happily in 1968, as in 1958, some of the finest surviving monuments of early Boston still fit harmoniously and sympathetically into the modern life of the North End. Happily too the South Cove and the South End have been more intelligently and sympathetically treated than was the West End.

The South Cove (Fig. 131) when filled in the 1830's [57] was chiefly concerned with the new railroads; today it contains two residential neighborhoods — Bay Village and Chinatown — a great medical center and a flourishing entertainment district. Bay Village is a good example of spontaneous historic preservation and rehabilitation. As houses on Beacon Hill became scarcer and more expensive in the fifties, various imaginative individuals began to buy and restore the small red brick nineteenth-century houses in Winchester, Fayette and Melrose Streets. Thus a pleasant residential area, within easy walking distance of the business district, was retrieved.[58] During the last quarter of the nineteenth century, in the vicinity of Beach and Kneeland Streets, a Chinatown evolved at the northern ends of Harrison Avenue, Tyler

Fig. 131. Aerial view of Boston in 1967

Street and Hudson Street. This district — modest in scale compared with its counterparts in New York and San Francisco — consisted of shops dealing in Chinese merchandise, curios and groceries, restaurants and living quarters in close juxtaposition. In spite of a recent proliferation of Chinese restaurants along suburban roads, this region still remains after three quarters of a century the center of the Chinese community, although its area has been constricted by the widening of Kneeland Street [59] in the thirties and the extension of the Massachusetts Turnpike into Boston in the sixties [60] (Figs. 131, 138). A highly significant element in the South Cove is the Tufts–New England Medical Center, established in 1930, a university teaching center, comprising three hospitals [61] and the Tufts University Schools of Medicine and Dental Medicine, that is spreading over blocks between Washington Street and Harrison Avenue. To the west along Tremont Street (between the Common and Broadway) is a concentration of theaters. The South Cove Project of the Boston Redevelopment Authority is designated to strengthen all four elements by eliminating muck where it exists, substituting additional housing,[62] and providing for an orderly expansion of the Medical Center, according to plans developed by The Architects Collaborative.

Across the Massachusetts Pike in the South End, the Boston Redevelopment Authority has substituted for the shambles of Castle Square (Fig. 131) five hundred units of new low-rental housing.[63] The construction of these buildings and the redevelopment of the New York streets have largely swept away the Harrison Avenue ghetto that Mary Antin described so vividly.[64]

Although other new housing projects and schools are basic elements in the BRA plan, efforts are being made to retrieve and to rehabilitate the pleasantly designed streets and squares of nineteenth-century houses, which, as we have seen in Chapter VI, began to slip into dinginess so short a time after their completion. As young families who cannot find moderately priced houses on Beacon Hill buy in the South End, a good deal of rehabilitation is occurring spontaneously, as it has in Bay Village. Moreover, the completion of the Prudential Center on the site of the railroad yards that had long been a "Chinese wall" between two parts of the city, is bringing the western portion of the South End for the first time into some accessible relation with the Back Bay.

In 1958, when Chapter VIII was written, the Prudential Center existed only on paper (Fig. 111) and the area was still a mass of railroad tracks (Fig. 110) as it had been since the filling of the Back Bay. By February 1965, when the city's War Memorial Auditorium was dedicated, the 52-story Prudential tower was in being and the adjacent 29-story Sheraton-Boston Hotel open. An aerial photograph taken in April 1967 (Fig. 132) shows two 26-story apartment towers completed and a third rising, thus bringing the drawing (Fig. 111) close to reality.[65] Today the Prudential Center is a windy world of its own where one can work or shop, live briefly or permanently. At the shopping level one is just enough above Boylston Street and Huntington Avenue to seem out of

Fig. 132. The Prudential Center in 1967

familiar Boston; from the upper stories of the towers one casually sees the sweep of the city as never before, and can appreciate how, in spite of numerous changes, the Back Bay and the South End have retained the character bestowed upon them by their nine-teenth-century planners and architects. The Prudential Center is a vast complex (Figs. 133–134), but as it was built almost entirely on railway yards the only important building that it supplanted was the Mechanics' Building. Many of the large gatherings which that rambling 1881 hall formerly accommodated now take place in the new War Memorial Auditorium.

The hope that I expressed a decade ago that with the comple-tion of the Prudential Center "the contagion of improvement may redeem many of the lost opportunities of Huntington and Massa-chusetts Avenues" is already being realized through the imagina-tive and daring plans of the First Church of Christ, Scientist.[66] Having foresightedly acquired adjacent buildings over the years,

Fig. 133. Aerial view of insurance district in 1967

the Church commissioned I. M. Pei and Associates in 1963 to make a comprehensive planning study of some thirty acres in the Huntington and Massachusetts Avenue area (Figs. 135–136) that would include not only the needs of the Church but the improvement of life in general in that part of Boston.[67] The whole of the north side of Huntington Avenue from the Prudential Center to Horticultural Hall has already been cleared, relieving the Mother Church and Publishing House of undistinguished neighbors. Work is already under way upon this portion of the site which will be devoted exclusively to Church use. At the Prudential end, parallel to Huntington Avenue, will rise a 26-story administration building, 350 feet in height. Across a new tree-lined garden, with an 80-foot fountain and a 700-foot reflecting pool, there will be a long lower building faced by 525 feet of columns 40 feet in height. This Colonnade Building will join (at an angle) the existing Publishing House, and will be used for offices and service

Fig. 134. Charles River Basin in May 1968

Fig. 135. Model of master plan of Christian Science Church Center
and perimeter

functions. At the west end of the new garden, next to Horticultural
Hall, will be a quadrant-shaped building for Sunday Schools and
conferences. Beneath the two-block area of this imaginatively
conceived development will be a 550-car one-floor garage with
access to all buildings, including the Church. This Church Center, covering approximately fifteen of the thirty acres, which is
entirely a private venture of the Church, solely for its own use, is
scheduled for completion by 1971.

The remaining perimeter of close to sixteen acres represents a
three-block area on the south side of Huntington Avenue, including the corners of Huntington and Massachusetts Avenues directly
across from Symphony and Horticultural Halls, and the northwest
side of Massachusetts Avenue from Westland Avenue to Boylston
Street.[68] Pei's plan shows three 34-story apartment towers on
Massachusetts Avenue, two at the Huntington Avenue intersec-

tion and one at Boylston Street, with long lines of lower apartments and retail stores along the northwest side of Massachusetts
and the southeast side of Huntington Avenues. This perimeter
property would be built and operated by private developers on
Church-owned land, leased by the Church to these developers on
long-term land leases, although the Church and the BRA would
retain design control of the buildings erected by the lessees. It
would, of course, pay taxes.[69] The three thousand apartments to
be built on Church-owned land would be for rental to middle-
income small families and single persons; there would be no lux-

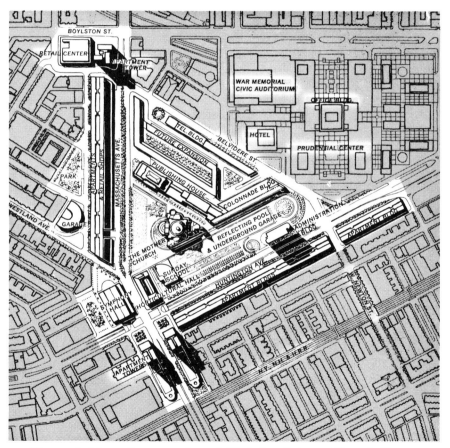

Fig. 136. Map of master plan of Christian Science Church Center
and perimeter

ury apartments, which are almost in excessive supply in other towers.[70] This development, which will run to at least $70,000,-000, is scheduled to be done in stages over a five- to seven-year period beginning in 1968.

This plan of the Christian Science Mother Church will do much to redeem the crowded surroundings of Symphony [71] and Horticultural Halls and to make the region — seventy-five years later — what it was intended to be when "the westward movement" of institutions began. Many of the colleges, hospitals and other institutions described in Chapter VIII have been busily expanding during the past decade. The creation of the Countway Library of Medicine, at the Harvard Medical School, was a notable

Fig. 137. Aerial view of Boston University below Boston University Bridge

Fig. 138. Aerial view of Boston University

event for it brought together the combined collections, staffs and services of the Harvard Medical Library and the Boston Medical Library in a fine building designed by Hugh Stubbins and Associates that was dedicated in the spring of 1965.[72] After nearly thirty years, the Museum of Fine Arts is resuming construction that will provide the space that Guy Lowell's plan of 1907 called for.

Boston University in 1963 took to the air with a 22-story tower, housing its Schools of Law and Education, which with the adjacent Mugar Library and Student Union, is now a conspicuous feature of the river front [73] (Fig. 137). Between this tower, I. M. Pei's 1964 Earth Sciences building at M.I.T., and Dean Sert's Francis Greenwood Peabody Terrace at Harvard there is hardly a point on the Charles River between the Longfellow and Eliot Bridges where one is out of sight of some institution of higher learning. Boston University has not only found a good use for Bay State Road, but has spread across Commonwealth Avenue, re- claiming areas once devoted to early automobile dealers. It now makes use of most of the land between the Charles River and the Massachusetts Turnpike, from Kenmore Square to the Cottage Farm (now Boston University) Bridge with numerous enclaves on the river side of Commonwealth Avenue beyond the bridge (Fig. 138). So a region that was too optimistically over-planned eighty years ago has at last come into its own.

Directly to the east of the Prudential Center, the Boston Public Library has cleared ground [74] for an addition that will occupy the remainder of the Dartmouth-Boylston-Exeter-Blagden Streets block. Plans have been completed by Philip Johnson [75] for a new building (Fig. 139), designed with the greatest respect for Charles F. McKim's masterpiece of 1888–1895. The exterior shape, mass and material will echo that of the earlier building, although the simple and massive design of the three visible façades [76] will be in the style of the third quarter of the twentieth century, as will the interior arrangements. Few great nineteenth-century buildings have received the loving care and consideration that Philip John- son has lavished upon the Boston Public Library in planning this addition.[77]

Ever since 1892 the proper treatment of Copley Square has been a perennial subject for discussion by the Boston Society of

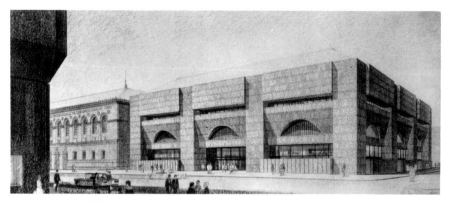

Fig. 139. Addition to Boston Public Library

Architects, the City Planning Board, and Bostonians in general. After more than seventy years of planning without execution, the city held a national design competition which was won in 1966 by Sasaki, Dawson, DeMay Associates, Inc., of Watertown.[78] The rerouting of traffic required for this design having already taken place, construction began in the summer of 1968. At long last a design has progressed from the drawing board into visible activity. But not even the attractive terraces and fountain of this plan can distract the eye from the gaping void that today exists at the southwest corner of Copley Square. The 1958 demolition of the S. S. Pierce building at the corner of Dartmouth Street and Huntington Avenue (Figs. 113–114) upset the balance of the square and made the Boston Public Library resemble a boat that was dragging its anchor. The even greater demolition entailed by the construction of the Massachusetts Turnpike compounded the damage, for today the entire square looks as if

Fig. 140. Southwest corner of Copley Square in 1968

it were washing away into a vast hole in the ground (Fig. 140). What is desperately needed in this site is a modern equivalent of the Admiralty Arch in London — a solid building on Turnpike air rights, no higher than the Boston Public Library, extending from Dartmouth to Blagden Street, pierced by great arches giving access to Huntington Avenue and the Massachusetts Turnpike. To design such a building would call for the imaginative skill of an I. M. Pei or a Philip Johnson, but it would redeem Copley Square and enhance the Boston Public Library by filling the present aching void.

The insurance district of 1958 (shown in an air view in Fig. 108) has not only spread westward to the Prudential Center, but is still suffering from growing pains (Fig. 133). The New England Mutual Life Insurance Company, having outgrown Ralph Adams Cram's "Urn Burial for a concern actuarial,"[79] has raised its lateral wings and filled its central court to the full height of the Newbury Street central section. The John Hancock Mutual Life Insurance Company, finding its Berkeley-St. James-Clarendon-Stuart Street block inadequate, announced in November 1967 its plan to build a 790-foot, 60-story tower on the adjacent block bounded by Trinity Place, St. James Avenue, Clarendon and Stuart Streets. Its relation to the Prudential Center is shown on the model of the Christian Science Church Center (Fig. 135). The architects, I. M. Pei and Associates, made every effort to design a building that, on a limited scale, would provide the two million feet of floor space required by the company, without overwhelming Copley Square. Their solution involved an 8-story base which from the street level would reinforce the building's relation to its near neighbors; from this would rise a slender 52-story tower in the shape of a rhomboid. To reduce the sense of massiveness the building was planned to be enclosed in anodized aluminum and glass, which would reflect the changes of light in the hours and the seasons as well as the city around it (Fig. 141). The company's present Clarendon Building would be razed and a new square created between the old (Fig. 109) and the new towers. From this new Hancock Place there would be admirable views of the apse and tower of Trinity Church. The prospect of the tallest building in New England rising beside Trinity Church caused a lively controversy among architects and others during the winter of 1967–1968. Mr. Pei, and his Boston-born associate, Henry N. Cobb, who has been the partner chiefly responsible for this design, are intimately acquainted with and have a deep feeling for this section of the city.[80] They have shown great imagination in attempting to provide their clients with a light and transparent building that will hopefully enhance the local scene rather than detract from and dominate it. The nineteenth-century Back Bay skyline of 5-story houses, accented by church spires, is gone. The point of no return was reached in 1927 when the 12-story Ritz Carlton Hotel was, by exception, permitted to violate the skyline of Arlington Street. One can no more justify "modest" violations of a height limit than to argue about the partial freshness of an egg or pregnancy of a girl. To me at least one slender 60-story tower clutters the skyline less than three 20-story buildings or four of 15.

Even though few of its houses are still occupied in the traditional manner, the Back Bay is still the handsomest and most consistent example of American architecture of the second half of the nineteenth century now existing in the United States. For the second half of that century it is every bit as typical as Beacon Hill is of the first. Although many Bostonians completely failed to realize this until very recently, the wind is changing. The Back Bay Neighborhood Association, under the leadership of the late Charles P. Howard and of Lawrence T. Perera, has made valiant efforts to restore the residential quality of the region, while the city has endeavored to discourage further expansion of schools and colleges.[81] Edward J. Logue described the latter measures:

During 1966, the zoning code was amended to further restrict the expansion of institutional uses by making dormitories a conditional use and fraternities a forbidden use. In addition, a design control bill to establish the Back Bay Architectural Commission was enacted by the Legislature. This legislation, which I believe is unique, will help to insure that all new construction and alternations in the Back Bay residential area will be in keeping with the area's distinctive architectural character. The area presently covered by this control includes Beacon Street, Marlborough Street, and Commonwealth Avenue.[82]

The publication in 1967 of Bainbridge Bunting's *Houses of Boston's Back Bay: An Architectural History, 1840–1917* by the Belknap Press of Harvard University Press further focused interest on the unique architectural quality of the Back Bay.[83] Its prospects seems brighter than they did a decade ago.

Beacon Hill, created a historic district by act of the Massachusetts Legislature in 1955, was designated as a Registered National Historic Landmark by the Department of the Interior in 1963. The boundaries of the district have twice been enlarged, so that today the external appearances of buildings between Beacon and Cambridge Streets, from Bowdoin Street to the Charles River are protected from thoughtless and inappropriate alteration. Although good new uses have been found for many buildings on Beacon Hill, Harrison Gray Otis's second house at 85 Mount Vernon Street (Fig. 34) is still a private residence.[84]

Boston has an excellent record for keeping handsome and worthwhile buildings in use as long as possible, and of finding new purposes for those that cannot be thus continued. Faneuil Hall still shelters butchers and civic meetings. The Governor, Executive Council and Senate of Massachusetts still transact their business in the handsome surroundings that Charles Bulfinch provided in the last decade of the eighteenth century. Christ Church in Salem Street (1723), King's Chapel (1750) and Park Street Church (1809) still function unchanged, while the West Church (1806), after seventy years as a library, has recently returned to religious use. While a few private houses of the nineteenth century are still occupied by single families, many more have been skillfully converted to institutional use or multiple occupancy. Harrison Gray Otis's first house provides excellent headquarters for the Society for the Preservation of New England Antiquities and his third houses the American Meteorological Association. The Colonial Society of Massachusetts occupies a Bulfinch house

at 87 Mount Vernon Street: the Colonial Dames are settled in
William Hickling Prescott's house at 55 Beacon Street, while the
Boston Bar Association has recently remodeled Chester Harding's
former studio at 16 Beacon Street.[85] The Somerset, Union, Tavern
and St. Botolph Clubs, and the Club of Odd Volumes, like the
distaff College, Chilton and Women's City Clubs, all occupy private houses, some of which are architecturally of great distinction.[86] In fact, one might claim that to the Bostonian a club is
ideally a large private house, for few clubhouses in the city were
specially built as such, or on a scale to accommodate a Peter Arno
"Club man." [87] The conversion of the century-old Boston Society
of Natural History building for retail use by Bonwit Teller will,
I hope, suggest a similar future for its contemporary, the old City
Hall in School Street. Great wharf warehouses, facing the harbor,
like Beacon Hill and Back Bay houses, have been converted in
plenty to apartment dwellings. The record of adaptation to new
uses in Boston has been varied and good, and I trust it will long
continue. A similar view was expressed by Cardinal Cushing on
18 April 1966 in an address at Christ Church, Salem Street —
the "Old North" — during a service commemorating the hanging
of Paul Revere's signal lanterns.

Wherever it is possible, our old buildings of historic and artistic importance should be kept, not just as relics of another time, not merely as
souvenirs of other days, but as a part of the City which still makes its contribution to the life of the community and its people. Old North Church is
an example of such a building, so too is St. Stephen's; so too is the West
Church, long a public library, and now a flourishing Methodist Church in
the West End of Boston. These are not just ornaments of the days of our
fathers; they are active, religious institutions which make their contribution in each generation. Elsewhere in the city we have been able to promote
similar projects and the effort should be encouraged. To be sure, new uses
will be found for some older buildings, but uses, as in the Old Corner
Bookstore, not incompatible with their original functions. Let me use this
occasion to plead for an ever wider interest in an intelligent preservation
of old Boston, one which does not stand in the way of true progress and
advancement, yet is ever mindful of events like the one we commemorate
here today.[88]

Fig. 141. The Back Bay from the State House with the
John Hancock Tower

The hopes of a decade ago have begun to be realized. If the plans concerted by the Boston Redevelopment Authority in recent years can be carried through to completion in the next decade, we shall be fortunate indeed in having a modern city that has kept its own traditional flavor and color. I hoped in 1958 that we should be spared both slavish antiquarianism and "Madison Avenue Colonial" in new construction, and we have been. What I should not have dared to hope then was that so many first-rate contemporary architects would be adding distinguished contributions to the Boston scene. Martin Meyerson and Edward C. Banfield in *Boston: the job ahead* remarked:

In the metropolitan area there are examples of the work of Aalto, Belluschi, Gropius, Koch, Le Corbusier, Pei, Rudolph, Saarinen, Sert, Stubbins, and Yamasaki. This is a greater concentration of work by outstanding living architects than is to be found anywhere else in the world. We should have a Beauty Trail as well as a Freedom Trail to lead tourists and, above all, Bostonians to the works of these men as well as to the architectural and civic design achievements of an earlier day.[89]

I have recorded elsewhere my misgivings about "trails" and tourists,[90] but I fully agree that Bostonians should become more aware of the variety and quality of recent buildings that surround them. Sometimes in Cambridge, at both Harvard and M.I.T., the works of outstanding architects seem to be packed in, like specimens in the cases of an overcrowded nineteenth-century museum, with little reference to their scale or their neighbors.[91] But in Boston, thanks to Edward J. Logue's emphasis on urban design,[92] the works of eminent contemporary architects, and of younger men who have come to the fore by their recent buildings here, have been related to each other and to the shape of the city in a singularly happy manner. Of all the work of this decade, I suspect that the plans of I. M. Pei and Associates for the Government Center (Figs. 118–120), the John Hancock and the Christian Science projects (Figs. 135–136) will have done more than anything to shape the future amenities of the city.

Appendix

A CHRONOLOGICAL LIST OF SOME OF THE SURVIVING HIS-
TORICAL SITES AND MONUMENTS MENTIONED IN
THE PRECEDING CHAPTERS

1631   KING'S CHAPEL BURYING GROUND, Tremont Street
        near School Street. The oldest burial place in the city, ante-
        dating the construction of the first King's Chapel by more
        than half a century.

1634   BOSTON COMMON. A tract of about forty-five acres pur-
        chased by the town from the Reverend William Blaxton, the
        first English inhabitant of the Shawmut peninsula.

1660   GRANARY BURYING GROUND, Tremont Street oppo-
        site Bromfield Street. Originally a part of the Common, this
        cemetery, known in the colonial period as the South Burying
        Ground, takes its name from the town granary, which for-
        merly stood on the site of the Park Street Church.

1660   COPP'S HILL BURYING GROUND, Hull Street. The
        earliest cemetery of the North End, situated on the summit
        of one of the ancient hills of the Boston Peninsula.

c.1680 PAUL REVERE HOUSE, North Square. A wooden dwell-
        ing house, bought in 1770, when approximately a century
        old, by Paul Revere, which is (although extensively re-
        stored) the only surviving example in Boston of seventeenth-
        century domestic architecture in wood.

1711– OLD STATE HOUSE, State and Washington Streets. The
1747   walls of a brick structure, built after the fire of 1711 to
       replace the wooden Town House of 1657, which was in its
       turn burned in 1747, survive in this building, which was
       occupied for half a century by the Massachusetts govern-
       ment, and later served as the town and city hall. It is now
       the headquarters of the Bostonian Society.

c.1711 MOSES PIERCE — HICHBORN HOUSE, North Square.
        A three-story brick dwelling house, separated from the Paul
        Revere House by a walled garden.

1711   OLD CORNER BOOK STORE, Washington and School
       Streets. A brick house, built after the fire of 1711, by
       Thomas Crease, an apothecary, that acquired literary con-
       notations during the following century when occupied by
       publishers and booksellers; the only surviving eighteenth-
       century house in this part of Boston.

c.1714 UNION OYSTER HOUSE, 41 Union Street. A brick build-
        ing, occupied before the Revolution by Capen's dry goods
        store, in which Isaiah Thomas published *The Massachusetts
        Spy* from 1771 to 1775; since 1826 an oyster house.

1723   CHRIST CHURCH, Salem Street. Built for Anglican wor-
       ship, and still used by an Episcopal congregation, this is the
       oldest extant church in Boston. From Longfellow's reference
       to the signal lanterns hung in its tower on the night of 18
       April 1775, Christ Church has become commonly known
       today as "the old North Church."

1729   OLD SOUTH MEETING HOUSE, Washington and Milk
       Streets. The second meeting house of the third Congrega-
       tional church in Boston, gathered in 1669; preserved since
       1876 as a historic monument by the Old South Association
       in Boston.

1742– FANEUIL HALL, Dock Square: John Smibert, architect.
1805   Erected in 1742 by the French Huguenot merchant Peter
       Faneuil as a market house, with a large hall above for
       public meetings, and, after various fires and rebuildings, en-
       larged to its present form in 1805 by Charles Bulfinch.

1750 KING'S CHAPEL, Tremont and School Streets: Peter Harrison, architect. The second building of the first Anglican congregation in Boston, organized in 1688, which became Unitarian after the Revolution.

c.1760 EBENEZER HANCOCK HOUSE, 10 Marshall Street. A brick house, which John Hancock inherited from his uncle, Thomas Hancock, in 1764; occupied during the Revolution by John's younger brother, Ebenezer Hancock; from 1796 to the 1960's a shoe store.

1795– STATE HOUSE, Beacon and Park Streets: Charles Bul-
1798 finch, architect. The cornerstone of this building, which replaced the Old State House as the seat of the government of Massachusetts, was laid in 1795.

1796 FIRST HARRISON GRAY OTIS HOUSE, 141 Cambridge Street: Charles Bulfinch, architect. The headquarters of the Society for the Preservation of New England Antiquities.

1797 U.S.S. CONSTITUTION, Boston Naval Shipyard, Charlestown. This frigate — the most historic surviving ship of the United States Navy — may be visited by way of a separate entrance to the Naval Shipyard.

1800 SECOND HARRISON GRAY OTIS HOUSE, 85 Mount Vernon Street: Charles Bulfinch, architect. This fine example of a detached mansion house is still occupied as a private residence.

1804 ST. STEPHEN'S CHURCH, Hanover Street: Charles Bulfinch, architect. Restored 1965 by Cardinal Cushing.

1804 THOMAS AMORY HOUSE, Beacon and Park Streets. This double brick house, part of which was subsequently occupied by George Ticknor, warrants notice even though it has been sadly mauled by rebuilders.

1805 COLONIAL SOCIETY OF MASSACHUSETTS, 87 Mount Vernon Street: Charles Bulfinch, architect. A four-story brick house, designed in relation to a comparable house at number 89, now destroyed.

1806 THIRD HARRISON GRAY OTIS HOUSE, 45 Beacon Street: Charles Bulfinch, architect. Occupied by Otis until his death in 1848; now the headquarters of the American Meteorological Society.

1806 WEST CHURCH, Cambridge and Lynde Streets: Asher Benjamin, architect. After more than sixty years as a branch library, now restored as a Methodist Church.

1809 PARK STREET CHURCH, Tremont and Park Streets: Peter Banner, architect. A Congregational church, built on the site of the town Granary, which gave its name to the adjacent burying ground.

1820 ST. PAUL'S CATHEDRAL, Tremont Street: Alexander Parris and Solomon Willard, architects. An Episcopal church; since 1908 the cathedral of the Diocese of Massachusetts.

1825– QUINCY MARKET, between North and South Market
1826 Streets: Alexander Parris, architect. Built by Mayor Josiah Quincy, as part of an imaginative and handsome redevelopment, to provide additional market space for a growing city.

1825– BUNKER HILL MONUMENT, Charlestown: Solomon
1843 Willard, architect. An obelisk of Quincy granite 220 feet in height, commemorating the battle that took place on 17 June 1775.

1847– BOSTON ATHENÆUM, 10½ Beacon Street: Edward
1849 C. Cabot, architect. The building of a proprietary library, founded in 1807; enlarged and rebuilt in 1913 by Henry Forbes Bigelow.

1859 ARLINGTON STREET CHURCH, Arlington and Boylston Streets: Arthur Gilman, architect. The first church to be built in the Back Bay for the Unitarian society formerly in Federal Street, of which William Ellery Channing had been the minister.

1861 CHURCH OF THE IMMACULATE CONCEPTION, Harrison Avenue: P. C. Keeley, architect. Built in the South End by the Jesuit Fathers, who soon after established Boston College in an adjacent building.

1862 CITY HALL, School Street: Gridley J. F. Bryant and Arthur Gilman, architects. The most conspicuous survival of the architectural influence of the French Second Empire in Boston.

1862 EMMANUEL CHURCH, Newbury Street: A. R. Estey, architect. The first Episcopal church to be built in the Back Bay.

1863 BONWIT TELLER, Berkeley and Boylston Streets: William G. Preston, architect. Built as a museum for the Boston Society of Natural History.

1865– FIRST CHURCH, Berkeley and Marlborough Streets: Ware
1868 and van Brunt, architects. A Gothic revival structure built for the oldest religious society in Boston; now Unitarian. In 1968 it was severely damaged by fire.

1867 CENTRAL CONGREGATIONAL CHURCH, Berkeley and Newbury Streets: Richard M. Upjohn, architect. Built of Roxbury Puddingstone, with a graceful spire.

1867– CATHEDRAL OF THE HOLY CROSS, Washington
1875 Street, corner of Waltham Street: P. C. Keeley, architect. A large Gothic revival building that replaced the first Bulfinch cathedral in Franklin Street.

1868 FRANKLIN SQUARE HOUSE, Franklin Square. Originally the St. James Hotel, the principal hotel of the South End; later the New England Conservatory of Music.

1871 FIRST BAPTIST CHURCH, Commonwealth Avenue and Clarendon Street: H. H. Richardson, architect. Built originally for the Brattle Square Church.

1875 NEW OLD SOUTH CHURCH, Boylston and Dartmouth Streets: Cummings and Sears, architects. The third meeting house of the Third Church, built after the society abandoned the Old South Meeting House in Washington Street.

1877 TRINITY CHURCH, Copley Square: H. H. Richardson, architect. An Episcopal church, built during the rectorship of Phillips Brooks, for a parish originally in Summer Street.

1879– CHURCH OF THE ADVENT, Mount Vernon and Brim-
1883 mer Streets: John H. Sturgis, architect. A brick Gothic revival church, built for an Episcopal parish founded in 1844 in the West End.

1888– BOSTON PUBLIC LIBRARY, Copley Square: McKim,
1895 Mead and White, architects. The most distinguished architectural monument of Boston built during the last quarter of the nineteenth century.

1894– CHRISTIAN SCIENCE CHURCH, Falmouth Street. To
1906 the Mother Church, occupied in 1894 was added in 1904–1906 a vast domed extension.

1899– FENWAY COURT, The Fenway and Worthington Street.
1903 Built by Mrs. John L. Gardner to house the paintings, sculpture and works of art that she collected for the Isabella Stewart Gardner Museum, now a public institution.

1899 MASSACHUSETTS HISTORICAL SOCIETY, 1154 Boylston Street. The oldest historical society in the United States, established in 1799, with an outstanding manuscript collection covering three centuries of Massachusetts history.

1900 SYMPHONY HALL, Massachusetts and Huntington Avenues: McKim, Mead and White, architects. Concert hall of the Boston Symphony Orchestra, founded in 1881 by Henry Lee Higginson.

1900 HORTICULTURAL HALL, Massachusetts and Huntington Avenues: Wheelwright and Haven, architects. The headquarters of the Massachusetts Horticultural Society, founded in 1829.

1909 MUSEUM OF FINE ARTS, 465 Huntington Avenue: Guy Lowell, architect. The collections include works of art from Egypt, Greece, Rome, the near east, China, Japan, India, medieval, renaissance and modern Europe and the United States.

Notes

Index

Chapter I

"Fittest for such as can trade into England"

1. Irving B. Crosby, *Boston Through the Ages, The Geological Story of Greater Boston* (Boston, 1928) gives a simplified popular account of the lands and shores of Boston and vicinity.

2. Charles C. Willoughby, *Antiquities of the New England Indians* (Cambridge: Peabody Museum, 1935), 6–10.

3. Frederick Johnson and others, *The Boylston Street Fishweir* (Andover, 1942) and *The Boylston Street Fishweir II* (Andover, 1949), which form volumes 2 and 4, number 1 of *Papers of the Robert S. Peabody Foundation for Archæology*. Fig. 1 in the 1942 volume is an excellent map of the Boston Peninsula and surrounding regions about 1700.

4. Nathaniel Ingersoll Bowditch's articles, contributed to the *Transcript, 1855*, were reprinted in *Fifth Report of the Record Commissioners, 1880*, cited henceforth as *B.R.C., V.*

5. This great series of close to forty volumes, beginning in the eighteen seventies and continuing into the present century, which contains town records, acts of the selectmen, vital statistics as well as many miscellaneous papers, is cited henceforth as *B.R.C.*

6. Nathaniel Bradstreet Shurtleff, *A Topographical and Historical Description of Boston,* first published by the City in 1870, with a second edition in 1871; a third and revised edition, with prefatory matter by W. H. Whitmore, appeared in 1891. References to this third edition are given simply as "Shurtleff."

7. Justin Winsor, *Memorial History of Boston,* a cooperative work, planned and edited by Winsor and published by James R. Osgood & Co., 1881–1883; cited henceforth as "Winsor."

8. Annie Haven Thwing, *The Crooked and Narrow Streets of Boston* (Boston, 1920).

9. William Wood, *New England Prospects,* Boynton ed. (Boston, 1898), 39–40.

10. Thomas C. Amory in *Bostonian Soc. Pub.,* I, 3–25; *B.R.C.,* V, 1–3.

11. James H. Stark, *Stark's Antique Views of ye Towne of Boston* (Boston, 1901), 163, 170.

12. Willis' Creek, later known as the Miller River, separated Cambridge from Somerville (Stark, 170).

13. Caleb H. Snow, *A History of Boston,* 2nd ed. (Boston, 1828), 46.

14. William H. Whitmore in *Bostonian Soc. Pub.,* I, 41.

15. Abel Bowen, *Bowen's Picture of Boston,* 3rd ed. (Boston, 1838), 10.

16. B.R.C., V, 61–67; Samuel C. Clough in *Publications of the Colonial Society of Massachusetts,* XX, 264–269; cited henceforth as C.S.M.

17. Nathaniel B. Shurtleff, ed., *Records of the Governor and Company of the Massachusetts Bay in New England* (Boston, 1853–1854), I, 137; cited henceforth as *Mass. Records.*

18. Winsor, III, opp. iv.

19. *Prints, Maps and Drawings, 1677–1822, A Massachusetts Historical Society Picture Book* (Boston, 1957), no. 20; Stark, 222–224.

20. B.R.C., V, 152–153. Dr. Edward Reynolds (1793–1881), *Reminiscences and Letters* (Boston, 1931), 36, wrote: "I see all of Mount Vernon from the back of Beacon Street down to Cambridge bridge, covered only with a few Negro huts and bearing the Euphonious name of Mount Horum."

21. *Discord and Civil Wars Being a Portion of the Journal kept by Lieutenant Williams of His Majesty's Twenty-Third Regiment while Stationed in British North America During the Time of the Revolution* (Buffalo: Salisbury Club, 1954), 5.

22. James K. Hosmer, ed., *Winthrop's Journal "History of New England" 1630–1649* (New York, 1908), I, 58.

23. *Winthrop's Journal,* I, 53.

24. Alexander Young, *Chronicles of the First Planters of the Colony of Massachusetts Bay* (Boston, 1856), 339.

25. Cf. Martin S. Briggs, *The Homes of the Pilgrim Fathers in England and America* (London, 1932).

26. George Francis Dow, *Every Day Life in the Massachusetts Bay Colony* (Boston, 1935).

27. *Mass. Records,* I, 116.

28. B.R.C., II; Clough in C.S.M., XXVII, 6–21.

29. C.S.M., XXV, 43–47.

30. B.R.C., II, 63–64.

31. B.R.C., II, 73.

32. B.R.C., II, 74–75. It should be remembered that "corne" in this sense applies to wheat and other cereals in general.

33. Winsor, I, 529.

34. B.R.C., II, 131.

35. *B.R.C.*, II, 70.

36. *B.R.C.*, II, 40, 60.

37. *B.R.C.*, II, 67.

38. Carl Bridenbaugh, *Cities in the Wilderness* (New York, 1938), and *Cities in Revolt* (New York, 1955).

39. Bernard Bailyn, *The New England Merchants in the Seventeenth Century* (Cambridge, 1955), 36–37.

40. *Ibid.*, 97–98. See Josiah H. Benton, *The Story of the Old Boston Town House 1658–1711* (Boston, 1908) and Charles A. Lawrence's reconstruction drawing done in 1930 for the Bostonian Society.

41. John Josselyn, *An Account of Two Voyages to New-England* (London, 1674), 20, 26–27.

42. *Ibid.*, 161–162.

43. Charles Shaw, *A Topographical and Historical Description of Boston* (Boston, 1817), 89–99.

44. *Handbook of the Paul Revere Memorial Association* (Boston, 1950) contains (pp. 17–25) Joseph Everett Chandler's notes on the restoration that he undertook for the Paul Revere Memorial Association, the present owners.

45. Snow, *History,* 206.

46. Identified in Winsor, III, 575, as the cook of a M. Dubuque, a French refugee from Martinique, who briefly occupied the Shirley-Eustis house in Roxbury.

47. For Shaw, opposite 291.

48. For Snow, 244. See also Shurtleff, 652–662, and Winsor, II, xxix, 524.

49. Shurtleff, 402; Winsor, I, 547–548; Edward G. Porter, *Rambles in Old Boston New England* (Boston, 1887), 87–89.

50. Shaw, opposite 73. See also Shurtleff, 683–689.

51. Shurtleff, 597–604; Porter, 373–378.

52. As to Captain Benjamin Gillam in 1668; *B.R.C.*, VII, 41.

53. Shurtleff, 116–117; *Mass. Records,* IV, ii, 297–299.

54. *B.R.C.*, VII, 79.

55. *B.R.C.*, VII, 82–83.

56. *B.R.C.*, VII, 84.

57. *B.R.C.*, VII, 83–84.

58. Shurtleff, 118–119. G. R. Payson, in *Proc. Bostonian Soc.* (1928), 23–24; *B.R.C.*, V, 11–13.

59. *Mass. Records,* V, 310–311.

60. Winsor, III, between vi and vii.

61. Winsor, II, 502.

Chapter II

The Eighteenth Century

1. *B.R.C.*, I, 99, Vote of 11 April 1650.

2. Reproduced in facsimile in *A Record of the Streets, Alleys, Places, etc., in the City of Boston* (Boston, 1910), a city publication that took 543 pages to record the kind of information that Green, 202 years earlier, could put on a broadside.

3. Shurtleff, 92.

4. Dewing, who arrived in Boston in 1716, engraved in 1717 Captain Cyprian Southack's "A New Chart of the English Empire in North America," which Lawrence C. Wroth described as the earliest map to be engraved on copper in this country. See L. C. Wroth and Marion W. Adams, *American Woodcuts and Engravings, 1670–1800* (Providence, 1946), 16–17, and John Carter Brown Library Annual Report 1942, pp. 26–38.

5. John H. Edmonds, in *C.S.M.*, XI, 246 ff.

6. John H. Edmonds, in *C.S.M.*, XI, 245–262, and John W. Farwell, in *C.S.M.*, XXV, 230–234.

7. The best copy is in the American Antiquarian Society. Others are in the Massachusetts Historical Society, the Boston Public Library, the Boston Athenæum (formerly owned by Herbert Foster Otis and Henry Lee Shattuck), and the private collection of the late Dr. James B. Ayer.

8. *C.S.M.*, XXV, 231–232.

9. Shurtleff, 92–93. A collotype facsimile of the Boston Athenæum copy was published in 1951.

10. John Carter Brown Library Annual Report 1946–47, pp. 5–11.

11. Winsor, II, xiv.

12. Winsor, II, xix–xx.

13. *Re-dedication of the Old State House, Boston, July 11, 1882* [commonly known by binding title of *Old State House Memorial*], (Boston, 1882), 43–44; Thomas Hutchinson, *The History of Massachusetts,* 3rd ed. (Salem, 1795), II, 181; Arthur E. Ellis, *History of the First Church in Boston* (Boston, 1881), 167. See Chapter IX, note 32.

14. *Old State House Memorial*, 45–46.

15. Ellis, *History of the First Church*, 167–173.

16. Clifford K. Shipton, *Sibley's Harvard Graduates* (Cambridge, 1933), IV, 306. The row which led to the founding of the New Brick or Revenge Church reached a height of vindictiveness perhaps never be-

fore or since known in Boston, with dissident occupants of the gallery relieving themselves upon the heads of their brethren on the floor.

17. Winsor, II, xi, 525–527, 548; Stark, 58–63.

18. Stark, 53–57.

19. E. Channing, *A History of the United States* (New York, 1916), II, 199–200.

20. M. A. DeWolfe Howe, *Boston Common* (Cambridge, 1910), 23.

21. Reynolds, *Reminiscences and Letters,* 15.

22. Carl Van Doren, *The Letters of Benjamin Franklin and Jane Mecom* (Philadelphia, 1950), 4–7.

23. Porter, 33–34; Walter Muir Whitehill, *A Brief Guide to Institutions and Sites of Historic Interest in Boston* (Boston: Bostonian Society, 1957), 15.

24. Susan B. Lyman, *My Early Home* (Boston, 1916). This narrative, written in 1893, contains a redrawing of a painting of the house by Vautin, then owned by the author. It is also reproduced as a headpiece to chapter I of Ellen Susan Bulfinch, *The Life and Letters of Charles Bulfinch, Architect* (Boston, 1896), 11. I am unable to discover what has become of the painting since Mrs. Lyman's death in 1898.

25. Shurtleff, 672–680.

26. B.R.C., V, 32.

27. This was the ninth church, and sixth Congregational society, to be established in Boston.

28. Shipton, *Sibley's Harvard Graduates,* VI, 490–495.

29. F. A. Gardner, *Gardner Memorial* (Salem, 1933), 127–133.

30. *A Home of the Olden Time* (Boston, 1872), reprinted from the *New-England Historical and Genealogical Register.*

31. H. W. Foote, *Annals of King's Chapel* (Boston, 1900), I, 8.

32. B.R.C., V, 7.

33. Winsor, II, 522–524.

34. Winsor, II, 521–522.

35. The first issue of the Bonner map in the New York Public Library gives the population as "near 15,000 people," a figure revised downward to "near 12,000 people" in the Massachusetts Historical Society's second issue, also of 1722. Seemingly Bonner had been too optimistic: at least Professor Carl Bridenbaugh accepts the lower in the following population figures, from his *Cities in the Wilderness,* 143, 303, and *Cities in Revolt,* 5, 216. The figures with asterisks he gives as from actual censuses [p. 3].

	Boston	Philadelphia	New York
1690	7,000	4,000	3,900
1700	6,700	5,000	5,000
1710	9,000	6,500	5,700

	Boston	Philadelphia	New York
1720	12,000	10,000	7,000
1730	13,000	11,500	8,622
1743	16,382*	13,000	11,000
1760	15,631*	23,750	18,000
1775	16,000	40,000	25,000
1776	3,500	21,767	5,000

36. *Record of Streets*, 214.

37. M. A. DeWolfe Howe, *Boston Landmarks* (New York, 1946), 53–70, for the chapters "Oldest North — Christ Church" and "An Old New North — St. Stephen's."

38. *Bowen's Picture of Boston*, 123–124.

39. Winsor, II, xxxix.

40. Shipton, *Sibley's Harvard Graduates*, VII, 472.

41. Hamilton A. Hill, *History of the Old South Church* (Boston, 1890), I, 461; Arthur W. H. Eaton, *The Famous Mather Byles* (Boston, 1914), 39.

42. *B.R.C.*, V, 24–26.

43. *B.R.C.*, V, 19–21.

44. Shipton, *Sibley's Harvard Graduates*, VII, 216–238. Upon Mather's death in 1785 his congregation reunited with the Second Church and the Bennet Street meeting house was sold to the Universalists.

45. *Sibley's Harvard Graduates*, VII, 227.

46. Robert M. Lawrence, *Old Park Street and its Vicinity* (Boston, 1922), 41–44.

47. Winsor, II, 264.

48. Reproduced in Winsor, II, 267; Stark, 101; *Old State House Memorial*, opp. 146.

49. For a Bowen engraving showing the relationship of the halls in size, see Stark, 103, or *Old State House Memorial*, opp. 146.

50. Walter Muir Whitehill, "Historical Continuity versus Synthetic Reconstruction," *Athenæum Items*, 67 (January 1958), 1–3.

51. 15 February 1958, 4.

52. 1 February 1958; reprinted as a broadside by the Stinehour Press, Lunenburg, Vermont.

Chapter III

The Boston of Bulfinch

1. M.H.S. *Collections*, III (1794), 241–304; cited henceforth as "Pemberton."

2. Pemberton, 249.

3. Pemberton, 250.

4. Oscar Handlin, *Boston's Immigrants: A Study in Acculturation, Revised Edition, 1790–1880* (Cambridge, 1959), 9–10. Table II gives population figures from 1790–1865.

5. Pemberton, 276–277, 279; Winsor, IV, 78.

6. Broadside reproduced in *Old State House Memorial,* opp. 97.

7. Pemberton, 245; Snow, 316–318; *Massachusetts Magazine,* I, no. 9 (September 1789), 533–534, where the engraving reproduced in Fig. 26 serves as a frontispiece.

8. *B.R.C.,* VIII, 145. Pemberton, 245, remarks that "it was then, according to Governor Hutchinson, looked upon as a Quixote enterprise."

9. Snow, 316. Pemberton, 245, pointed out that "the river over which this bridge is built is broader and deeper than the Thames at London or Westminster."

10. Pemberton, 269–273.

11. C. A. Place, *Charles Bulfinch, Architect and Citizen* (Boston, 1925), 5; cited henceforth as "Place."

12. Place, 15.

13. Place, 20–24.

14. Ellen Susan Bulfinch, *The Life and Letters of Charles Bulfinch Architect* (Boston, 1896), 48; cited henceforth as "Bulfinch."

15. Snow, 318; Pemberton, 245–246.

16. Joseph Coolidge (1747–1829) married as his first and second wives Elizabeth and Katherine Boyer, who were Charles Bulfinch's second cousins. His son Joseph Coolidge (1773–1840) married Bulfinch's sister, Elizabeth, in 1796.

17. The drawing of the west front, owned by the Boston Athenæum, is reproduced in Whitehill, *A Boston Athenæum Miscellany* (Boston, 1950), 9–10; Place, 41; *B.R.C.,* V, 47–49.

18. Bulfinch, 301.

19. 1789 directory in *B.R.C.,* X, 179; presumably with shop and house together. The 1796 directory in *B.R.C.,* X, 236 gives him as "merchant, No. 8, Kilby street, house Cambridge street."

20. Place, 159–163; S. E. Morison, *The Life and Letters of Harrison Gray Otis, Federalist, 1765–1848* (Boston, 1913), I, 44.

21. Place, 141; Snow, 332.

22. Place, 218, 281 (which reproduces a reconstruction drawing of Bowdoin Square in 1825 from the frontispiece of *Proc. Bostonian Soc.* for 1922, showing these houses as well as Bulfinch's birthplace). *Proc. Bostonian Soc.* for 1922 also contains, opp. 10, a view of the Kirk Boott

house, built in Bowdoin Square in 1806, which in 1847 was incorporated in the Revere House.

23. *Memoir of the Life of Eliza S. M. Quincy* (Boston, 1861), 60–61.

24. Snow, 321.

25. Massachusetts Historical Society *Proceedings,* I (1791–1835), 58, 65, 67, 143; Boston Library Society Record Book (in Boston Athenæum), minutes of 3 March 1794, 14 July 1794, 24 April 1858. Both recipients of space had to finish and furnish their quarters at their own expense. The deed to the Massachusetts Historical Society property was executed 1 May 1794, and the Society first met in the 40-by-27-foot room on 11 June 1794. Bulfinch was elected a resident member on 1 October 1801 and exempted from admission fee and dues "in consideration of the generous donation of the library room." The Boston Library Society (today merged with the Athenæum) promptly elected Bulfinch a trustee on 14 July 1794. That Society first met in its "new room" on 2 March 1795.

26. Place, 38; B.R.C., XXXI, 253, 276, 319, 349, 384, 391.

27. Place, 94–117; B.R.C., XXXV, 59, 79, 96, 118, 141, 160, 175, 191, 207, 226, 246, 260, 279, 297, 329; XXXVII, 1, 24, 49, 65. In 1815 when he was defeated for re-election, the gentlemen elected declined to serve, and he was triumphantly returned to office on a second ballot. In 1818 when he moved to Washington to become architect of the Capitol, the town voted him thanks "for his able and faithful services as a Selectman for twenty two years nineteen of which he with great ability discharged the duties of Chairman of that board"; B.R.C., XXXVII, 93.

28. B.R.C., XXXIII, 16–17.

29. B.R.C., XXXIII, 459–460.

30. Place, 114.

31. Shurtleff, 355–356.

32. B.R.C., XXXI, 366–371; Snow, 322.

33. *Memoir of the Life of Eliza S. M. Quincy,* 87.

34. Drawn in 1910 from studies by C. K. Bolton and Alexander Corbett as illustrations for *Anthology Society* (Boston: Boston Athenæum, 1910), opposite 72, 74, 76.

35. Stark, 64–69.

36. Stark, 117–120; Snow, 329–331.

37. Place, 20, 86.

38. B.R.C., XXXI, 317.

39. B.R.C., XXXI, 383, 396–397.

40. Ellen M. Burrill, *The State House* (Boston, 1914), 6–7.

41. Shurtleff, 325–326.

42. Drawn by George N. Woodward for the President of the Common Council's office in City Hall; reproduced in Stark, 291–293, and in the

Boston Public Library *Bulletin*, new series V (1894–1895). The full set shows Tremont Street from Court to Carver Streets. The Boston Athenæum has a partial set, extending only to Boylston Street, given by Dr. George C. Shattuck in 1956; see Boston Athenæum *Reports . . . 1956, 9.*

43. The Knox watercolor is reproduced in M. A. DeWolfe Howe, *Boston Common,* opposite 22, and by Place, 196. Both are reproduced in Stark, 154–156.

44. Morison, *The Life and Letters of Harrison Gray Otis,* I, 42–44; B.R.C., V, 152–163; Allen Chamberlain, *Beacon Hill Its Ancient Pastures and Early Mansions* (Boston, 1925), chapters IV and V.

45. Chamberlain, *Beacon Hill,* 70; Carl J. Weinhardt, Jr., "The Domestic Architecture of Beacon Hill, 1800–1850," *Proc. Bostonian Soc.* (1958), 11–32.

46. *B.R.C.,* V, 163.

47. Chamberlain, *Beacon Hill,* 80.

48. Place, 163–165.

49. Place, 152–153.

50. *B.R.C.,* V, 165–166.

51. Place, 164–167.

52. Morison, *Otis,* I, 232. This house has now become the headquarters of the American Meteorological Society, and so it is hoped will be permanently preserved.

53. Hugh Whitney and Walter Muir Whitehill, "The Somerset Club," *The Somerset Club 1851–1951* (Boston, 1951), 18–20.

54. *B.R.C.,* XXXI, 239.

55. *B.R.C.,* XXXI, 398–399.

56. Place, 98; Snow, 324.

57. *B.R.C.,* XXXV, 65.

58. Lawrence, *Old Park Street,* 81–97.

59. *Prints, Maps and Drawings,* no. 24; Lawrence, *Old Park Street,* 51–63; Place, 168.

60. Walter Firey, *Land Use in Central Boston* (Cambridge, 1947), 161–165.

61. Place, 188–189.

62. M. A. DeWolfe Howe, *The Articulate Sisters* (Cambridge, 1946), 13–14.

63. Place, 60–61; Snow, 333.

64. Walter Muir Whitehill, *A Memorial to Bishop Cheverus* (Boston, 1951); Place, 125–129.

65. Winsor, III, 536.

66. Howe, *Boston Landmarks,* 67–70.

67. Place, 141–142.

68. Place, 212–215. Shubael Bell, writing in 1817, noted that Chelms-ford granite was brought via the Middlesex Canal to the Charlestown prison, where convicts prepared the blocks for the builder's use; *Bostonian Soc. Pub.*, 2nd ser., III, 36–37.

69. Place, 143–145; Snow, 331–332.

70. Place, 122–125.

71. Place, 138–139; Snow, 332.

72. Place, 141; Snow, 332.

73. Edwin M. Bacon, *King's Dictionary of Boston* (Cambridge, 1883), 210–211; Nathaniel Dearborn, *Boston Notions* (Boston, 1848), 301.

74. Bulfinch, 271–272.

75. Bulfinch, 314.

76. Place, 115; Bulfinch, 187.

77. *B.R.C.*, XXXVIII, 113.

78. Josiah Quincy, *A Municipal History of the Town and City of Boston, during Two Centuries* (Boston, 1852), 26–27.

79. Place, 199.

80. *A brief account of the origin and progress of the Boston Female Society for Missionary Purposes, with extracts from the reports of the Society in May 1817 and 1818* (Boston, n.d.), 7–8.

81. Mr. Roger Butterfield has given me an undated clipping "Boston's Beautiful Quadroons" from the *Boston Courier* regarding Ira Gray, "the handsomest quadroon of his day, and the most accomplished gambler ever seen in Boston," who with his brother-in-law, Coburn, kept at the corner of Southack and North Russell Streets a "private place" that was "the resort of the upper ten who had acquired a taste for gambling."

82. Their whereabouts are easy to trace, as the Boston Directories during the first half of the nineteenth century segregated "Africans" or "People of color" at the end. See Handlin, *Boston Immigrants*, 95, 97, for maps of the distribution of the colored population in 1813 and 1815.

83. Edward H. Savage, *Police Records and Recollections; or, Boston by Daylight and Gaslight for Two Hundred and Forty Years* (Boston, 1872), 57.

84. Quincy, *Municipal History*, 102–105, "The chief officer of the former police said to the Mayor soon after his inauguration: 'There are dances almost every night. The whole street is in a blaze of light from their windows. To put them down, without a military force, seems impossible.' He was asked if vice and villany were too strong for the police? He replied, 'I think so; at least it has long been so in that quarter.' He was answered, 'There shall be at least a struggle for the supremacy of the laws.'" The method that he chose was characteristic in its simplicity; first, acting under an old provincial ordinance never repealed, he arrested

the fiddlers in the dance houses, and then took away the licenses of the bar-rooms in the region. "Deprived at once of music and drink, the enemy succumbed to the authority of law without resistance." See also Edmund Quincy, *The Life of Josiah Quincy* (Boston, 1868), 396–397. On another occasion, when rioters were engaged in destroying some bawdy houses, without hindrance from the constabulary, the Mayor assembled a force of burly draymen, and, placing himself at their head, "swept the rioters out of the street by mere force of muscle, and sent them about their business."

85. Place, 237–240; Bulfinch, 191.

86. Quincy, *Municipal History*, 26–27.

Chapter IV

Cutting Down the Hills to Fill the Coves

1. Josiah Quincy, *Figures of the Past* (Boston, 1883), 103–104.

2. B.R.C., XXII, v.

3. Winsor, III, 217–236.

4. On 4 April 1785 a town meeting had turned down proposals for the improvement of the Neck in view of "the present straitened Finances of the Town"; B.R.C., XXXI, 65–67. By 1797 it was concluded that "previous to a general disposition of the very valuable property of the Town, lying on each side of the neck, it is expedient that an accurate map of the same should be taken"; B.R.C., XXXV, 16.

5. Shurtleff, 381–382; B.R.C., XXXV, 101.

6. Hon. Thomas Dawes, George Richards Minot, John Winslow, William Tudor, Deacon William Brown and Josiah Knapp were appointed to serve with the nine Selectmen, of which Charles Bulfinch was Chairman; B.R.C., XXXV, 105.

7. B.R.C., XXXV, 108–109.

8. B.R.C., XXXV, 286.

9. Chamberlain, *Beacon Hill*, 59–60.

10. Winsor, IV, 29–31; III, 597–598.

11. Susan B. Lyman, *My Early Home* (Boston, 1916), [14].

12. Quincy, *Figures of the Past*, 334–335.

13. Mary Caroline Crawford, *Famous Families of Massachusetts* (Boston, 1930), II, 247–249.

14. Winsor, IV, 31.

15. The anonymous author of *Considerations on the Public Expediency*

of a Bridge from one part of Boston to the other (Boston, 1806) justifies his plea by a preliminary advertisement, stating that "no apology will be considered requisite for a calm and respectful examination of the merits of a public question, by those who are informed, that on the day of the last public town-meeting on the question relative to a Bridge from South-Street, a pamphlet of 62 pages was distributed by the Front-Street Corporation." This advocate of a new bridge confined himself to 33 pages, but tedious reading they are!

16. Winsor, IV, 30–31; Morison, *Life and Letters of Harrison Gray Otis,* I, 243–244.

17. Snow, 320; Shaw, 122. Snow lists the persons named in the act of 27 February 1807 incorporating the Canal Bridge as John C. Jones, Loammi Baldwin, Aaron Dexter, Benjamin Wild, Joseph Coolidge, Jr., Benjamin Joy, Gorham Parsons, Jonathan Ingersoll, John Beach, Abijah Cheever, William B. Hutchins, Stephen Howard and Andrew Craigie.

18. *B.R.C.,* XXXV, 159.

19. Shurtleff, 109–110.

20. *B.R.C.,* XXXV, 169.

21. *B.R.C.,* XXXV, 215–218.

22. *B.R.C.,* XXXV, 223–225.

23. *B.R.C.,* XVI, 10, 14.

24. *B.R.C.,* XVI, 119.

25. *B.R.C.,* XVI, 149; XVIII, 72, 80, 90, 172, 179, 196–197; XXVI, 57.

26. William W. Wheildon, *Sentry, or Beacon Hill; the Beacon and the Monument of 1635 and 1790* (Concord, 1877), 27.

27. Winsor, IV, 27–29.

28. *B.R.C.,* V, 99.

29. Shurtleff, 172–180; *B.R.C.,* V, 121–123, where a letter from Charles Bulfinch's son, Thomas, is reprinted; Place, 31–32.

30. *B.R.C.,* XXXI, 59, 134, 143, 154, concerning a petition of 1785 that Hancock finally withdrew.

31. *B.R.C.,* XXXIII, 349–350.

32. *B.R.C.,* XXXIII, 350.

33. Winsor, IV, 28; Place, 104.

34. *B.R.C.,* XXXIII, 462–463.

35. *B.R.C.,* XXXIII, 462–463.

36. See the report of a committee of representatives of the twelve wards, presented at the 27 May 1811 town meeting; *B.R.C.,* XXXV, 286–292, where the town's land on Beacon Hill is valued at $12,000.

37. Winsor, IV, 28; Shurtleff, 179.

38. Winsor, IV, 64–65.

39. See *B.R.C.*, V, 99–100, where N. I. Bowditch expresses his dissatisfaction with the decision in *Thurston* vs. *Hancock* (12th Mass. Rep., 220) that "no action lay for the owner of the house for damage done to the house; but that he was entitled to an action for the falling of his natural land into the pit so dug."

40. Shurtleff, 180; Winsor, IV, 29.

41. Bunker Hill Monument Association, *Proceedings,* 1899, 8–9, 16–17.

42. Winsor, IV, 29.

43. Snow, 325–326; *B.R.C.*, XXXIII, 409; Dearborn, *Boston Notions,* 223.

44. Shurtleff, 113.

45. Snow, 326.

46. *B.R.C.*, V, 53.

47. Winsor, IV, 479; Dearborn, *Boston Notions,* 224–225.

48. *Bostonian Soc. Pub.,* 2nd ser., III, 30–32, cited henceforth as "Bell."

49. When demolished by private owners to make a parking lot.

50. Winsor, IV, 156.

51. Bell, 44–45.

52. *B.R.C.*, XXXV, 340–341. Both reports, and the act of incorporation submitted to the legislature, were printed in a 28-page pamphlet, without imprint or date, bearing the caption title of *Report of the Town's Committee On the Petition of Isaac P. Davis and others, for liberty to build a Mill Dam and Turnpike Road from the bottom of Beacon-Street, and for other Mill improvements.*

53. *Report . . . On the Petition of Isaac P. Davis and others,* 10–11. He continued, in the proper vein of a China Trade merchant: "The question would seem to be, therefore, not whether a provident Legislature will discountenance the forming of large factories; their establishment, or not, will be left to the clearsightedness of private interests, unrestrained by prohibitions or monopolies; a policy which, in the opinion of the best writers on political economy, will be found to consist best with the public prosperity; wisely considering that, in general, a disposition in the people, to change the channels of their industry, is the best possible evidence of the necessity or utility of such change."

54. *Ibid.,* 17–20.

55. *Ibid.,* 21–28.

56. Winsor, IV, 33, reproduced opposite 34. This is, incidentally, an interesting example of letter-press printing in color.

57. Quoted in Winsor, IV, 33.

58. Shurtleff, 357–358, 423–425.

59. Twenty-four pages, without imprint, with the caption title *Boston and Roxbury Mill Corporation.*

60. Winsor, IV, 33.

61. John G. Hales, *A Survey of Boston and its Vicinity* (Boston, 1821), 24–26, with an excellent folding map.

62. Shurtleff, 424.

63. Quoted in Winsor, IV, 34.

Chapter V

Railroads and Immigrants

1. Walter Muir Whitehill, *Boston Public Library, A Centennial History* (Cambridge, 1956), 40.

2. *Bostonian Soc. Pub.*, IV, 112–113. I happily ate shellfish under similar circumstances for many years at the southeasternmost stall in Quincy Market, until the death of the proprietor caused the closing of the stall. Oysters and quahaugs always seem to taste better "on the hoof" than in more elegant surroundings.

3. *Ibid.*, 118.

4. Quincy, *Municipal History,* 74–75, 415–418; Abram E. Brown, *Faneuil Hall and Faneuil Hall Market* (Boston, 1901), 171–188.

5. Quincy, *Municipal History,* 113–116; Shurtleff, 355–357.

6. Winsor, IV, 116–120.

7. *Bowen's Picture of Boston,* 226–229; Winsor, IV, 126 ff; Francis B. C. Bradlee, *The Boston and Lowell Railroad* (Salem, 1918).

8. Francis B. C. Bradlee, *The Eastern Railroad* (Salem, 1917).

9. Francis B. C. Bradlee, *The Boston and Maine Railroad* (Salem, 1921).

10. Wilbur W. Davis, "The History of Boston As Disclosed In the Digging of the Commonwealth Avenue Underpass and Other Traffic Tunnels," *Bostonian Soc. Proc.,* 1938, 33.

11. Winsor, IV, 34.

12. Caroline Gardiner Curtis, *Memories of Fifty Years in the Last Century* (Boston, 1947), 20–21.

13. Winsor, IV, 129.

14. Davis, in *Bostonian Soc. Proc.,* 1938, 35.

15. Winsor, IV, 129.

16. Winsor, IV, 140. This line, through consolidations in 1854 and

1862, became successively the Old Colony and Fall River Railroad Company and the Old Colony and Newport Railway Company, with connections for Fall River Line steamers to New York.

17. Winsor, IV, 141. This completed the entry of railway lines into Boston, for the narrow-gauge Boston, Revere Beach and Lynn, chartered in 1874, and opened to Lynn in 1875, had its terminus in East Boston, with ferry connection into Boston proper.

18. Winsor, IV, 39–40; Boston Athenæum, *Reports,* 1953, 11–12.

19. Edward C. Kirkland, *Men, Cities and Transportation* (Cambridge, 1948), I, 125–137.

20. For this region, see Lawrence, *Old Park Street,* 133–151; Chamberlain, *Beacon Hill,* chapter 1; B.R.C., V, 54–94.

21. The two houses were occupied by the American Congregational Association from 1872 until the completion of their present building at 14 Beacon Street in 1898. The houses were removed in 1904 to make way for the ugly building first occupied by the not very glamorous department store of Houghton & Dutton Company and later by the Veterans Administration; demolished in 1967.

22. Winsor, IV, 67, 610–611.

23. *B.R.C.,* V, 55–56. The print of the garden, owned by the Boston Athenæum (Fig. 58), was brightly colored in 1832 by E. Dexter, presumably a schoolgirl. Robert Salmon's vast painting of the view from Pemberton Hill in 1816, reproduced as the frontispiece to Winsor, IV, and mentioned, IV, 66–67, as owned by William H. Whitmore, is now in the Society for the Preservation of New England Antiquities.

24. Asa G. Sheldon, *Life of Asa G. Sheldon: Wilmington Farmer* (Woburn, 1862).

25. Sheldon, *Life,* 171.

26. Sheldon, *Life,* 181.

27. Sheldon, *Life,* 211. Sheldon was always ready to be obliging in the course of his work. When the United States Marshal had five Spanish pirates to hang, Sheldon allowed him to erect a gallows on the land he was clearing. The execution drew such a crowd that spectators, climbing for a better view onto the roof of a barn in which Sheldon kept fifty oxen, caused the barn to collapse. The sequel is best told in his own words; *Life,* 188. "The next day I made out a bill like this, — 'United States Marshal, Dr., To A. G. Sheldon: To damage done to barn, . . . $50;' and presented it to the Marshal. He looked at it and said, 'I can pay no such bills.' I then requested the use of a slip of paper, pen and ink, and then wrote, — 'United States Marshal, Dr., To A. G. Sheldon, To use of land to hang 5 pirates, and damages sustained thereby, . . . $75.' This suited him, and he paid the money."

28. *Conditions of Sale of Building Lots on Phillips Place, and Tremont and Somerset Streets, on Tuesday, October 6th, 1835, at Ten o'clock, A.M. under a Pavilion on the Premises. Whitwell, Bond & Co., Auctioneers.* (Boston, 1835).

29. Abner Forbes and J. W. Greene, *The Rich Men of Massachusetts containing a Statement of the Reputed Wealth of about Fifteen Hundred Persons* (Boston, 1851), 28, credits him with a fortune of three million dollars, which was only matched by that of Abbott Lawrence. Although this, like other "scandal sheets" before and since, must have derived much of its "information" from gossip, it at least furnishes evidence of what was popularly believed in 1851. It has been useful as a guide to the city directories in discovering where supposedly rich men lived in mid-century. It will be cited henceforth as *Rich Men.*

30. *B.R.C.,* V, 54–56.

31. *Nathaniel Goddard A Boston Merchant* (Boston, 1906), 143–150, 253. The account of Goddard's life in Summer Street makes the region sound very pleasant. We learn that he was "an early riser, often working in his garden before breakfast, pruning the fruit trees or trimming the grapevines and training them over a trellis. After breakfast and on his way to the counting-room he did his marketing at the Quincy Market, principally with Messrs. J. & H. Bird (who also supplied his ships with fresh meats), his servant Michael Larkin following with a large basket to take home the purchases."

32. Louisa Crowninshield Bacon, *Reminiscences* (Boston, 1922), 32, 46.

33. Bulfinch, *Life,* 301. Joseph Coolidge for whom the house was built died in 1820; his son Joseph Coolidge, who was Charles Bulfinch's brother-in-law, died in 1840; his grandson, also Joseph, settled in Pemberton Square, moving to 184 Beacon Street in the seventies.

34. *Selections from the Court Reports originally published in the Boston Morning Post, from 1834 to 1837* (Boston, 1837), 134.

35. *Boston's Immigrants,* 56.

36. *Boston's Immigrants,* 95, for a map showing the distribution of the Irish in Boston in 1850 by streets.

37. Quoted by Howe, *Boston Landmarks,* 69.

38. See William Lawrence, *Memories of a Happy Life* (Boston, 1926), 302–310, for a vivid account not only of the church when "its condition became a source of scandal and its usefulness as a house of worship meagre" but of the steps that he took to insure its preservation.

39. Savage, *Police Records,* 107–112. This invasion by supposedly outraged citizens, who had disguised themselves as for a second Tea Party, can best be explained by an observation of Josiah P. Quincy's in Winsor,

IV, 23, concerning Boston habits of the early nineteenth century: "A degree of license was permitted to men in their relations with women of an inferior caste; but the moment the conventional limit was exceeded a wholesome public opinion outlawed the transgressor. 'A man may repent, and God may forgive him; but his fellow-sinners never will!' bitterly exclaimed one who had felt the ostracism of his generation for an offense of this nature."

40. Savage, *Police Records*, 254–262.

41. *A Trip to Boston in a series of letters to the Editor of the United States Gazette* (Boston, 1838), 207–208.

42. Curtis, *Memories of Fifty Years*, 5.

43. Curtis, *Memories of Fifty Years*, 6.

44. Josiah Quincy, *The History of the Boston Athenæum* (Cambridge, 1851), 70–72, 78–85.

45. Thomas G. Cary, *Memoir of Thomas Handasyd Perkins* (Boston, 1856).

46. The map in Firey, *Land Use*, 56, entitled "Residences of Wealthy Persons in Boston, 1846" shows dramatically the shift away from Fort Hill.

47. Harold Schwartz, *Samuel Gridley Howe, Social Reformer* (Cambridge, 1956), 62.

48. Quincy, *History*, 148.

49. Quincy, *History*, 122, 211.

50. *Boston's Immigrants*, 94.

Chapter VI

The Flight from the South End

1. John P. Marquand, *The Late George Apley* (Boston, 1937), 25–26.

2. William Dean Howells, *The Rise of Silas Lapham* (Boston, 1885), 31.

3. The term is, however, often used today to describe anything south of the Park Square area.

4. The merchant Nathaniel Goddard, in his impecunious twenties, had, as captain of a gundalow, wielded pick and shovel in this operation. See *Nathaniel Goddard*, 92–94.

5. "A Plan of lots for sale on Boston Neck," manuscript map of 1803 or 1804 in Boston Athenæum (Δ 64B = 64 = c).

6. Manuscript map in Boston Athenæum (Δ 64B = 64 = ca).

7. Shurtleff, 121–122.

8. Curtis, *Memories of Fifty Years*, 22, 25; Walter H. Kilham, *Boston After Bulfinch* (Cambridge, 1946), 65.

9. *King's Dictionary of Boston*, 322.

10. Shurtleff, 385–386.

11. *Ballou's Pictorial*, IX, no. 9 (1 September 1855), 129.

12. Winsor, IV, 34–38.

13. "The Development of Franklin Street," *Sketches and Business Directory of Boston and its Vicinity for 1860 and 1861* (Boston, 1860), 155–161.

14. Edward Stanwood, *Boston Illustrated* (Boston, 1872), 85–86; Charles S. Damrell, *A Half Century of Boston's Building* (Boston, 1895), 41; Kilham, *Boston After Bulfinch*, 48.

15. *King's Handbook*, 163–165; Stanwood, *Boston Illustrated*, 84–85.

16. *King's Handbook*, 174.

17. *King's Handbook*, 171–172; Damrell, *Half Century*, 42; *Sketches and Business Directory*, 21.

18. *King's Handbook*, 176–177.

19. *King's Handbook*, 180.

20. *King's Handbook*, 178.

21. *King's Handbook*, 172.

22. *King's Handbook*, 179.

23. *King's Handbook*, 168; Stanwood, *Boston Illustrated*, 86.

24. *King's Handbook*, 174–175.

25. *King's Handbook*, 186, 187.

26. Winsor, III, 424.

27. *King's Dictionary*, 47, 86–87; Winsor, III, 424.

28. *Bowen's Picture of Boston*, 152–153; *King's Handbook*, 184; Damrell, *Half Century*, illustration opp. 246.

29. *King's Handbook*, 184.

30. Stanwood, *Boston Illustrated*, 86–87; Kilham, *Boston After Bulfinch*, 65–66.

31. Stanwood, *Boston Illustrated*, 83–84; *King's Handbook*, 47; *King's Dictionary*, 311–313.

32. *King's Handbook*, 119–120.

33. *King's Handbook*, 118–119.

34. Whitehill, *Boston Public Library*, 134–137.

35. Mr. Ebenezer Gay very kindly undertook to track the five hundred names listed by Forbes and Greene through the Boston directories of the fifties and sixties.

36. John Albree and Sidney B. Morse, merchants.

37. Samuel Bradlee, retired hardware dealer, Josiah M. Jones, a shoe and leather dealer from Athol, Edward A. Raymond, retired grocer, William H. Spear, retired merchant, and John G. Torrey, President of the Columbian Bank.

38. Jacob Bacon, "miscellaneous business," William Beals and Charles G. Greene, publishers of the *Boston Post,* George A. Curtis, retired type and stereotype-founder, Noah Lincoln, wood-wharfinger from the North End, John C. Proctor, retired hardware dealer, Uriah Ritchie, mason from the North End, Henry B. Smith, lawyer, and Otis Tufts, manufacturer of steam engines.

39. Curtis, *Memories of Fifty Years,* 11–12.

40. Albert B. Wolfe, *The Lodging-House Problem in Boston* (Cambridge, 1906), 15.

41. One of the few South End addresses in the 1899 *Social Register.*

42. Winsor, IV, 46–48.

43. Mary Antin, *The Promised Land* (Boston, 1912), 286–287.

44. *Ibid.,* 298.

Chapter VII

The Filling of the Back Bay

1. Lawrence, *Memories of a Happy Life,* 3–4.

2. Other photographs taken from the dome at the time show the view to the east (Fig. 76), the south (Fig. 77) and the southwest (Fig. 79). The Boston Athenæum has a copy of the photograph reproduced in Fig. 78 mounted with another view looking toward the southwest, which thus supplies a panorama of the entire Back Bay, including the crossing of the Worcester and the Providence Railroad tracks. This was reproduced by Bainbridge Bunting, "The Plan of the Back Bay Area in Boston," *Journal of the Society of Architectural Historians,* XIII (1954), 19–24, cited henceforth as Bunting, *Plan.*

3. See Chapter V.

4. This engraving, dated 1824, which shows wide tree-lined avenues, comparable to Commonwealth Avenue, was presumably prepared before Mayor Quincy's views against the sale of the land had prevailed. It was apparently not generally included in Snow's *History,* for a catalogue of Goodspeed's Book Shop, circa 1908–1909, mentions it in the description of a copy of Snow as follows: "This copy is so far as I can learn made unique by the insertion of an outline engraving — 'View of the proposed

buildings west of the Common, Boston,' signed *A. Bowen, Aquat, 1824.* I have not seen another copy of the book containing this interesting print, which foreshadowed almost exactly the ultimate development of that section of the city."

5. *Report of the Joint Committee on Public Lands in relation to the Public Garden, July 1850* (Boston, 1850). See also Winsor, IV, 37, 614–617, and Shurtleff, 359–367. Edward Stanwood suggested (Winsor, IV, 36) that "many of the city fathers were mechanics, who saw a chance for good building jobs in case the land were sold."

6. According to Bainbridge Bunting's *Houses of Boston's Back Bay: An Architectural History, 1840–1917* (Cambridge: Belknap Press, Harvard, 1967), 50, 401, which contains a detailed appendix, street by street, of Back Bay houses with dates of construction, and names of architects, builders and original owners, where they can be ascertained. Mr. Bunting's study of the Back Bay began with a Harvard Ph.D. thesis, submitted in 1952.

7. Lawrence, *Memories of a Happy Life,* 3.

8. A. S. Wheeler, *Address on Boston, Fifty Years Since Delivered before the Commercial Club of Boston, November 21, 1896* (Boston, 1896), 14.

9. Robert Fleming Gourlay, *Plans for Beautifying New York, and for Enlarging and Improving the City of Boston, Being Studies to Illustrate the Science of City Building* (Boston, 1844), 17. The Boston Athenæum copy was presented by the author on 16 October 1844.

10. *Ibid.,* 37.

11. The Athenæum also has a manuscript map of similar content prepared for submission to Governor Lincoln.

12. The plan bears the inscription: "Boston   June 4th 1849. By an amicable agreement between the cities of Boston and Roxbury, the Water Power Company and the owners of the flats in the Back Bay, this plan is respectfully submitted to the City Authorities, for removing the nuisance of the Empty Basin and ornamenting the City of Boston. David Sears, Owner in part of the Flats in the Back Bay."

13. Winsor, IV, 35.

14. *Report of the Committee Appointed under the Resolves of 1856, Chap. 76, in relation to Lands in the Back Bay, with accompanying documents, also, the Fifth Annual Report of the Commissioners on the Back Bay* [Senate No. 17] (Boston, 1857), which includes a map by S. P. Fuller of the Commonwealth's lands; *Commonwealth of Massachusetts, Acts and Resolves relating to the Lands in the Back Bay, with a List of the Commissioners and Reference to the Reports* (Boston, 1859), cited henceforth as *Lands in the Back Bay.*

15. *Lands in the Back Bay,* 10–11, where Act 1857, chapter 169, and Resolve 1857, chapter 70, are quoted.

16. Kilham, *Boston After Bulfinch,* 63; Bunting, *Plan,* 20; *Report of the Committee Appointed under the Resolves of 1856, Chap. 76,* 15.

17. Albert Matthews, in *Boston Evening Transcript,* 22 June 1935, 7; "Improvements on Back Bay, Boston," *Ballou's Pictorial Drawing-Room Companion,* XV (2 October 1858), 209; "Scene on the Back Bay Lands," *ibid.,* XVI (21 May 1859), 328.

18. I owe the photograph of Souther's steam shovel (Fig. 84) and my information about his career to the fortunate accident of his granddaughter Miss Marguerite Souther, of Jamaica Plain, having attended one of the early lectures in this series. Through her kindness I was able to show this unusual view, at its proper place in the lectures. Souther's career, which involved building the machinery for the sloop of war *Guerriere* and sixteen naval vessels during the Civil War, as well as demolishing Fort Hill, was summarized in his obituary in the *Boston Evening Transcript,* 12 September 1911.

19. In his *Transcript* article, Mr. Matthews noted that in 1933 "When pipes for steam heat were being laid, I found on the sidewalk at the corner of Huntington Avenue and Irvington Street a pile of oyster shells two or three feet high; and when the trench was refilled a little later, it pleased me to see that the oyster shells were carefully replaced in it."

20. *Lands in the Back Bay,* 12–17.

21. Mr. William Doogue's 1889 *Annual Report of the Superintendent of Common and Public Grounds* (City of Boston Document 76–1889) contains fine photogravures of the Public Garden and an amusing account of his quarrels with Professor Charles S. Sargent and a "lady art-critic" [Mrs. Schuyler Van Rensselaer], who found his gardening deficient in taste. Mr. Doogue's account of going to Marion to call on Mrs. Van Rensselaer, and going away without doing so on finding "Oscar Wilde sunflowers" and "bilious-looking geraniums . . . among the triumphant weeds" in her dooryard, is a classic that should not remain buried in a public document.

22. In his *Proposed Modification of the Plan of Building on the Back Bay Territory* (Boston, 1860), ii, Snelling recalls how he buttonholed Governor Banks one afternoon on the Common, and "pointing to the wide expanse of water, on which the afternoon sun was glistening," said to him, "Instead of that water, you are giving us dry land, on which the sun will be beating all day, and accumulating heat to be given out all night. Hot days and hot nights will be our doom."

23. *Ibid.,* 3.

24. Letter of 20 June 1936 to David McKibbin, in Boston Athenæum.

25. In Boston Public Library. I am grateful to Mr. William Bradford

Osgood for his kindness in allowing me to use blueprints of these plans that he had made.

26. Morris Carter, *Isabella Stewart Gardner and Fenway Court* (Boston, 1925), 23–24, 51, 175.

27. As the contents were scattered and the building became a lodging house soon after Mrs. Endicott's death, one can only recall the interiors through the illustrations in Diana Whitehill Laing, "The Cushing-Endicott House: 163 Marlborough Street," *Proceedings of the Bostonian Society, 1960,* 15–52.

28. N. A. Thompson & Co., auctioneers, who conducted this sale at the Merchant's Exchange Reading-Room, issued a catalogue with a lithographic plan of the Commonwealth lands. I have seen their catalogue of similar sales on 24 December 1868, 30 April 1869, 2 February 1870 and 7 March 1871.

29. Kilham, *Boston After Bulfinch,* 68–69; *King's Dictionary,* 28–29. The church had in 1846 considered moving to Somerset Street and having Richard Upjohn build them a church. Upjohn's staunch Anglican principles prevented him, in the end, from designing a building for a Unitarian group, which led to a good deal of rather absurd newspaper comment, summarized in Everard M. Upjohn, *Richard Upjohn, Architect and Churchman* (New York, 1939), 81–87.

30. Winsor, III, 462.

31. Upjohn, *Richard Upjohn,* 135.

32. *Ibid.,* 178; *King's Handbook,* 161.

33. Ellis, *History of the First Church in Boston,* 306–313.

34. *King's Dictionary,* 420–421.

35. The church's account of the transaction which contains notable omissions, is given in A. Hamilton Hill, *History of the Old South Church (Third Church) Boston 1869–1884* (Boston, 1890), II, 513–548. *Freedom and the Old South Meeting House (Old South Leaflets,* no. 201) contains some useful material on the history of the building. I hope, in the predictable future, to publish an account of the campaign for the preservation of the meeting house, in which nearly all the great Boston figures of the seventies participated.

36. *King's Handbook,* 86–87; Henry-Russell Hitchcock, Jr., *The Architecture of H. H. Richardson and His Times* (New York, 1936), 110–113; Kilham, *Boston After Bulfinch,* 81.

37. *Trinity Church in the City of Boston, Massachusetts 1733–1933* (Boston, 1933), 67–77, 185–198; Hitchcock, *H. H. Richardson,* 136–144.

38. Richard Herndon, *Boston of Today* (Boston, 1895), 70; Kilham, *Boston After Bulfinch,* 83.

39. Samuel C. Prescott, *When M.I.T. was "Boston Tech,"* 1861–1916 (Cambridge, 1954), 3, 30–32, 55, 59, 97.

40. P. S. Gilmore, *History of the National Peace Jubilee and Great Musical Festival held in the City of Boston, June 1869* (Boston, 1871).

41. William Arms Fisher, *Notes on Music in Old Boston* (Boston, 1918), 46–47; M. A. DeWolfe Howe, *The Boston Symphony Orchestra* (Boston, 1914), 4.

42. Samuel Eliot Morison, *The Development of Harvard University since the Inauguration of President Eliot,* 1869–1929 (Cambridge, 1930), 562–563.

43. Whitehill, *Boston Public Library,* chapter VII.

Chapter VIII

The Westward Movement

1. *Boston's Immigrants,* 105.

2. Winsor, III, 272.

3. Shurtleff, xlvii–liii.

4. William Lawrence, "Rev. Phillips Brooks, D.D., Ninth Rector of Trinity Church 1869–1891," *Trinity Church in the City of Boston* (Boston, 1933), 71–78; Hamilton A. Hill, *History of the Old South Church (Third Church) Boston 1669–1884* (Boston, 1890), II, 525–529.

5. Robert A. Woods, ed., *Americans in Progress, A Settlement Study* (Boston, 1903), chapter III.

6. *King's Handbook,* 45–46, published in 1878, indicates that in addition to having housed such guests as President Grant, the Prince of Wales, King Kalakaua, the Emperor Dom Pedro, the Grand Duke Alexis, "club and class dinners are made a specialty, and the house has the reputation of serving them in the most elegant manner."

7. Wallace Goodrich, ed., *The Parish of the Advent in the City of Boston A History of One Hundred Years 1844–1944* (Boston, 1944), 6–70.

8. Whitehill, *Boston Public Library,* 125–126.

9. *King's Handbook,* 273–274; *King's Dictionary,* 110–111; Kilham, *Boston After Bulfinch,* 85.

10. *Annals of the Massachusetts Charitable Mechanic Association 1795–1892* (Boston, 1892), 294.

11. Holbrook and Fox, auctioneers, for example, conducted an auction for the Trustees in the Mechanics' Building on 16 June 1886, at which

they offered some seventy lots between Huntington Avenue and the Boston and Providence tracks. A priced catalogue in my possession indicates that 154,183 square feet of land were sold on this day for $313,363.30. *Fifth Statement of the Trustees of Huntington Avenue Lands to the Proprietors* (Boston, 1889), 12–13, shows receipts of $732,953.66 from sales of land during the years 1871–1889, with 776,578 square feet of land sold and 534,478 square feet remaining for sale.

12. *Boston After Bulfinch,* 85–86.

13. E. W. Howe, quoted in *Proc. Bostonian Soc.* (1938), 34–35.

14. The situation is clearly shown in Bunting, *Plan,* figure 2.

15. See Bunting, *Plan,* figure 1. The scope and imagination of Olmsted's planning is shown in his "Report of the Landscape Architect Advisory" published as an appendix to City of Boston Department of Parks, *Thirteenth Annual Report of the Board of Commissioners for the year 1887* (Boston, 1888), 51–71. Sylvester Baxter, *Boston Park Guide including the Municipal and Metropolitan Systems of Greater Boston* (Boston, 1895), is also helpful.

16. *A Record of the Streets, Alleys, Places, Etc., of the City of Boston* (Boston, 1910), 232, 301.

17. The Riverbank Improvement Company, according to their record book, to which John Adams, Esq., gave me access, was incorporated by Chapter 109 of the Acts of 1890. It held its first meeting on 2 May 1890, and by June 1892 was executing deeds to land.

18. *Handbook of the Massachusetts Historical Society* (Boston, 1949), 6–7.

19. John W. Farlow, *The History of the Boston Medical Library* (Boston, 1918), 109–126. *Celebration of the Fiftieth Anniversary of the Boston Medical Library* (Boston, 1926), contains pictures of all the homes of the library.

20. Morris Carter, *Isabella Stewart Gardner and Fenway Court* (Boston, 1925), 171–172, 174–175, 182–188.

21. M. A. DeWolfe Howe, *The Boston Symphony Orchestra: An Historical Sketch* (Boston, 1914), 8.

22. *Ibid.,* 192–201.

23. *Ibid.,* 197.

24. Albert Emerson Benson, *History of the Massachusetts Horticultural Society* (Boston, 1929), 78–87, 141, 146, 357, 342, 349–350, 366–367.

25. *The Commemoration of the Founding of the House of Chickering & Sons* (Boston, 1904), 91.

26. Henry Morton Dunham, *The Life of a Musician* (Boston, 1931), 90–98.

27. Frank H. Jackson, *Monograph of the Boston Opera House MDCCCCIX* (Boston, 1909).

28. Plans are reproduced in Perkins Institution, *Eighty-first annual report of the Trustees* (Boston, 1913).

29. David R. Dunigan, *A History of Boston College* (Milwaukee, 1947), 268.

30. William Marshall Warren, "Beacon Hill and Boston University," *Bostonia: The Boston University Alumni Magazine*, IV (November, 1930), 3–21.

31. Arthur Mann, ed., *Growth and Achievement: Temple Israel 1854–1954* (Cambridge, 1953), 34, explains the use of marble thus: "The modern Moorish-style tabernacle, constructed of blemished white marble, was originally to have been built in brick. However, Coolidge and Walker, the architects of Temple Israel, were also the architects of the Harvard Medical School. They were able to take advantage of an opportunity to acquire the handsome but blemished white marble from the Harvard Medical School, which had ordered but could not use it."

32. Eugene C. Hultman, "The Charles River Basin," *Proc. Bostonian Society* (1940), 39–48. Commonwealth of Massachusetts, *Report of the Committee on Charles River Dam* (Boston, 1903), contains detailed reports of Chief Engineer John R. Freeman and numerous valuable photographs and drawings. The plan "Relation of the Fens Basin to the Former Tide Mill Ponds," opposite 192, is particularly useful for anyone interested in the history of the Massachusetts Avenue–Kenmore Square–Fenway region.

33. David McCord, *About Boston* (New York, 1948), 90.

34. John Albree, *A Blight on Boston* (Boston, 1906), is a vigorously written, privately printed polemic on the waste of this land, with good illustrations.

35. Margaret Williamson, *The Mother Church Extension* (Boston, 1939), which is, incidentally, illustrated by one of Rudolph Ruzicka's wood engravings, and by "before" and "after" photographs.

Chapter IX

A Decade of Renewal

1. The *Report made to the Boston Society of Architects by its Committee on Municipal Improvements* (Boston, 1907), of which Robert S.

Peabody was chairman, contains a number of thoughtful and dramatic suggestions for the making of a "New Boston" that are reminiscent of Burnham's and McKim's thoughts on the regeneration of Washington and Chicago. For the history of this society, see my "Boston Society of Architects, 1867–1967, a Centennial Sketch" in Marvin E. Goody and Robert P. Walsh, eds., *Boston Society of Architects, The First Hundred Years, 1867–1967* (Boston, 1967), 15–70. On pages 59–62 are reproduced studies made in 1909 by Robert S. Peabody and Arthur A. Shurcliff for a new city hall in various locations: Copley Square, the Public Garden and Park Square. A 1919 scheme of Ralph Adams Cram's for a municipal center at the intersection of Stuart Street and Columbus Avenue is mentioned on page 58.

2. For a sketch of Parker, see *Boston Society of Architects, The First Hundred Years,* 87–88.

3. In 1949, 1951 and 1955 elections John B. Hynes defeated that hardy perennial, James Michael Curley. During the decade in which he held office, Mayor Hynes did much to restore the confidence of Boston citizens in their government. Furthermore he took the first steps toward many of the topographical changes of the 1960's.

4. My characterization of Mayor Collins in *Boston in the Age of John Fitzgerald Kennedy* (Norman, Oklahoma: University of Oklahoma Press, 1966), 47–48, was quoted in his political advertisements when he was seeking nomination as United States Senator later in that year. He received an honorary LL.D. from Harvard University in 1964, the first twentieth-century Boston mayor to be thus honored. The last previous instance was Nathan Matthews, Mayor 1891–1895, who was awarded a Harvard LL.D. in 1909.

5. See pages 105 and 195. This 22-acre project, involving new streets, in which ten buildings were constructed, was completed in April 1964.

6. Although, as I pointed out on page 195, the best things in the West End had already gone, there were streets and courts that were quite as suitable for economical living in the center of the city as the streets of the north slope of Beacon Hill or of Bay Village. In Poplar Court, for example, a number of young physicians and their families lived pleasantly in nineteenth-century red brick houses converted into apartments. They were near the Massachusetts General Hospital, and their wives made full use of the nearby foreign groceries and bakeries. The West End had many of the virtues that Jane Jacobs found in New York's Greenwich Village.

7. Restored to religious use by Methodists in 1962, after more than sixty years as a branch of the Boston Public Library. A new West End Branch Library in Cambridge Street was completed in 1968 next to the Harrison Gray Otis house.

8. This brick Greek Revival structure on Chambers Street was built in 1824 to relieve overcrowding at the West Church, then presided over by Rev. Charles Lowell. The group that formed it was incorporated in January 1824 as "The Twelfth Congregational Society in the city of Boston," although its theology was Unitarian and it was, as pointed out in *Bowen's Picture of Boston* (Boston, 1838), 149, "in fact the eighteenth Congregational church formed regularly in Boston, and is the fifteenth of those now in existence; we know not why it was called the twelfth." Nor do I, but the matter is of no great consequence, for the "Congregational Society" died, with population changes in the West End, and the building was bought by the Catholic Archdiocese and renamed St. Joseph's Church. Kilham, *Boston After Bulfinch,* 38, mentioned its "front composed of a pediment with wooden Doric columns and wooden cornices" and noted that "standing as it does in the curve of a street [it] has considerable impressiveness." That was lost when, thanks to the first efforts of the Boston Redevelopment Authority, the curve, the street and all neighboring buildings disappeared, leaving poor St. Joseph's forlorn and isolated in a great dump, later to become a parking lot. Cardinal Cushing has recently built *Regina Cleri,* an apartment house for retired clergy, beside the church, which is reached from Staniford Street by a new street, Cardinal O'Connell Way, so named because that prelate had served as curate of St. Joseph's Church in early life.

9. This somber building, designed by Gridley J. F. Bryant and completed in 1851, is as impressively handsome from the exterior as it is unsanitary and miserable within.

10. Construction began on the first of these complexes, designed by Victor Gruen Associates, in March 1960. Gruen's plan eliminated all through streets in the area, substituting footpaths and cul-de-sac roads to service the groups of buildings.

11. He resigned in the summer of 1967 to seek (unsuccessfully) the Democratic nomination for mayor to succeed John F. Collins, who did not wish to serve a third term. The accomplishments of his years as administrator are set forth concisely in an 80-page book, *Seven Years of Progress, A Final Report by Edward J. Logue, Development Administrator* (Boston: BRA, 1967). Good bits of contemporary reporting may be found in "The Battle for Boston," *The Economist* (11 March 1961), 952–953, and the extensive section on Boston redevelopment in the June 1964 issue of *Architectural Forum.* Early in 1968 Mayor Kevin H. White appointed as Redevelopment Administrator, Hale Champion, formerly an administrative assistant to the Governor of California.

12. The ten original general renewal areas were modified into nine renewal projects: (1) Government Center; (2) Washington Park; (3)

Charlestown; (4) Waterfront; (5) South End; (6) South Cove; (7) Fenway; (8) Central Business District; and (9) Madison Park; a tenth, Back Bay, is being undertaken as a private project sponsored by the Back Bay Council, and Back Bay Planning and Development Association with the cooperation of the BRA. 2, 3 and 9 lie outside the scope of this book.

13. This involved a wide terraced mall, wandering uphill from Faneuil Hall to the Suffolk County Court House. A sketch is reproduced in *The Economist* (11 March 1961), 952.

14. *Seven Years of Progress,* 58. In accordance with this, Logue sought the services of the ablest architects available for BRA projects, and in the BRA Urban Design Department created a Design Advisory Committee, an unpaid group of internationally recognized architects who live and work in the Boston area. This committee, consisting of Hugh Stubbins chairman, Dean José Luis Sert of Harvard, Dean Lawrence B. Anderson of M.I.T., Pietro Belluschi and Nelson W. Aldrich, meets monthly to consider the projects under review by the BRA staff.

15. *Seven Years of Progress,* 17

16. *Boston Society of Architects, The First Hundred Years,* 85–86, contains a brief sketch of Dean Emerson, who was president of the society in 1940–42.

17. In the colonial period Hanover Street had been the principal thoroughfare between the center of Boston and the North End. As it had ceased to be that when bisected by the overhead roads of the John F. Fitzgerald Expressway, the elimination of the section between Court and Union Streets passed almost unnoticed.

18. The idea of such a competition was put forward by the society in June 1958, James Lawrence, Jr. (president, 1962–1963) being its foremost advocate. *Boston Society of Architects, The First Hundred Years,* 69, 95–96.

19. Although afflicted with the horrid designation of One, Two and Three Center Plaza, this building, through its graceful curve and the play of light and shade upon its façade, is a pleasing addition to the region. It was designed by Welton D. Becket of Los Angeles.

20. Designs for this Center Hotel and Office Building (by the firm of Raymond and Rado) and for the parking garage (by Samuel Glaser Associates and Kallman and McKinnell) are reproduced in Logue, *Seven Years of Progress,* 19.

21. Subway stations have changed their names confusingly. SCOLLAY SQUARE is now GOVERNMENT CENTER; MECHANICS BUILDING is PRUDENTIAL; MASSACHUSETTS AVENUE is now AUDITORIUM. The Massachusetts Bay Transit Authority is, however, now posting decent maps, assigning distinctive colors to different transit lines, and generally trying

to make information about public transportation as intelligible in Boston as it has long been in the London Underground or the Paris Metro.

22. The Boston Welfare Department's building of the 1920's remains. A new police station is under construction on Sudbury Street. Two private insurance buildings and quarters for WNAC–TV (Channel 7) and the Jewish Family and Children's Service are under construction.

23. Designed by Emery Roth & Sons of New York and Hoyle, Doran, and Berry of Boston.

24. Abbott Lowell Cummings, "Charles Bulfinch and Boston's Vanishing West End," *Old-Time New England,* LII (October, December 1961), 30–49, discusses certain buildings destroyed in this 1960–1961 clearing.

25. I. M. Pei's plan had called for three separate buildings on the tract. The Boston firm of Desmond & Lord, with Paul Rudolph as consultant, was retained to design the Mental Health building; Shepley, Bulfinch, Richardson & Abbott were engaged for the Employment Security Division headquarters; and M. A. Dyer and Pedersen & Tilney were commissioned to design the Health Welfare and Education Building. As Charles Hilgenhurst, the BRA Project Designer, recalled it (reported by Philip Herrera in *Architectural Forum* (June 1964), 92: "Under Ed Logue's and the State Government Center Commission's prodding, the five firms tried to come up with a comprehensive scheme for the whole complex, and arrived at a solution which looked like an Italian town, full of small buildings. None of the firms was completely satisfied, though the BRA and State Commission tentatively accepted the plan. Then one day, at a meeting of the architects, Rudolph walked in with what he called 'a stake with a tail.' Everyone became enthusiastic about the tower (though it exceeded Pei's height limits) and the low buildings enclosing a plaza; Rudolph was named design coordinator for the project. All the firms collaborated from then on, producing three buildings merged into one monolithic, monumental whole."

26. Characteristically his *Seven Years of Progress* notes in each project not only "substantial achievements" but "setbacks," and states both "where we are now" and "what remains to be done." Few public administrators have recorded their activity in as forthright a manner.

27. *Seven Years of Progress,* 18.

28. The reader will recall from Chapter IV how Mayor Quincy cleaned up Mount Whoredom in the 1820's, yet Scollay Square became its spiritual descendant.

29. Herrera in *Architectural Forum,* 92.

30. Richard R. Wood of Hunneman & Co. assembled the site and found the major tenants. The building was designed by the Pearl Street Associates (Stahl and Hugh Stubbins, architects; William Le Messurier, struc-

tural engineer). Robert Adams, "The Building Maker," *Boston,* LVII (November 1965), 24–27; Walter Muir Whitehill, *History of the site of the State Street Bank Building,* an illustrated folder published by the bank in 1966.

31. Designed by Edward L. Barnes and Emery Roth & Sons. A piece of sculpture by Henry Moore has been commissioned for the area between this building, the Boston Company Building and the Old State House.

32. Designed by Pietro Belluschi and Emery Roth & Sons. The 1640–1808 site of the First Church (see page 27) was long recalled by the survival of Cornhill Square, which ran on three sides of the twentieth-century office building where the Ehrlichs sold pipes and tobacco. This has now been merged in the site of the Boston Company Building. The century-old David P. Ehrlich Company, an esteemed Boston institution with a fondness for historic sites, moved in 1967 to Tremont Street, beside King's Chapel Burying Ground.

In the first edition I attributed the 1711 fire which destroyed the First Church, following earlier secondary sources, to "the carelessness of a poor drunken Scottish woman in a backyard tenement." Just as the revisions were going to press, Wendell D. Garrett, Managing Editor of *Antiques,* sent me a transcription of the account of the fire in the 1–8 October 1711 issue of the *Boston News-Letter,* which begins: "On Tuesday the second of *October,* about Eight a Clock in the Evening, a Fire broke out in an old Tenement within a back yard in *Cornhill,* near to the First Meeting-House, occasioned by the carelessness of a poor Sottish Woman, by using Fire to a parcel of Ocum, Chips, and other combustible Rubbish, which soon raised a great Flame." Although some Scots are sots, it by no means follows that all sots are Scots; therefore I have amended this line in the second edition. Mr. Garrett encountered this entry during a systematic search of Boston colonial newspapers for a work on the arts and crafts in Boston. As a careful editor, he sent me a note of the discovery, with the comment that, although he "did not think it worth taking the trouble to change," it did illustrate how earlier editors "in transcribing their notes in longhand, later distrusted their transcriptions and tended to amend and correct spellings with occasional serious changes in meaning."

33. Designed by Campbell, Aldrich, and Nulty.

34. Demolished when that firm moved to the State Street Bank Building.

35. A partner in the law firm of Ropes and Gray, for thirty years a member of the Harvard Corporation, and in 1960–1961 president of the Greater Boston Chamber of Commerce.

36. Victor Gruen Associates, Inc., *Boston/Central Business District Planning Report,* October 30, 1967 (Boston: BRA, 1967). The recom-

mendations of this 192-page report are briefly summarized in *Boston/The Plan for the Central Business District* (Boston: BRA, 1967).

37. Although the report says "suitable for pedestrian use," I prefer (in accordance with David McCord's distinction set forth in the preface, pages viii–ix) to use "walker," for "pedestrian" has come to mean to me "a man in danger of his life.'"

38. The Port Authority is seeking legislative approval for an extensive redevolpment in this area for which plans have been made by Sert, Jackson, and Associates.

39. Built, like the Prudential Center, by private investors in accordance with chapter 121A of Massachusetts General Laws, which provides certain tax concessions to encourage new construction.

40. Raymond's, the long-established Boston prototype of the discount house, specializing in bargains announced in misspelled advertising, featuring a mythical New England hayseed known as Uncle Eph, long occupied a rabbit-warren of buildings in Washington Street between Franklin and Milk Streets. In August 1966 the store moved to temporary quarters elsewhere, pending construction of a new building (with an 800-car garage) designed by Samuel Glaser Associates.

41. *Seven Years of Progress,* 3.

42. On a vast billboard, wrapped around the corner of the building, a dachshund with a purse in its mouth, led its owners to the Boston Five Cents Savings Bank in School Street, while most of the rest of the façade was concealed by signs informing the passer-by that sliced crispy pizza was to be had within for 15¢.

43. Walter Muir Whitehill, "The Old Corner Book Store Building," *Athenæum Items,* 72 (November 1960), 1–2.

44. The early nineteenth-century ell running up School Street has been leased to the Liberty Bank and Trust Company. When it takes possession, presumably in 1969, Historic Boston Incorporated, will complete the exterior restoration of the ell. Historic Boston Incorporated also owns the adjacent building at 277 Washington Street, which is the only old structure between the Old Corner and the parking garage and Boston Company Building that are in 1968 under construction; it hopes soon to reconstruct the eighteenth-century façade that this building once had.

45. Although the realignment of School Street, which is part of this plan, may begin in 1969, the park will necessarily be some years away, for it involves a Chauncy/Arch Streets by-pass which can only be achieved when the full CBD plan is in motion.

46. *Seven Years of Progress,* 24.

47. One of Logue's last acts as Redevelopment Administrator was to approve a contract with Architectural Heritage Incorporated for a feasi-

bility study of the reuse of these buildings that would involve their external restoration to the original design of Alexander Parris.

48. See George Caspar Homans, "The Harbor and Shipping of Boston, 1880–1930," *Fifty Years of Boston: A Memorial Volume Issued in Commemoration of the Tercentenary of 1930* (Boston, 1932), 279–290.

49. See James B. Connolly, "The Fishing Industry of Boston," *Fifty Years of Boston,* 291–294.

50. The Boston Yacht Club had delightful quarters in a Rowes Wharf warehouse, and India Wharf long housed the India Wharf Rats, from whose 1916 publication *The Story of India Wharf* by Herbert F. Otis, figure 45 is reproduced. Z. William Hauk, *T Wharf Notes and sketches collected during a quarter century of living on Boston's Waterfront* (Boston: Alden-Hauk, Incorporated, 1952) gives a delightful account of Larry O'Toole (1908–1951) and other T Wharf inhabitants.

51. *Report on the Downtown Waterfront-Faneuil Hall Renewal Plan* (Boston: BRA, 1962). In November 1960 the Greater Boston Chamber of Commerce provided $150,000 for the planning studies for this project, which were carried out during the next eighteen months.

52. A $7,000,000 New England Produce Center, Inc. located at Beacham Street on the Chelsea-Everett line was opened in April 1968. Plans were being made for a new wholesale meat market in South Bay, and negotiations were underway in 1967 for a waterfront location for the seafood wholesalers, according to *Seven Years of Progress,* 24.

53. This building, designed by the Cambridge Seven, has been built by a recently formed New England Aquarium Corporation. See *Seven Years of Progress,* 24–25, where mention is made of the construction of a bulkhead between Central and India Wharves as the first step toward the construction of an apartment complex (designed by I. M. Pei) and parking garage on the site of India Wharf, and of plans for the construction by the Employers Group of Insurance Companies of an office building on air rights over the Central Artery.

54. Demolished by private owners who acted on the principle of the lord of the vineyard in Matthew xx. 15: "Is it not lawful for me to do what I will with mine own?" The best record of the wharf, published shortly before the warehouses were pulled down is Abbott Lowell Cummings, "The Beginnings of India Wharf," *Proceedings of the Bostonian Society* (1962), 17–24.

55. *St. Stephen's Church, Boston, Mass.* (Boston: St. Stephen's Church, 1966), 3. The architect for the restoration was Chester Wright, A.I.A. Since 1800 the North End has had four successive groups of residents. On page 113 I noted how the New North Church was complaining in 1822 that some of its congregation found the region "ungenteel." By

the middle of the nineteenth century, Irish immigrants had taken over the North End; hence the purchase of the New North by Bishop Fitzpatrick and its transformation into St. Stephen's. President Kennedy's grandfather, Mayor John F. Fitzgerald (1863–1950), in the days when he was Democratic boss of the North End, lived in Garden-court Street, and was a parishioner of St. Stephen's. In the last three decades of the nineteenth century it became the center of the first exclusively Eastern European Jewish community in Boston; see Arnold A. Wieder, *The Early Jewish Community of Boston's North End* (Waltham: Brandeis University, 1962). In this century the Irish and Jews have been supplanted by Italians.

56. *Final Report of the Boston National Historic Sites Commission,* 87th Congress, 1st Session, House Document No. 107 (Washington: U.S. Government Printing Office, 1961), 130–136.

57. See pages 104–105.

58. Church Street (see pages 138–139) runs from Columbus Avenue to Tremont Street through the heart of Bay Village.

59. This was part of a plan devised by the City Planning Board from 1916 onward for a "Western Artery to the Boston Central District" that would link Huntington and Atlantic Avenues by the widening and extension of Stuart, Eliot and Kneeland Streets with a view to expediting traffic and encouraging real estate development.

60. Although the Massachusetts Turnpike was opened from Lee to Weston in 1957, it ended at route 128 for five years while the question of continuing into Boston as a toll or free road was heatedly argued. In 1962, when the Legislature authorized the Boston extension as a toll road, it was built alongside the right of way of the Boston and Albany Railroad, with considerable demolition as it chewed its way into the heart of the city. Where the road is depressed, it does less visual damage to its surroundings than the elevated Central Artery; nevertheless in recent aerial photographs (Figs. 128, 133) this vast gully is a conspicuous feature.

61. The Boston Dispensary, established in 1796, which was the first medical service in New England and the third oldest in the country, serves outpatients; the Boston Floating Hospital, established 1894, has now come ashore; and the Pratt Clinic–New England Center Hospital (1948) established first in 1938 as the Pratt Diagnostic Hospital and Clinic.

62. *Seven Years of Progress,* 26–27. Over two hundred units of cooperative housing, sponsored by the local Chinese Urban Renewal Committee, are underway, while the Massachusetts Housing Association (a subsidiary of the Morgan Memorial) has plans for still more units of rental housing.

63. *Seven Years of Progress,* 28–29.

64. See pages 139–140.

65. The Prudential Center was designed by Charles Luckman who, after nearly two decades in the soap business (president of Lever Brothers, 1946–1950), returned to the practice of architecture. This $200,000,000 project was a private venture using chapter 121A of the Massachusetts General Laws. I am grateful to Daniel F. Becker, Director of Public Relations, Prudential Insurance Company of America, Northeastern Home Office, for his kindness in furnishing some of the illustrations of this chapter.

66. I am indebted to Erwin D. Canham and to Carl B. Rechner, Development Consultant of the First Church of Christ, Scientist, for furnishing me information about the Church's plans.

67. The Church and Araldo A. Cossutta, the Pei partner in charge of the project, have worked closely with the Boston Redevelopment Authority staff to integrate the needs of the Church with the BRA plans for the Fenway Project (*Seven Years of Progress,* 32–34; described also in F. Peter Model, "The Healers and the Wreckers," *Boston,* LVIII [June 1966], 22–25). This area contains over seventy medical and educational institutions. Over the past fifteen years increased institutional property in the Fenway has caused the total taxable property to decline by more than 20 per cent. Logue states: "Our primary goal is to reverse these trends, to encourage new taxable development within the institutional area, to coordinate the development plans of various institutions with each other and with the residential area, to redevelop and rejuvenate the commercial center on Massachusetts Avenue, and to provide attractive housing in medium and high-rise developments including housing for the elderly."

68. In a statement about the plan made at the Boston Citizen Seminar of 5 December 1967, Carl B. Rechner, Development Consultant for the Church, stated: "Our master plan includes a limited area the Church does not own. This decision was based on the premise that since the Church project is in an active Urban Renewal area and the BRA plans require acquisition and redevelopment of these properties, the Church anticipates sponsoring a redevelopment which will fully measure up to the required standards and feasibly tie in with the design accommodations and services of the adjoining properties on land which the Church owns. The Church does not seek nor want the government to take the property of others for itself. However, if the BRA is going to acquire adjoining property anyhow and sell it to a qualified bidder for the best new redevelopment plan offered, then the Church simply desires to be considered impartially as a potential bidder in order to sponsor and assist in an orderly redevelopment which we feel would benefit the entire community including the Church."

69. Mr. Rechner stated in his Boston Citizen Seminar paper: "All of

the new construction shown in the master plan will be tax-paying. The Church edifice is the only tax-exempt property in the entire plan."

70. The number of apartments projected, like the parking arrangements, represents a three-to-one increase over the existing use of the land.

71. The Pei plan includes the creation of open space beyond Symphony Hall and reversing the entrance to the hall off of crowded Massachusetts Avenue; see page 185.

72. David McCord, *Bibliotheca Medica: Physician for Tomorrow, Dedication of the Countway Library of Medicine, May 26 & 27, 1965* (Boston: Harvard Medical School, 1966). With the completion of the Countway Library, the Boston Medical Library sold its 1901 building in the Fenway (page 183) to a music school.

73. Designed by Sert, Jackson and Gourlay in association with Edwin T. Steffian. I am grateful to Professor Robert E. Moody for obtaining photographs of recent Boston University Developments for me.

74. Demolishing in the process the 1883 Harvard Medical School (see page 172) that had, after that institution's move to Longwood Avenue, been used by Boston University.

75. As Philip Johnson felt an association with a Boston firm would be helpful, Architects Design Group, Inc. was selected and a joint venture formed. The architects selected William J. LeMessurier to be structural engineer and Francis Associates to be mechanical engineer for the project.

76. The east wall of the new building will join the west wall of the old one, although with the architectural device of a narrow connecting pavilion — an elegant and sublimated version of the familiar "breezeway" — to mark the transition.

77. The only other comparable example in Boston is the 1913–1915 enlargement by Henry Forbes Bigelow of Edward C. Cabot's 1847–1849 Boston Athenæum.

78. *Boston Society of Architects, The First Hundred Years,* 55, 57; *Seven Years of Progress,* 36–37.

79. Page 189.

80. Pei's first years as an architectural student at M.I.T. were happily spent in the Rogers Buildings in Boylston Street.

81. Schools and colleges proliferated in the Back Bay as large houses, assessed at astronomical values, were put on the market at very low prices by owners who wished to live in the country and be rid of Boston real estate taxes.

82. *Seven Years of Progress,* 37.

83. A party given at the College Club on a very hot summer day in 1967 to celebrate the publication of this book indicated a new appreciation

of the Back Bay, for architectural historians, householders (represented by the Back Bay Neighborhood Association) and the Boston Redevelopment Authority (represented by Mr. Logue in person) joined with the Harvard University Press in recognizing the significance of the area. To supplement Professor Bunting's book, Mrs. Ropes Cabot and I prepared for the 1967 *Proceedings* of the Bostonian Society a picture book, *Back Bay Churches and Public Buildings,* also issued separately. Some copies got loose with the captions of the First Church and the Central Congregational Church interchanged. The First Church is the Gothic edifice, designed by Ware and Van Brunt, that appears beyond the Lutheran Church in Fig. 112. Unhappily it burned in the spring of 1968, only the exterior arcades and the tower surviving.

84. After the death late in 1966 of Miss Evelyn Sears, who had lived in the house for most of her ninety-some years, it was bought by Mr. and Mrs. Lawrence Coolidge who are young enough to have many years ahead of them. Nathaniel Dexter has made himself an apartment in the later kitchen and stable wing.

85. Designated by the Department of the Interior in 1966, like the neighboring Boston Athenæum, as a National Historic Landmark.

86. For the Somerset Club, see page 63. The Union Club occupies the former houses of Abbott Lawrence and John Amory Lowell in Park Street; the Tavern Club three small red brick houses in Boylston Place; the St. Botolph Club a house at 115 Commonwealth Avenue; the Odd Volumes a house at 77 Mount Vernon Street once owned by Mrs. Henry Whitman and, later, Dr. John C. Phillips. The College Club in 1919 united two houses, built in 1862, at 38–40 Commonwealth Avenue. The Chilton Club has greatly enlarged a house at the southeast corner of Commonwealth Avenue and Dartmouth Street. The Women's City Club occupies two very fine Greek Revival houses at 39–40 Beacon Street.

87. The finest clubhouse built as such is that of the Algonquin Club at 219 Commonwealth Avenue, designed by McKim, Mead and White, 1887.

88. *St. Stephen's Church, Boston, Massachusetts,* 17.

89. (Cambridge: Harvard University Press, 1966), 113. For details, see Joan E. Goody, *New Architecture in Boston* (Cambridge: M.I.T. Press, 1965) and Kenneth John Conant, "The New Boston Architecture in an Historical Setting," *Boston Society of Architects, The First Hundred Years,* 89–98.

90. "Tourist Stay Home!," *Saturday Evening Post* (12 August 1967, 8–10.

91. At Harvard Le Corbusier's Carpenter Center for the Visual Arts and neighboring buildings in Quincy Street do each other very little good.

At M.I.T. Eero Saarinen's Kresge Auditorium and Chapel and Alvar Aalto's Baker House Dormitory seem unrelated to each other or Welles Bosworth's central group of 1916. Curiously enough I. M. Pei's 23-story Center for Earth Sciences — the first departure from a low skyline at M.I.T. — seems in happier relation with its neighbors than other recent buildings there.

92. *Seven Years of Progress,* 58–61.

INDEX